The Kent coalfield, its evolution and development

AE Ritchie

TO

M. R.

An Acknowledgment and a Token.

R. A. C. Godwin-Austen, Esq., F.R.S., etc.

(From a hitherto unpublished photograph (1860) kindly lent to the author by his son, Colonel H. H. Godwin-Austen.)

[*Frontispiece.*

THE KENT COALFIELD

ITS EVOLUTION AND DEVELOPMENT.

BY

A. E. RITCHIE.

"The strength of Great Britain lies in her iron and coal beds; the Lord Chancellor now sits upon a bag of wool, but wool has long ceased to be emblematical of the staple commodity of England. He ought to sit upon a bag of COALS."—*George Stephenson.*

THE IRON AND COAL TRADES "REVIEW,"
Bessemer House, Adelphi
LONDON, W.C. 2.

"Amongst the solved problems and remarkable discoveries of the nineteenth century will rank, as not least of importance, that of the real existence of a 'Kent coalfield.'"—G. D. HULL, LL.D., F.R.S., F.G.S.

FOREWORD.

The time has surely come when the scepticisms so generally evidenced towards the Kent Coalfield should give place to belief in its actuality, and to faith in its future. To the long delay in the sinking of the pits at Shakespeare Cliff, and the many unfulfilled prophecies concerning them, must be attributed the lack of public interest in, not to say ignorance of, the economic revolution that is now in progress in Kent.

Two collieries have entered upon the producing stage, and are raising a quarter of a million tons of coal per annum; a quantity which would probably be doubled but for the disabilities imposed by the war. A third colliery has recently got both shafts into a 5-ft. seam of excellent coal, from which, in the early part of 1920, a fairly substantial output should speedily be produced. Yet another colliery has its shafts sunk almost down to the Coal Measures: so that by the end of 1920 there should be four producing collieries in Kent—the forerunners of many more that will follow as rapidly as post-war conditions of labour permit.

Not only collieries, but steel works on a large scale will be in operation in the near future; for the Channel Steel Company has been formed by a powerful group, as will be seen hereafter, to work the extensive beds of iron ore, first proved at Shakespeare Cliff, and, later, in several borings put down to test their continuity between Dover and Folkestone.

It remains to be added that some of the coal borings provided, incidentally, beds of valuable fire-clay, from which specimen pieces of high-grade pottery ware have been made, giving promise of the establishment in due course of manufactories of all classes of these goods, from sanitary ware to a wide range of artistic productions.

In these circumstances a review of the facts which have led up to the present position in East Kent, and upon which its future developments are based, should be both interesting and instructive.

A glance at the bibliography of Kent Coal will be sufficient to make it apparent that, in attempting to deal with the subject within reasonable limits, great restraint must be exercised. It is quite obvious that it would be impossible to traverse in detail the accumulation of incidents, geological and financial, that have led to the establishment of the Kent Coalfield as it exists to-day. This must be my answer in advance to any criticisms that my omissions may evoke.

Castle Avenue,
Dover.
31st Oct., 1919.

ILLUSTRATIONS.

MAPS, PLANS AND SECTIONS.

SIR EDWARD WATKIN, BART., M.P.,
Chairman of the Channel Tunnel and South-Eastern Railway Companies in 1890.

Photo. Lambert-Weston, Folkestone.

CONTENTS.

Part I.—Evolution.

CHAPTER I.

Evolution, 1826-1875.—The Discovery of the Pas de Calais Coalfield. The Lens, Bruay and Courrières Collieries. Godwin-Austen's Paper "On the Possible Extension of the Coal Measures beneath the South-East Part of England." Joseph Houldsworth supports Godwin-Austen's Theories. The Royal Commission on Coal Supplies, 1871. Meeting of the British Association at Brighton. The Sub-Wealden Committee.

"The best of prophets of the future is the Past."
—BYRON.

No account of the discovery and development of the East Kent Coalfield can be complete without reference to its nearest neighbour, that of the Pas de Calais. The opening up that famous field, from which in pre-war days France obtained more than 50 per cent. of her home supplies, emphasised the importance of a subject that for some years previously had been exercising the minds of our leading geologists. This was as to the probability of a continuation on our side of the channel, of the Coal Measures of Belgium and of the Boulonnais district of France.

1826.

The physical similarity of the coalfields of Somerset with those of the Departement du Nord, and of Belgium, was noted by Buckland and Conybeare so far back as the year 1826; but the first suggestion of the possibility of a buried coalfield in the South of England came from Sir Henry de la Beche, some twenty years after that date, and was published in the first "Memoir of the Geological Survey" in the year—

1846.

I quote the following extract:—"From the movement of the older rocks many a mass of Coal

Measures may be buried beneath the Oolites and Cretaceous rocks on the east, the remains of a great sheet of the accumulations connecting the districts we have noticed, the Mendip Hills, with those of Central England and Belgium, rolled about and partially denuded prior to the deposit of the New Red Sandstone."

In this same year came the discovery that was to prove the germ of the Pas de Calais coalfield, and which decided the hitherto debatable question as to the extension of the coalfield of the Nord, viz., the accidental finding of coal in an artesian boring at Oignies.

1847—1849.

The pointer thus given was followed up, post-haste, by a series of borings to test the extent and value of the discovery, and to trace the trend of the seams indicated; with the result that the scope of these explorations was rapidly extended.

Workable coal was proved at Escarpelle in 1847, and later at Courrières and Lens; while towards the end of 1849 the development stage had been reached, shafts had been started, and applications lodged with the Government for mining concessions.

In France, as most of my readers are probably aware, the minerals belong to the State, which has always dealt liberally with the pioneers whose enterprise and money have been the means of opening-up new districts for development. Substantial areas are granted to explorers, and the Government is content with a modest royalty.

A chapter might easily be written here on the different manner in which similar enterprise is treated in this country. Landlords who have never raised a finger, nor spent a penny, even towards ascertaining the existence of minerals under their properties, in many instances act as if those who adventure their money in the quest were legitimate subjects for plunder.

In this connection I should like to interpolate some almost identical remarks by Whitaker, in 1890, which came to my notice only some months after the preceding paragraph had first appeared in print. "If the national wealth is to be largely increased by the scientific exploration of the South-

East of England, surely it is not too much to ask that those who carry out the costly work should have a goodly share in the profit thereof; but the laws of this enlightened country make it possible that after having spent thousands of pounds, used up a good amount of brain-power, and got through much valuable time, explorers may find that they have done little else than increase the property of neighbouring land-owners, who have stood by with their hands in their pockets, until such time as they could practically put the said hands into the pockets of other people, legally."

Developments in the Pas de Calais progressed with remarkable rapidity, but apparently attracted little or no attention amongst us; the only circumstance to be recorded being the publication by Dunn, in 1848, of a little-known work entitled "Winning and Working Coal," in which he remarked upon the continuity of the chalk overlying the Coal Measures of Belgium with that of Kent. He stated that this "raised the very curious and important question as to whether or not the carboniferous coalfields of Belgium exist under similar chalk formation in Britain."

1852.

In this year were established the three undermentioned collieries which were destined to prove so phenomenally successful. The history of Lens, Bruay and Courrières is famous in the annals of the coal industry, and, indeed, world-wide celebrity attaches to their names. The Lens Colliery, in particular, is deserving of more than a passing mention, as my readers may not all be aware of its romantic financial history.

1853.

The commercial career of these celebrated Pits began in the year 1853, when 223 tons of coal were raised. The original capital of the Company was £120,000, in shares of £40 (1,000 fcs.), of which only £12 was called up. Exactly 50 years later the output of coal was more than 3¼ million tons per annum, and the market value of the original shares had reached £3,000; the dividend on which represented 1,000 per cent. on the amount called up. Lucky shareholders!

It was only natural that the operations in the Pas de Calais should at last have attracted the attention of British geologists, and led them to devote much study to the problem of the possible extension of that field into England. Science was ahead of Industry in this; for, so far, our great coalowners, firmly established in their Northern fastnesses, had not taken any thought as to the effect of these novel geological conditions across the Channel. It cannot truthfully be said that this aloofness has been modified to any appreciable extent up to the present day, for the cream of the South-Eastern coalfield—the logical outcome of the discoveries we are considering—bids fair to pass under the control of our more enterprising neighbours, the French.

1855.

The first important move from the scientific side was made in the year 1855 when Godwin-Austen presented his now historical Paper, "On the Possible Extension of the Coal Measures beneath the South-Eastern Part of England," before the Geological Society. His starting point was the assumption, based on an exhaustive study of the geological phenomena of Belgium, and of the Bristol Coalfield, that the "Axis of Ardennes" (now more usually referred to as the "Axis of Artois") is identical with our Mendip Hills. To quote his own words:—

> "The depression of the Thames represents, and is physically a continuation of, that which, extending from Valenciennes by Douai, Bethune, Therouanne and thence to Calais, includes the great coal trough of those countries. At an early time a line of disturbed surface was produced, having a general east and west direction, traversing a portion of the area of the fossil coal-growths. This disturbance placed all the rocks of that series along its course, either at or near the present surface. Thus we have a strong *a priori* reason for supposing that the course of a band of Coal Measures coincides with, and may some day be reached along, the line of the Valley of the Thames."

Godwin-Austen's arguments in support of this thesis created a stir in scientific circles, but the opposition his theory encountered from certain of his compeers effectually prevented any practical steps being taken to put the issue to the test.

Sir Roderick Murchison, then head of the Geological Survey, was largely responsible for this, as he stoutly maintained, even up to his death, that it was quite hopeless to expect to reach coal in the direction indicated by Godwin-Austen.

1858.

Notwithstanding that Murchison was generally regarded as a Colossus in his particular sphere, Godwin-Austen stuck to his guns. He returned to the charge in another Paper before the Royal Institution in 1858, in which he elaborated his views, and urged that exploratory borings should be put down to determine the existence, or otherwise, of coal beneath the Secondary Rocks in the South of England. In his judgment, the principle on which the existence of a band of Coal Measures might be conjecturally placed along the North-East Counties of England was that "like physical features have a like significance." So that the question as to the probability of coal in this part of England depended on the relation between the physical configuration of the present surface with that of the older surface.

An examination of the problem from this point of view led Godwin-Austen to the following conclusion :—

> "The precise probability of the continuity of the coal band along our South-East area is great, and every fresh point of agreement adds strength to that probability; so that when these amount to three or four, the evidence may be deemed conclusive."

To interrupt my narrative for a moment, I should like to point out that there has been a great deal of ink spilt over the question as to whom should be given the palm for forecasting the existence of that mineral basin now known as the East Kent Coalfield. Having a full knowledge of all the work done in this connection for the last 20 years, I am satisfied that the discovery of this hidden wealth—so far as Godwin-Austen's successors are concerned—was but the outcome of a process of elimination.

Successive borings were put down, particulars of which will be given in due sequence, that merely proved where workable coal was *not*. Even so late as 1903 we find Whitaker, in his evidence before the Royal Commission on Coal Supplies, stating:—

> "The trials should steadily progress from parts where we have certain information, and be carried gradually thence into the benighted region where ignorance reigns."

It is unfortunate for Kent that it took so many successive borings before the benighted region was left behind. Had Godwin-Austen's recommendation of 1858 been acted upon the advent of the coalfield would have been advanced by more than half a century. This is a demonstrable fact.

To return to my text, despite the opposition of so commanding a personality as Murchison, many geologists gave their allegiance to Godwin-Austen; but still nothing of a practical nature was done.

1866.

In this year Joseph Houldsworth, a much lesser light than either Godwin-Austen or Prestwich, whose name, so far as I can gather, is little known in connection with the problem, made a notable contribution to the discussion. His book entitled "On the Extension of English Coalfields beneath the Secondary Formations" was published by "The Mining Journal" to whose columns some twelve years previously he had contributed a series of articles upon which this work was based.

After enumerating and tracing the course of the series of coal basins from Southern Russia through Poland, Germany, Belgium and the north of France, and thence—with a skip over unknown and unexplored territory—to Somersetshire, he says:—

> "And the inference is a fair one, that the Chalk ranges and Coal Measures of France and England, adverted to, are co-extensive."

Further that—

> "The more important coalfields of England, and those we have alluded to in the Continental

border countries of the German Ocean and Straits of Dover, are too commonly viewed as distinctive, and inevitably unconnected, as though the intervening oceanic waters formed a positive barrier between these home and foreign coal deposits, whereas, in a geological sense, certain of them may deducibly well be supposed to constitute one vast subterraneous and subaqueous deposition of the Coal Measure series."

Having marshalled all the then known facts, Houldsworth emphatically states his belief in a buried coalfield linking up Somersetshire with the recently opened-up Pas de Calais, in the following words:—

"The evidences, direct and inferential, now adduced in reference to the existence of the old coal-formation series, beneath the newer depositions of the South of England, are, we imagine, of a character not to be disregarded even by the most sceptical; and in the minds of those who are duly prepared to appreciate geological phenomena, they must, altogether, be considered to present testimony of much weight and importance."

"The Mining Journal" of January 6, 1866, in the course of a preliminary notice of Houldsworth's book, pointed out, as many writers have since done during the long evolutionary period, the national importance attaching to the subject, thus:—

"We are glad to perceive that at length one or two other of our notable geologists are beginning to direct their attention to the matter, and trust ere long to see it thoroughly discussed in all its essential bearings, and the public generally attracted to the practical solution of a problem of such vast consequences to the national welfare."

But nothing happened! Then came the Royal Commission on Coal Supplies, when the subject was, literally, much "in evidence," and the protagonists had ample scope for the display of their personal bias.

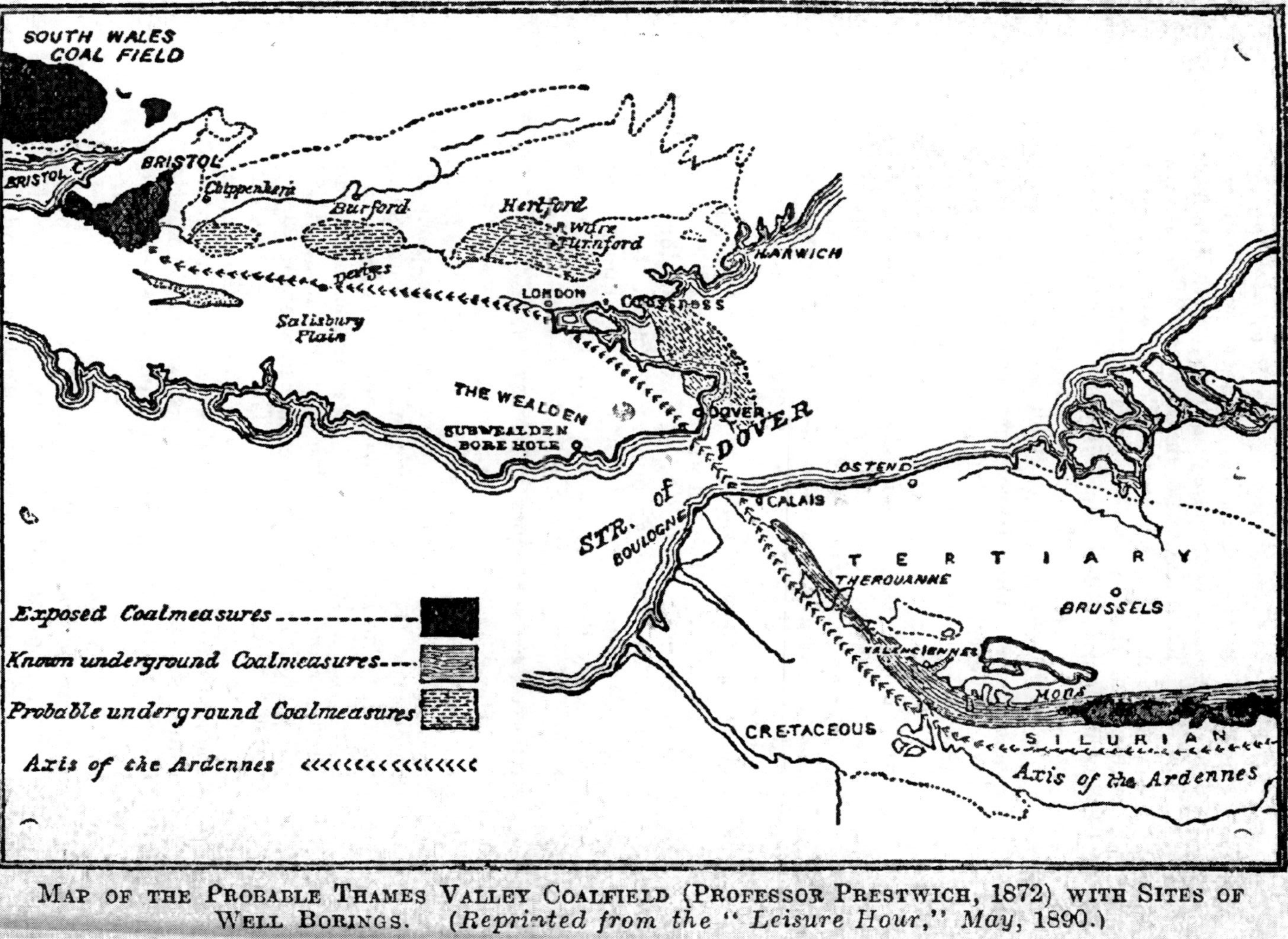

MAP OF THE PROBABLE THAMES VALLEY COALFIELD (PROFESSOR PRESTWICH, 1872) WITH SITES OF WELL BORINGS. (*Reprinted from the "Leisure Hour," May, 1890.*)

1871.

One of the Commissioners was Prestwich, an Ex-President of the Geological Society, who had evidently become thoroughly imbued with Godwin-Austen's views, and who in the year 1871, in the course of a "Report of the Commissioners to inquire into the Several Matters relating to Coal," was responsible for the following further contributions to the momentous question:—

> "Everywhere along that old tract of Carboniferous and Devonian rocks, extending from Westphalia to Bristol and South Wales, there appears to have been an old growth of coal-producing vegetation of great luxuriance and persistence. Everywhere along the immediate flanks of the great axis traversing that old tract we find rich and productive measures. however much they may deteriorate as they recede from that line; and there is no reason to believe but that we should find the same productiveness along the flanks of the same underground ridge, although at a distance of 20 or 30 miles from it a falling-off might possibly be found. On these grounds we believe that the Coal Measures, should they exist under the Secondary Rocks of the South of England, would be found in full force and productiveness."

Further, Prestwich goes on to say that:—

> "The divisions of the Coal Measures into separate basins are subordinate to the great east and west axis, and so far as experience teaches us they are never wide nor long maintained. The length of those portions of the axis included between West Pembrokeshire and Frome and between Calais and Dortmund is 472 miles, and in this distance we find eight separate and distinct coalfields. The combined length of these eight coalfields is about 350 miles, leaving only about 122 miles occupied by intervening tracts of older rocks, so that nearly three quarters of the whole length is occupied by coal strata. We consider that a structure which is constant so far as the axis of disturbance can be traced above ground is, in all probability, continued underground along the range of the same line of disturbance, and we

see no reason why the coal strata should not occupy as great a proportionate length and breadth in the under-ground (South of England) and unknown as in the above-ground and explored area."

In the final Report of the Royal Commission on Coal Supplies (1871) the theories of Godwin-Austen and Prestwich were given due prominence, as is evidenced by the following extract:—

"Reasoning on theoretical considerations connected with the formation of coal in the West of Europe, Mr. Godwin-Austen concluded that Coal Measures might possibly extend beneath the South-Eastern part of England. . . . Upon a general review of the whole subject, Mr. Prestwich adopts, with slight variations, the views of Mr. Godwin-Austen, and is led to the conclusion that there is the highest probability of a large area of productive Coal Measures existing under the Secondary Rocks of the South of England. He shows that the thickness of these overlying rocks is not likely to exceed 1,000 to 1,200 ft. and considers that there is reason to infer that the underground coal basins may have a length of 150 miles, with a breadth of two to eight miles—limits within which are confined the rich and valuable Coal Measures of Belgium. . . . As the existence of coal under the unexplored areas of the South of England is still a question of theory, no attempt has been made to estimate its quantity."

Looking backward one cannot help reflecting on the lack of enterprise exhibited by those landowners who should have been so vitally interested in the solution of this question—to say nothing of the lethargy of the general public. But with us the voice of science has ever fallen on deaf ears, and it has always been more difficult to interest people in matters of Home import than in schemes —wild-cat or otherwise—in remote countries.

The public is an inveterate gambler—it seemingly enjoys providing funds for extracting gold from sea-water; or for recovering golden images said to have been thrown by Aztecs or Incas into the waters of some Central American lake; or for salving gold doubloons from some long sunken Spanish galleon! So, nothing happened!

1872.

The first milestone on the road to practical results was reached consequent upon the visit to Brighton of the British Association in the year 1872, when, at the instigation of Mr. Henry Willett, F.R.S., and in commemoration of the visit of this illustrious body, a committee was formed, under the title of "The Sub-Wealden Committee," with the following declared objects:—

(1) To ascertain, by the experiment of a boring, the actual thickness of the unknown geological strata which exists beneath the Wealden area.

(2) To endeavour to reach Palæozoic Rocks, if such exist within 2,000 ft. of the surface.

(3) Subordinately, to ascertain whether Carboniferous strata (as in Belgium and the Boulonnais district of France) extend across the Channel in this direction.

(4) To notify the subterranean temperature.

It is questionable whether an equally powerful and representative committee has ever before, or since, been formed in this country, having similar objects. And, in view of later events, it is interesting to recall its constitution.

Patrons.

Her Majesty's Lords Commissioners of the Treasury.

The Royal Society.

His Imperial Majesty the Ex-Emperor of the French.

His Grace the Duke of Norfolk, E.M.

His Grace the Duke of Richmond and Gordon, K.G.

His Grace the Duke of Devonshire, K.G., F.R.S.

His Grace the Duke of Argyll, K.T., F.R.S., F.G.S.

The Rt. Hon. the Earl of Ashburnham.

The Rt. Hon. the Earl of Chichester.

The Rt. Hon. the Earl of Ducie, F.R.S., F.G.S.

The Rt. Hon. the Earl of March.

The Rt. Hon. the Earl De La Warr.

The Rt. Hon. Lord Talbot de Malahide, F.R.S., F.G.S.

The Rt. Hon. Viscount Walden, F.R.S.
The Rt. Hon. Lord Leconfield.

Committee.

Professor Ramsay, LL.D., F.R.S., Director General of the Geological Survey of the United Kingdom.

Sir Philip de Malpas Grey-Egerton, Bart., M.P., F.R.S., F.G.S.

Sir John Lubbock, Bart., M.P., D.C.L., F.R.S., F.L.S., F.G.S.

Sir John Hawkshaw, C.E., F.R.S., F.G.S.

F. J. Bramwell, Esq., C.E., F.R.S.

John Evans, Esq., F.R.S., President of the Geological Society

R. Godwin-Austen, Esq., F.R.S., F.G.S., President of Section C, British Association, 1872.

Professor Joseph Prestwich, F.R.S., Ex-President of the Geological Society.

W. Warrington Smyth, Esq., F.R.S., F.G.S., Chief Inspector of Crown Mines.

H. W. Bristow, Esq., F.R.S., F.G.S., Director of the Geological Survey of England and Wales.

Thomas Hawkesley, Esq., F.G.S., Ex-President of the Institution of Civil Engineers.

Professor W. Boyd Dawkins, M.A., F.R.S., F.G.S.

W. Topley, Esq., F.G.S., Geological Survey of Great Britain.

Professor T. Rupert Jones, F.R.S., F.G.S.

H. Woodward, Esq., F.R.S., F.G.S., British Museum.

S. Owens, Esq.

Robert Etheridge, Esq., F.R.S., F.G.S., Palæontologist to the Geological Survey of England and Wales.

Henry Willett, Esq., F.G.S., Hon. Sec.

Subscribers.

Amongst the subscribers the following well-known names appeared:—

British Association for the Advancement of Science.

F. Goldsmid, Esq., M.P.

The Royal Society.

The South-Eastern Railway Company.

The London Treasury.

H. Bessemer, Esq., F.R.S.
Brighton Railway Company.
Charles Darwin, Esq., M.A., F.R.S., F.G.S.
Erasmus Darwin, Esq.
Warren De La Rue, Esq., M.A., D.C.L., F.R.S.
Professor Flower, F.R.S., F.G.S.
Francis Galton, Esq., F.R.S., F.G.S.
Professor T. McKenny Hughes, F.G.S.
Professor E. Hull, F.R.S., F.G.S., Director of the Geological Survey of Ireland.
Samuel Laing, Esq., M.P.
D. Larrach, Esq.
Sir Charles Lyell, Bart.
J. Montefiore, Esq.
Professor G. Rolleston, M.D., F.R.S.
C. W. Siemens, Esq., C.E., F.R.S.
The Rt. Hon. W. H Smith, Esq., M.P., First Lord of the Admiralty.
The Rt. Hon. the Speaker of the House of Commons.
W. Spottiswoode, Esq., M.A., LL.D.
Rear-Admiral T. A. B. Spratt, C.B., F.R.S., F.G.S.
The Baron de Tessier.
John Van Voorst, Esq., F.L.S.
Charles B. Vignoles, Esq., C.E., F.R.S.
Major T. F. Wisden.

The site for the boring was selected by Henry Willett, in conjunction with Boyd-Dawkins, at Netherfield, near Battle, Sussex.

1872—75.

The greater part of the above years was consumed in taking the hole down to a depth of 1,905 ft., when operations were brought to an abrupt close owing to the boring tool becoming jammed in the borehole. The Kimmeridge Clay here was nearly 1,100 ft. thick, and the boring terminated in Oxford Clay.

In view of the great known thickness of the Oolites in this district, it was quite evident that it was hopeless to expect to reach the Palæozoic Rocks, or even Coal Measures, should they exist, at any reasonable depth.

The cost of this boring was little short of £7,000. It is somewhat strange that this site should have been selected, because, according to Boyd-Dawkins, Godwin-Austen always maintained that Netherfield was too far to the south.

Following upon the failure of this boring to determine the vexed question, a Sub-Committee consisting of Godwin-Austen, Ramsay, Prestwich and Evans, was formed to consider what further steps should be taken. With this Sub-Committee the views of Godwin-Austen prevailed, and their report to the Committee concluded thus:—

> "We therefore recommend this trial to be made in the neighbourhood of Dover or the valley of the Stour, a short distance south of Canterbury, where it is probable that the thickness of the chalk and gault will not be found to exceed 700 to 1,000 ft., and where the other secondary strata may be expected to be comparatively thin."

Had any of the members of this Sub-Committee lived to see the results of the numerous borings ultimately put down in the districts thus indicated, they would have been, I think, highly gratified, perhaps even astonished, at the extraordinary accuracy of their figures forecasting the maximum thickness of the chalk and gault. In no single instance was their limit of 1,000 ft. exceeded, and the following actual results of some of the borings nearest to Canterbury, to the south, surely establish their forecast as being almost uncanny in its exactitude:—

Ropersole	Boring	953 ft.	chalk and gault
Fredville	,,	947 ft.	,, ,,
Barfrestone	,,	879 ft.	,, ,,
Bourne	,,	923 ft.	,, ,,
Trapham	,,	877 ft.	,, ,,

Even making every allowance for the depressing effect of the failure of the Sub-Wealden boring, it must seem strange to the present generation, more educated in financial matters, that such a powerful Committee, many individual members of which could easily have furnished all the funds needed, should have failed to raise sufficient money for the further boring so strongly advocated by the Sub-Committee. Yet such was the case.

The events of 1909 prove that, had the Sub-Committee's report been acted upon, this boring must inevitably have ante-dated the Kent Coalfield by more than a quarter of a century.

Each of us may find occasion here for the exercise of his imagination as to what Kent, not to say London, would have been had this golden opportunity for adding to the known mineral wealth of the Kingdom been grasped at this juncture.

In parenthesis I might mention that where that glorified, and surely unique, Committee failed, the Sondage Syndicate (particulars of which will be given in due course) with its modest capital of £5,000, and equally modest and unimportant shareholders, achieved a success of far-reaching importance.

The negative result of the Sub-Wealden Boring, and the failure to secure funds for another experimental bore, apparently sufficed to damp the ardour of that noble array of rank, fashion, finance and science. Such great names and high-sounding titles should, surely, have prompted their aristocratic and learned possessors to prosecute their aims to a successful issue, instead of knuckling under, as they did, on a single failure.

Veritably, the cynic who defined "Committee" as a "Noun of multitude, signifying Many but not signifying Much," had ample justification in this case!

CHAPTER II.

Evolution continued, 1877-1878.—*Pas de Calais Developments. Godwin-Austen's Paper on Meux's Boring in Tottenham Court Road. More Committees.*

"What ado here is to bring you together."
—MERRY WIVES.

1877.

We have now arrived at the year 1877, and while we in England have been forming committee after committee, holding meetings of learned Societies, and almost burying the question of this probable great national asset under a mass of verbiage, our more practical neighbours across the Channel had gone steadily ahead; the output of the Pas de Calais having risen to 4,000,000 tons per annum, and the number of workmen employed to 25,000.

1878..

An important factor bearing upon the question as to whether the Palæozoic floor might be met at a reasonable depth in the South of England, was the boring put down for water at the well-known Meux's Brewery in Tottenham Court Road, London. So much interest was aroused by this that at a meeting of the British Association in Dublin, in the year 1878, Godwin-Austen read a Paper "On the Geological Significance of the Result of the boring at Messrs. Meux's, Tottenham Court Road," in the course of which he stated that:—

"It is now very well known that this undertaking in quest of water, after passing through 653 ft. of chalk, met with insignificant representations of the sands and clays which usually underlie it in the South-East of England, and thence passed into strata, which by characteristic fossils, were identified as Palæozoic, and of Upper Devonian age."

And further that—

> "The importance of determining the exact line of the Palæozoic band was this—that along the whole exposed part of its course, as from the extreme east to near Valenciennes, it had dependent on it and part of it, the band of productive Coal Measures of Westphalia, Belgium and the North of France."

His final conclusion was as follows:—

> "This much has now been ascertained, that in one direction or the other, part of London very nearly overlies a band of Coal Measures."

The result of the Meux's boring evidently confirmed, if, indeed, he needed such confirmation, Godwin-Austen in his previously expressed judgment. The conclusions to be drawn from it pointed so strongly to the importance of further exploration, that efforts were made to interest the landowners of North Kent, bordering upon the Thames Valley, in the proposed work. With a view to giving an impetus to the movement, the Committee of the British Association adopted the following resolution:—

> "That Mr. Godwin-Austen, Professor Prestwich, Mr. Davidson, Mr. Etheridge, Mr. Willett and Mr. Topley be a Committee for the purpose of assisting the Kentish Boring Exploration; that a sum of £100 be placed at their disposal for that purpose."

It should be understood, however, that it was with reference to the solution merely of the scientific point of the underground physical structure that the British Association contributed this £100 towards the "Kentish Boring Researches."

Enter now another Committee, that was destined to carry on the tradition of failure so well established by its predecessors. It was entitled "The Kentish Exploration Committee," and had as its Hon. Secretary Major Fred Beaumont, M.P., who did all that was humanly possible to arouse public interest in this important question as to the existence, or no, of a buried coalfield in the South of England.

While this Committee was seeking funds for carrying out its programme, an alternative scheme

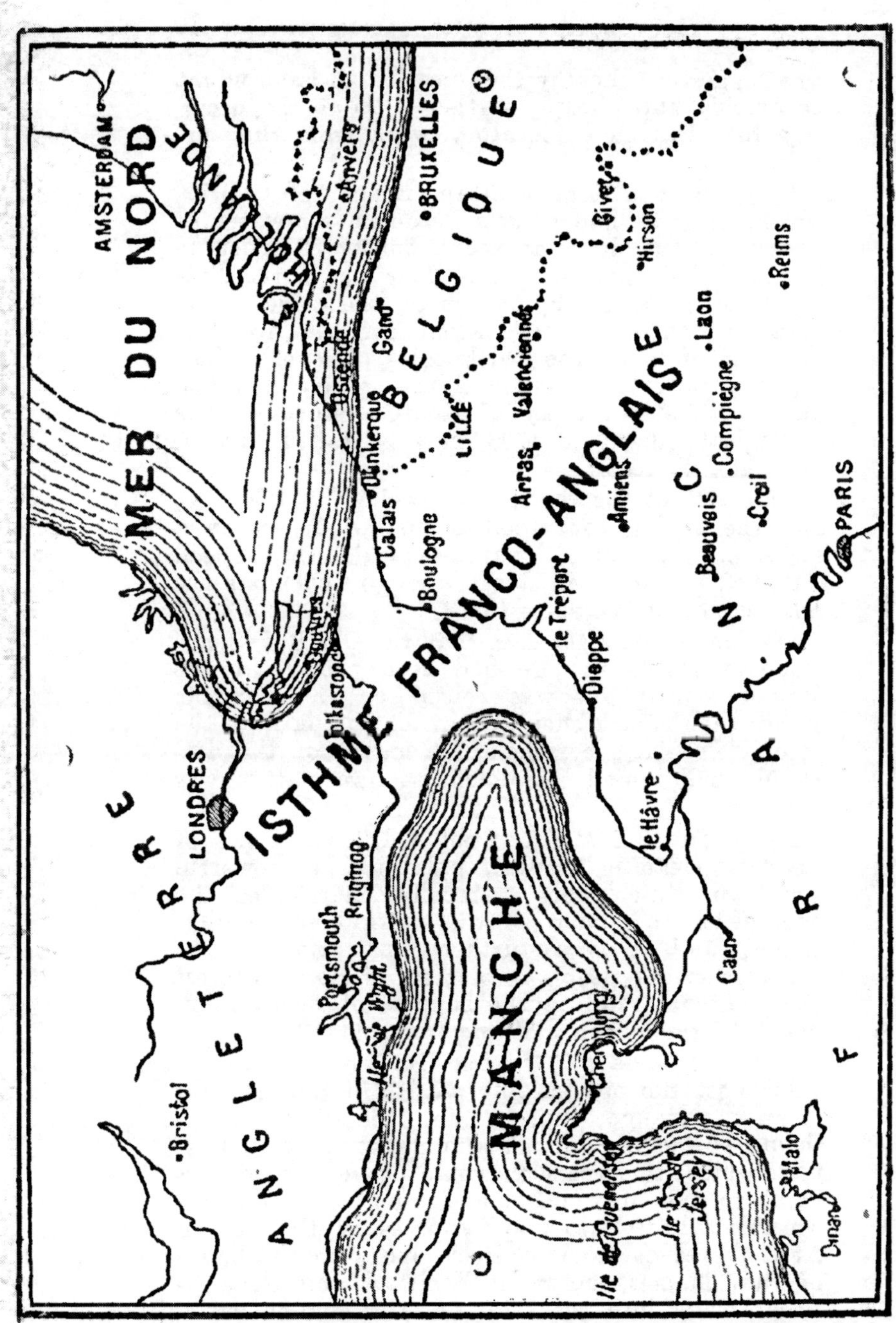
MER DU NORD
AMSTERDAM
BRUXELLES
Anvers
BELGIQUE
Gand
Ostende
Dunkerque
Calais
Boulogne
LILLE
Valenciennes
Arras
Givet
Hirson
Reims
Laon
Compiègne
Creil
Beauvais
Amiens
PARIS
le Tréport
Dieppe
le Hâvre
Caen
Cherbourg
ISTHME FRANCO-ANGLAISE
FRANCE
MANCHE
ANGLETERRE
LONDRES
Portsmouth
Bristol
Jersey
St Malo
Dinan

was suggested whereby the question at issue might be quickly and cheaply settled without the necessity for starting exploratory work from the surface.

In 1878 the Metropolitan Board of Works, which, in 1869, had sunk a bore-hole for water at Crossness, put down a second boring in order to increase their supplies. This hole was bored to a depth of 1,060 ft. by means of the chisel. The data furnished are insufficient for the accurate determination of the thicknesses of the various strata penetrated, but the figures given in Whitaker's "Water Supply of Kent," issued by the Geological Survey in 1908, may be taken as substantially correct.

The base of the Gault was reached at 1,008 ft, and the boring continued a further 52 ft. in a series of shales and quartzose which have been classified as New Red Rocks, though geologists are not very emphatic as to this.

Having in view the fact that the Old Red Sandstone of Devonian age had been proved at the Meux's boring, it was considered in scientific circles that efforts should be made to continue the second Crossness bore-hole, by means of the diamond drill, until some definite information was obtained.

Early in 1878 "The Standard," then one of London's leading dailies, published a powerful article in which were carefully marshalled the arguments in favour of this work being undertaken; and it is a further illustration of the lethargy of our people in matters of Home interest that, notwithstanding the support of such an important Press organ, nothing happened!

"The Standard" opened its appeal thus:—"Amongst the outstanding wealth of this country it seems strange that a few thousand pounds should be lacking for the completion of an enterprise which, if successful, would prove of enormous value to the Metropolis, and would even make a sensible addition to the resources of the nation. At the present moment there exists on the banks of the Thames, between Woolwich and Erith, a deep boring into the strata of the London basin, which only needs to be carried down one or two hundred feet farther in order to throw light on one of the most interesting problems of the day. . . . . Some disappointment has indeed been felt that the rocks which have been reached are of so early a period, and a conclusion has been somewhat hastily formed in some quarters that the intervening beds containing coal will never be found in the south-eastern counties. But the authorities which take a more hopeful view of the case are quite sufficient to counterbalance those whose conclusions are adverse." It was further pointed out that there was a marked uncertainty with regard to the age of the rocks in which the boring terminated, but that the Metropolitan Board of Works being only interested in obtaining a water supply, they were not justified in spending the ratepayers' money in the settlement of a scientific question.

It was obvious that a satisfactory conclusion would greatly enrich the large landowners in the neighbourhood, who might reasonably be expected to furnish the necessary funds. As regards the Metropolis itself, the advantages of a coal supply at its front doors would be not only of great benefit to domestic consumers, but would favourably affect a large number of industrial enterprises, such as the iron shipbuilding industry on the Thames, for instance.

The article proceeds:—"The case as it now stands calls for speedy action. In their second search for water at Crossness the Metropolitan Board have carried their exploration down to a depth exceeding 1,000 ft. The last 50 or 60 ft. consist of a mysterious mass of red clay, or marl, as to the identity of which there is a great amount of uncertainty. Unlike the well at Tottenham Court Road, the Crossness boring exhibits none of the lower green sands. Respecting the abnormal beds at its base, scientific opinion agrees that they belong to a series very far down below the chalk, but whether the stratum appertains to a series below the coalbeds or above them is a point which cannot be considered settled. Mr. Etheridge, who was clear and decided as to the geological results at Messrs. Meux's well, hesitates as to the character of the final stratum at Crossness. The absence of fossils in this latter instance deprives the boring of the data required for its absolute determination. . . . .

"To a nation like England and to a city like London coal is only another name for gold; and we might even say that the presence of gold in Kent would be of far less importance to London than the existence of coal. The theory which looks for the latter result is not a mere dream, nor without facts to support it. The name of Mr. Godwin-Austen has long been known in connection with the hypothesis that coal may be found in the south-east of England, and at the present time a proposal to explore the Kentish strata by means of a deep boring receives the approval of many other geologists of celebrity. The fate of the Wealden boring was unfortunate, though not without results of interest. But in the case now before us the search has been carried to the very threshold of that knowledge which it is so important to obtain. . . . . Surely here is an opportunity which individuals or corporate bodies possessed of wealth might seize with credit to themselves, if not with profit. A less sum than was expended on the Wealden boring might suffice in this case. An appeal to the Government for pecuniary aid would not be desirable. The grant made from the Imperial funds to assist the Sussex exploration was a grievance in the eyes of the northern coalowners."

Apparently there was no idea in the writer's mind that the funds might be raised by means of a public company; nor is there any reason to suppose that they would have been forthcoming through such a medium. The venture, as experience before and since has shown, was too near home to prove attractive to the general public. Had it been a question of proving and developing coal at, shall I say, Spitzbergen? there would, of course, have been no difficulty whatever in finding the money. I quote again :—

"With such a great commercial problem pressing for solution and lying at their very doors, why should not some of the great city companies—those Guilds with princely revenues—unlock their coffers to aid so suitable an enterprise? The members of the coal-ring might raise objection, but the enterprise of the City of London ought not to be baffled by any opposition of that kind. Are there no civic funds available to promote the search for that which London so pre-eminently wants—a ready and cheap supply of coal? If the boon is to be obtained, who will have the honour of showing precisely where it is to be found? *He who strikes coal in the south-east of England will make himself famous for ages to come.*" . (The italics are mine.)

After pointing out that coal was being worked in France almost up to the chalk cliffs near Calais, and that it was but a step from chalk to coal in some parts of the Continent, the article concluded thus :—" But it seems clear that if neither private enterprise nor public liberality will grapple with the question, the probability of getting at Coal Measures in the vicinity of the Metropolis must remain as a mere hypothesis until some lucky chance throws further light upon it."

Major Beaumont wrote to the Editor of "The Standard" with reference to the article from which I have so liberally quoted, intimating his anxiety that it should be widely known that his committee was appealing for subscriptions to carry out a further search for coal in Kent, under the direction of the foremost geologists in England. With regard to the suggestion to deepen the Crossness boring, Major Beaumont stated that this had received careful consideration, but that, having in view the difficulty of continuing with the diamond drill a hole begun with another system, it was decided to start *de novo*. The following extract from his letter, to which I give the emphasis of italics, is, I think, of great historic interest :— "*The exact spot chosen by the Committee for the new Kentish exploration is not yet decided upon, but the Committee have settled that it shall be in the neighbourhood of Dover, or the Valley of the Stour, a short distance from Canterbury.* And certainly the wisdom of this decision can hardly be doubted, as it is in line with the coalfields of Calais and Belgium, and the prolongation of what are believed to be the same measures forming the Somersetshire coalfields."

The Kentish Exploration Committee, of which Major Beaumont, was the Hon. Secretary, issued a circular addressed " To the landowners of North Kent bordering on the Thames Valley," in which an appeal was made for funds for an experimental boring, and in which the great commercial possibilities were enlarged upon. Godwin-Austen's Paper at Dublin was reproduced and other geological data submitted, some of which I rescue from the obscurity of a 40-year-old pamphlet, very few copies of which, I should think, are now extant :—

"Up to an early period of the last century it was generally held by German and Belgian mining authorities that coal was not to be expected to occur beneath chalk. The question at that time was: Does the Condé coalfield cease at the chalk escarpment at Valenciennes, or is it continued onwards beneath? The prevalent opinion was confirmed by certain abortive trial shafts, the southern deflection of the band at that place not having been ascertained at that time. Fortunately for France and its future resources a local proprietor, Le Vicomte Desandroin, was not satisfied with this common opinion, and, acting perseveringly on his convictions he, after many trials and disappointments, was ultimately successful in discovering coal. What guided Desandroin was this, that up to Valenciennes the coal-band and its subordinate beds was traceable at the surface in an east and west course for 250 miles, and he reasonably argued that the deposition of the chalk at a long subsequent period could not have any influence on the Coal Measures should their course be continued westwards. Since Desandroin's day the coal band has been proved for 60 miles from Valenciennes to the Boulonnais.

"The consideration of the continuity of the coal-band beneath the chalk of the north of France in its like steady direction from Westphalia across Belgium, for a distance of 310 miles, is sufficient to warrant the speculation that it is in like manner continued on beneath our own South-Eastern area of Kent, Essex and Middlesex. It is true that some geologists of repute have discountenanced this supposition (see Communication to the Geological Section of the British Association at Nottingham, 1866, by Sir Roderick Murchison, Bart.). Let us see what bearing the discovery at Meux's may have on these objections. It is now ascertained that: First, a Palæozoic rock underlies the very heart of London; secondly, that it is of 'Upper Devonian' age, and thirdly, with a dip of 35 deg. The significance of these points is the subject of Godwin-Austen's Paper, read at the Dublin meeting of the British Association, hereto subjoined. It may suffice to add that the Devonian series, in all its subdivisions, is continuous from Liège to the Boulonnais, both on the south and west of the Coal Measure band."

But no appeals, neither to the cupidity of landowners nor to the civic patriotism of rich corporate bodies, "those Guilds with princely revenues," nor even to the intelligence of the general public, produced the desired result, and the Committee died a natural death. I feel somewhat as though I were assisting at a disinterment in thus removing the shroud that has so long enveloped it.

My press-cuttings book shows that the error of the German and Belgian authorities of the 18th century was perpetuated in the writings of some of the opponents of Kent Coal down to quite recent years. This is scarcely excusable seeing that past theories had been exploded by practical demonstrations; and from quarters to which the public looks for guidance, and from which it derives so much of its education in these days, a little more up-to-date knowledge might reasonably have been expected.

The man in the street has little or no knowledge of the history of the earth's surface, and to him it would probably appear that the existence of the Channel in itself settled the question as to the extension of the Continental Coal Measures into England. That, in the Carboniferous epoch, Great Britain and the Continent were one huge land area, and that the water now separating us from France is of quite recent origin — geologically speaking — are matters beyond his ken, and, I might add, care.

The accompanying map (see page 18), which was published by the well-known French magazine, "Je Sais Tout," in an article on the Channel Tunnel, illustrates this land connection in times prehistoric, though millions of years later than the laying down of coal.

CHAPTER III.

Evolution concluded. 1886-1896. *Channel Tunnel Works near Dover. Coal proved in the Brady Boring. Godwin-Austen's Theories confirmed. The Coal Search Committee. Attitude of the South-Eastern Railway Company. Shaft sinking recommended by Engineers and Geologists. Whitaker in* 1890 *accurately forecasts the extension of the productive Coal Measures. Six years wasted. Colliery to be established at foot of Shakespeare Cliff.*

> "There is a cliff, whose high and bending head
> Looks fearfully in the confined deep."
>
> —KING LEAR.

1886.

Another eight years must be passed over as barren of results—barren even of endeavour—which brings us to the year 1886, when, more by accident than design, wheels are set in motion which were destined to carry the issue over many a rutty road to the goal of success. I refer to the Brady Boring.

It is an incontrovertible fact, in my opinion, that the Kent Coalfield of to-day owes its existence primarily to the workings of chance.

Had it not been for the works at the foot of Shakespeare Cliff, Dover, in connection with the proposed Channel Tunnel, who can say when, if ever, Godwin-Austen's prophecies would have been realised? Had the Channel Tunnel work been allowed to proceed there would have been no Brady Boring, which owes its inception merely to the chance fact that in 1882 the Government, acting on the advice of military big-wigs, vetoed the Tunnel scheme. Plant and labour were thus rendered idle, which Sir Edward Watkin, chairman of both the South-Eastern Railway Company and the Channel Tunnel Company, wished to keep available in the expectation that Parliament would remove the veto.

Mr. Francis Brady, engineer to the same two Companies, thereupon advanced the suggestion that here was a ready-made opportunity for putting the theories of Godwin-Austen in 1858, and those of Prestwich in 1873, to the test. There is, unfortunately, no evidence to prove to what extent Brady's views commended themselves to Sir Edward Watkin; one thing only is certain—that the bacillus of procrastination, so universally present in all matters relating to the Coal-in-Kent problem, delayed any practical steps being taken for nearly four years.

Boyd Dawkins, who strongly resents any claim for precedence on behalf of Mr. Brady respecting the inception of the boring which bears his name, in a Paper before the Manchester Geological Society, February 9, 1897, said:—

> "The suggestion (of Mr. Brady) was still-born, was not acted upon, and as I have shown above had no share in the 'institution of the enterprise,' the claim may safely be left without further comment to the judgment of those who are interested in the discovery."

But, surely, still-born or very much alive, the facts as to paternity remain the same!

Apparently Whitaker was the next to suggest the Dover site. In his evidence before the Royal Commission on Coal Supplies (see Part X. Minutes of Evidence, page 28) Boyd Dawkins stated that "Whitaker also pointed out in 1885 that Dover was a good place for a further trial."

Although Whitaker's suggestion was made before such an eminent scientific body as the Geological Society of London, and must therefore have obtained wide publicity, no material results followed. It was Boyd Dawkins, however, who undoubtedly gave the final impetus to Sir Edward Watkin, and who was responsible for galvanising into life Brady's still-born offspring. I will let him tell the story himself, quoting from his article, entitled "The Discovery of Coal near Dover" in "The Contemporary Review," April, 1890:—

> "In 1886 I presented a Report to Sir Edward Watkin, Chairman of the South-Eastern Railway, and the Channel Tunnel Company, on the general question, and recommended on both

scientific and commercial grounds that a boring should be made in South-East Kent, in the neighbourhood of Dover, and that the Channel Tunnel works, now so unfortunately suspended, offered the best site for a trial."

The only other instance that has come under my personal notice of so long a delay in putting the opinion of experts to the practical test, was that of the Murchison Goldfield in Western Australia. In 1851 the then Surveyor General of that Colony, whose name is perpetuated in that of Lake "Austin," on his return from what in those days was an adventurous trip inland, made the following remarkable statement in the course of his official report—I quote from memory:—

> "We have in this remote, and hitherto imprudently neglected, portion of our territory what is probably destined to prove one of the richest goldfields in the world."

Nearly forty years had to elapse before it was possible to witness, as I did, an army of men equipped only with the most rough and ready tools, winning gold from the surface sands. Gold that had lain "hitherto imprudently neglected," just waiting to be picked up!

1890.

Four years elapsed before the Brady Boring proved the existence of Coal Measures, to be followed by several seams of coal of workable thickness This was the first of a long series of borings in Kent, it was the first to achieve success and to prove that the nearly half-century old theories of Godwin-Austen had been based on a sure foundation, that the possibilities which he had forecasted, and which the commercial community had so signally failed to appreciate, were established beyond question. As such it demands attention in some detail.

The work commenced in the Grey Chalk, at the foot of Shakespeare Cliff, starting at the bottom of a shaft which had been sunk for convenience in handling the rods, to a depth of 44 ft.

It will save confusion later if I mention here that some authorities whom I shall have occasion to quote, take their figures as to depths from the

"THE KENT COAL HOLE."

Finding coal in the Channel Tunnel Works. Rush of S.F.R. shareholders to Shakespeare Cliff.

" . . . . half way down
Hangs one that gathers samphire, dreadful trade!"—KING LEAR.

bottom of this shaft, some reckon from the surface, and others as from O.D. which at this spot is 50 ft.

The actual depth from the surface at which the Coal Measures were struck is 1,157 ft., to which point the hole had been put down with the chisel, but thereafter the diamond drill was used in order that cores might be obtained.

At 1,180 ft. from the surface what is generally referred to as the 2 ft. 6 in. seam was met with; it is in two sections of 1 ft. 3 in. each, with a parting of 1 ft. From thence to the bottom of the bore-hole at 2,330 ft., six seams of 2 ft. and over, aggregating 15 ft. 6 in. of coal, were proved; the most substantial one being 4ft. in thickness, at a depth of 2,221 ft.

Section of Dover Coal Boring.

	Surface of Ground.	Depth below. H.W.M. Feet.	Thickness. Feet.
1,113 *feet of Secondary Rocks to Coal Measures.*	UPPER CRETACEOUS (259 ft.)—		
	Lower Grey Chalk and Chalk Marl.	H.W.M.	130
	Glauconitic Marl	130	8
	Gault	138	121
	LOWER CRETACEOUS, NEOCOMIAN, OR LOWER GREENSAND (246 ft.)		
	Folkestone Beds	259	64
	Sandgate Beds	323	77
	Hythe Beds	400	87
	Atherfield Clay	487	18
	OOLITIC (608 ft.)—		
	Portlandian Oolitic	506	32
	Kimmeridgian	537	73
	Corrallian	610	159
	Oxfordian, Cullovian	769	188
	Bathonian	957	156
	COAL MEASURES	1,113	—

COAL MEASURES.

DEPTH BELOW HIGH WATER MARK	DESCRIPTION.

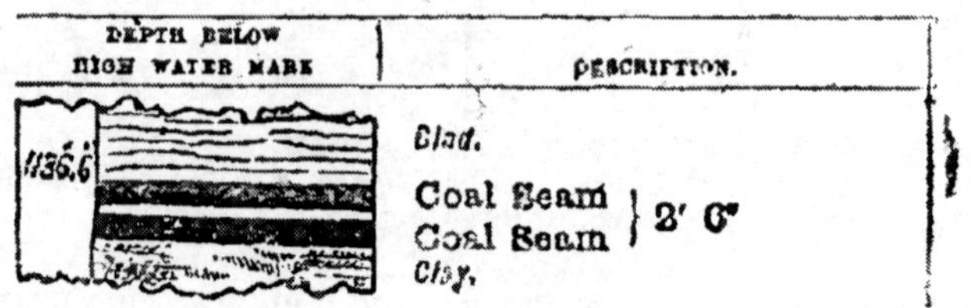

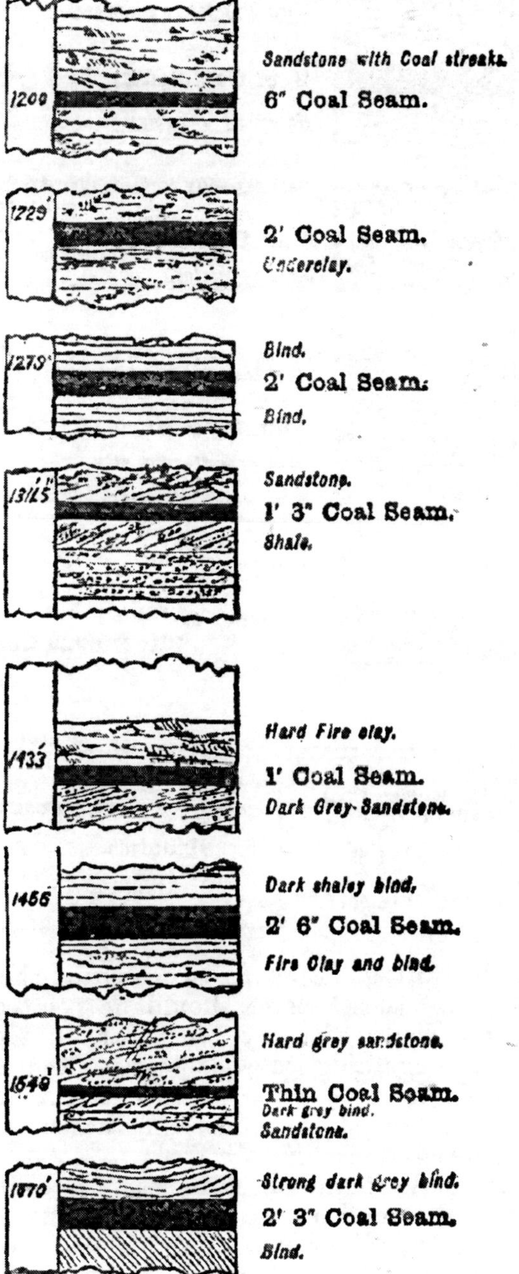
1200
Sandstone with Coal streaks.
6" Coal Seam.
1229'
2' Coal Seam.
Underclay.
1279'
Bind.
2' Coal Seam.
Bind.
1311' 5"
Sandstone.
1' 3" Coal Seam.
Shale.
1433'
Hard Fire clay.
1' Coal Seam.
Dark Grey Sandstone.
1456'
Dark shaley bind.
2' 6" Coal Seam.
Fire Clay and bind.
1549'
Hard grey sandstone.
Thin Coal Seam.
Dark grey bind.
Sandstone.
1570'
Strong dark grey bind.
2' 3" Coal Seam.
Bind.

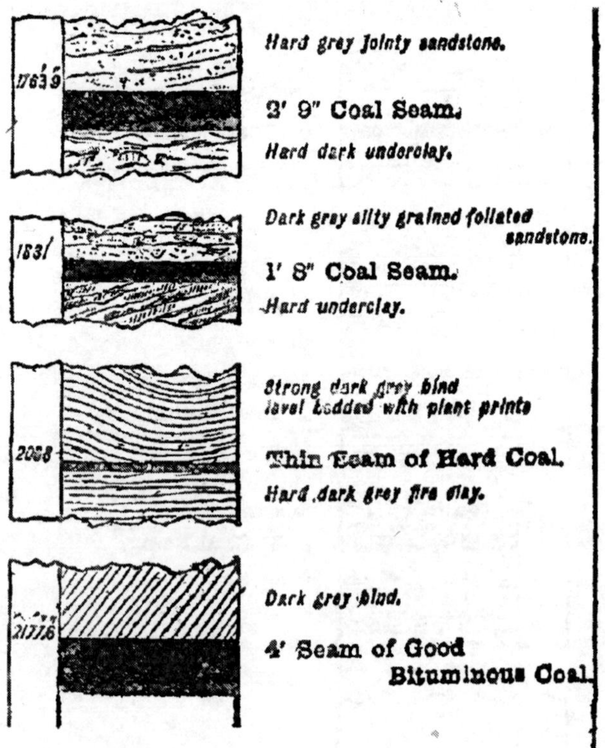

2 ft. 6 in. seam at 1,456 ft, Clear Bright Navigation Coal Composition.		Composition of 37 Samples of Welsh Coal.	
Carbon ..	83.80	Carbon	83.78
Hydrogen ..	4.65	Hydrogen ..	4.79
Oxygen	3.23	Oxygen	4.75
Heating Power..	14.867	Heating Power ..	14.858

The important question as to which of the Coal Measure series these seams should be related was exhaustively dealt with by Monsieur R. Zeiller, Lecturer on Vegetable Palæontology to the School of Mines, Paris, in a Paper before the Academie des Sciences, 1890, from which I make the following excerpts:—

"The coal found in the seams contains, according to analyses made by Monsieur Victor Watteyne, Ingenieur Principal des Mines of Belgium, 25 per cent. of volatile matters, and partly resembles in composition the *charbon gras* of the Pas de Calais, and partly those of Wales. In spite of the apparent correspondence in structure between some of the sandstones met with in the boring and those of the lowest region of the Coal Measures of Belgium, Monsieur Watteyne rejects the idea that the Dover coals belong to the base of the formation, on account of their high quantity of volatile matters, and Mr. Brady for his part sees in the system traversed by the boring the equivalent of all or most of the coals belonging to the upper division of the Somerset basin; that is to say, the beds of Farrington and Radstock. As, however, the quality of a coal in volatile matters does not constitute an absolute criterion for the determination of the level these opinions could not, without more ample information, be accepted except with reserve; but it was permitted to hope that amongst the vegetable imprints collected in the course of the boring operations specimens would be met with susceptible of furnishing more precise indications on this important question.''

After dealing in detail with the specimen cores sent to him for his examination, Monsieur Zeiller concludes his report thus:—

" It may therefore be concluded that, as presumed by Mr. Brady, the beds traversed by this boring rightly belong to the upper region of the Middle Coal Measures, and, if one may state it more precisely, that they cannot be either more recent than the beds of Radstock in Somerset or more ancient than the deepest beds of the upper zone (*charbon gras et flénus*) of the Pas de Calais.''

The Brady Boring also penetrated some beds of iron ore of a total thickness of 12 ft., at a depth of 600 ft.; but they do not seem to have received much attention until they had been further disclosed in the shafts at a later date. Even then their real value was not appreciated, though the great importance of the discovery was to become fully recognised in the future, as will be shown later in this narrative.

The announcement of the first seam of Kent Coal caused quite a stir in City circles, and the prospect of developing a new coalfield, so near to London, appealed to the imagination of the city magnates; to the extent, at any rate, of prompting either the then Lord Mayor, Sir Henry Isaacs, or some such worthy, to convene a meeting of notables for the purpose of considering how best the discovery might be turned to account. I can find no published record of this meeting, but from one who was present I learn that much talking took place, and something was going to be done.

Boyd-Dawkins, whose name will constantly recur in the course of my narrative, emphasised the importance attaching to the Brady Boring, thus:—

> "The discovery of coal near Dover is one of those events which mark a new era in our industrial development, and which promises in the not very remote future to effect the same changes in South-Eastern England as those which have been caused by similar discoveries in France and Belgium in the eighteenth and nineteenth centuries. The story of the discovery is full of interest, not merely from the commercial point of view. It is the story of a scientific idea originated many years ago, taking root in the minds of geologists, developed into theory, and ultimately verified by facts. It offers a striking example of the relation of faith to works in the scientific world. The faith has been proved by experiment to be true, and the works necessary for the proof would not have been carried out without the faith. The idea, which when first started was in advance of the evidence, has been the centre round which the facts have clustered, until, from the standpoint of to-day, it appears almost as the result of a strict and rigid induction, without any trace of 'scientific imagination, or *à priori* argument."

But still nothing happened, save the formation of yet another Committee which, like its predecessors, was composed of names of high standing in various sections of the scientific community, headed by certain Peers of the Realm.

I use the word "names" advisedly in describing the constituents of this committee, for had it been composed of live men something would surely have resulted from their association. The fact remains, however, that once more nothing happened!

The circumstances were these: -Mr. J. T. Day, F.G.S. had for some time been pondering upon the question, "Is there Coal under the London Basin?" and it seemed to him that the answer might be forthcoming if the trend of the Coal Measures at Dover was satisfactorily determined. He accordingly formed the "Coal Search Committee," at the head of which appeared the names of the Right Hon. the Earl Amherst and the Right Hon. the Earl of Winchelsea and Nottingham.

A circular was issued stating that the Committee had been formed "for the purpose of investigating the distribution of the Coal Measures in the South-East of England by means of borings, sinkings, or other devices which may become available, and a public appeal is now made in order to obtain the necessary funds to carry out these operations. With a view, therefore, to a systematic investigation of the matter, it is proposed to raise a fund of 2,000 guineas to meet the cost. Promises of support should be sent to J. T. D., 12, Albert Square, Stepney, London, E."

Several names which had figured in connection with the Sub-Wealden and Kent Exploration Committees appeared on this "Coal Search Committee," and Professors Prestwich and Judd were said to approve of its programme.

It is scarcely necessary for me to say that promises of support were not forthcoming to the required extent, and the whole thing fizzled out. I am tempted to wonder under what conditions the obsequies of these deceased committees are conducted. A crematorium suggests itself as being the most appropriate means of disposing of such defunct bodies.

In any event, 2,000 guineas would have been totally inadequate for the investigation foreshadowed in the Committee's circular. Not one of the borings since made in East Kent has been put down for so small a sum, while the total expenditure on "systematic investigation" exceeds Mr. J. T. Day's suggested amount by about £98,000!

Mr. H. Hall, in the course of his presidential address to the Manchester Geological Society in 1889, said:—

"With regard to the probability of coal under the Cretaceous Rocks in the South of England, it seems hardly possible to conceive that the commercial enterprise of Englishmen could have failed to discover it long ago if it had been in existence."

I have shown that, so far as the search for "hidden treasure" in South-East England was concerned, the commercial enterprise of Englishmen for a long stretch of years had been conspicuout by its absence. Nevertheless, there was one man who did not share the pessimistic conclusions to which this fact had brought Mr. Hall, and it is refreshing to feel the spirit of confident optimism that inspired Whitaker in 1890 when he wrote:—

"As a geologist I must decline to be in any way bound by the lamentable failure, or, one may say, heartrending absence, of commercial enterprise amongst my fellow-Englishmen. I have elsewhere given a lengthy account of what has been published on the subject of the old underground rocks of the London Basin, and, in summing up the general conclusions that, to my mind, may fairly be drawn as to the possible occurrence of Coal Measures, have ventured to say '*it seems to me that the day will come when coal will be worked in the South-East of England.*"

In stirring up the waters of oblivion under which so much of the past history of this coalfield has lain submerged, certain facts come to the surface which needs must be presented, however much they may conflict with the claims put forward by certain individuals whose names have figured largely in the literature of the subject. Such, for instance, as the following recommendation made by Whitaker in 1890 after the first coal seams had been struck in the Brady Boring:—

"Another likely site, for the continuation of the work already done, is St. Margarets, north-eastward of Dover, where a boring made for the former Channel Tunnel Company has reached the gault, and where probably less of the Jurassic Rocks would be found than at the Dover Boring, though the two are not five miles apart."

In the course of my narrative it will be seen that had this advice been acted upon a large expenditure upon many abortive borings, for which other eminent geologists were responsible would have

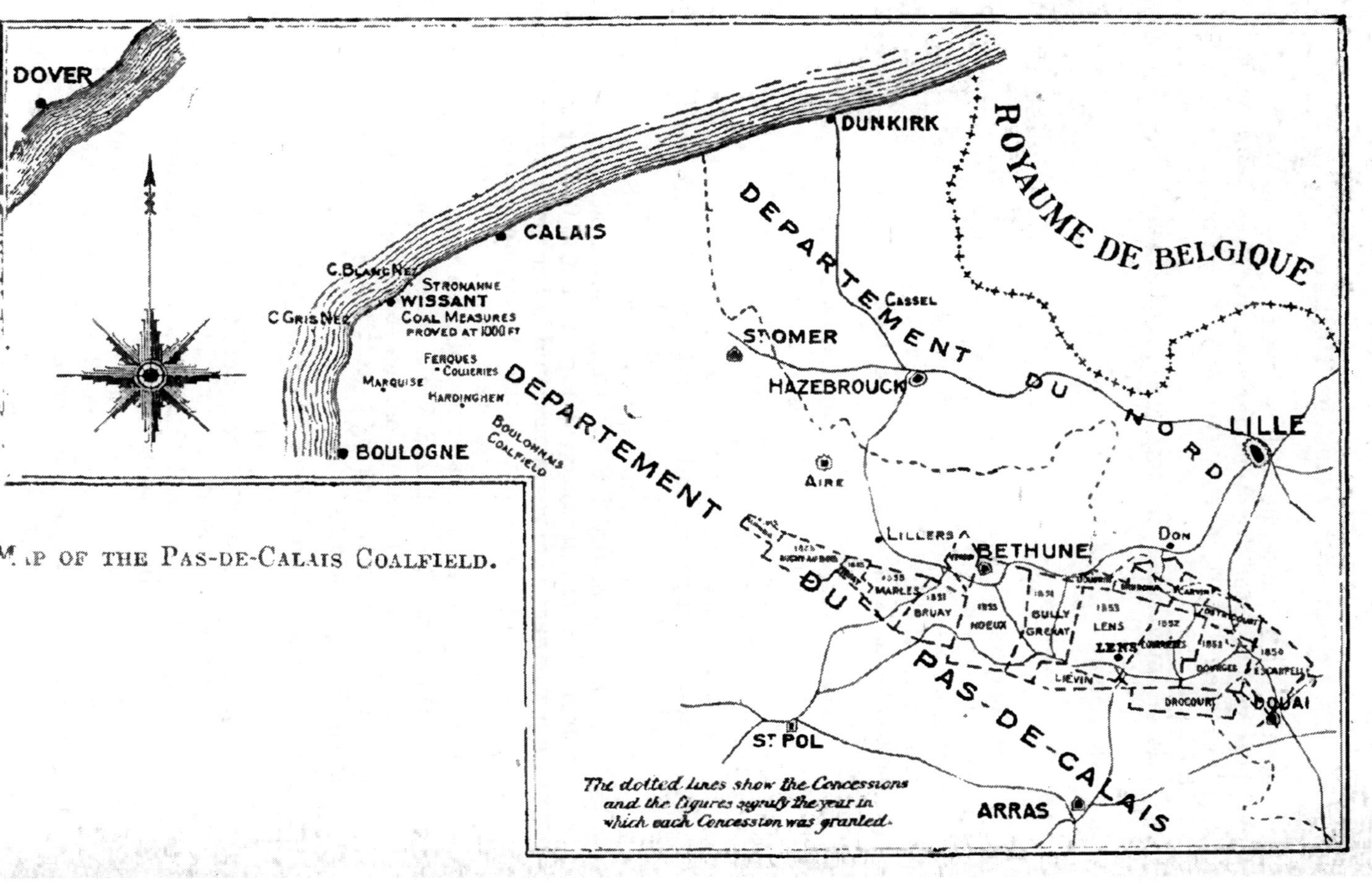

MAP OF THE PAS-DE-CALAIS COALFIELD.

been avoided, and the rich seams that lie in the locality indicated by Whitaker would have been discovered nearly twenty years sooner than was the case.

It is interesting to note, *en passant*, that the Pas de Calais output about this time amounted to approximately 10,000,000 tons per annum.

1891.

The Annual Meeting of the South-Eastern Railway Company was held this year on July 23, when the chairman, Sir Edward Watkin, speaking before the lowest seam of 4 ft. in thickness had been proved in the Brady Boring, made the following reference to Kent coal—I quote from a Press report:—

> "At a cost of some £10,000 they had already come upon some good seams and were boring to a lower depth. The discovery of a great coal seam in the South of England would mean a commercial revolution and be in favour of the South-Eastern Company, and he thought the shareholders ought to thank him and the others who advanced the money for this work without charging them a penny for it. They were now contemplating the sinking, at a cost of £30,000, of a permanent shaft, which would settle once for all the question of the South of England Coalfields. Towards this he was prepared to subscribe £1,000 if the balance could be raised."

At the time Sir Edward Watkin was speaking thus he had in his possession the following report upon the question of sinking to test the coal proved in the Brady Boring:—

> "*Coal at Channel Works, Dover.*
>
> "July 1, 1891.
>
> "Having carefully considered the general question and examined the sections, and the several samples of coal that have been obtained, we are of opinion that the evidence in favour of workable coal is sufficient to justify a trial shaft being put down immediately on the site of or near to the present boring.
>
> "(Signed) W. BOYD DAWKINS.
> C. TYLDEN WRIGHT.
> FRAS. BRADY."

The desirability of sinking a shaft had also been urged by Whitaker (see "Journal of the Society of Arts," April 25, 1890), whose voice also was that of one crying in the wilderness, but whose words are none the less worth recalling, thus:—

"It is always open to any disciple of St. Thomas to cast a doubt on what has been brought up from a bore-hole, on the ground that it may have been dropped down beforehand. Probably many of you know the story of a trial boring from which coal was brought up one day, but only to be followed by bread and cheese the next day; a succession quite out of geologic sequence of formations, and not to be explained by any disturbance of the beds, even an over-thrust fault. Now, with a shaft, if anyone doubts the occurrence of coal, he can be taken down to see for himself, with the further advantage that, if his doubts still last, he can be left down for reflection. . . . Without wishing to touch on a subject so provocative of discussion as the Channel Tunnel is, I cannot but say that it would be useful if Sir E. Watkin's well-known weakness for tunnelling could be turned, for a time at least, from a horizontal to a vertical direction, so that a shaft might be at once sunk at Dover."

Still nothing happened!

1896.

It was not until the year 1896 that any practical steps were taken to turn the momentous discoveries at Shakespeare Cliff to commercial account.

Readers may well wonder, and South-Eastern Railway Company shareholders may more than wonder, at the apathy with which the proving of workable coal was treated by those whose duty it surely was to assist, in so far as it lay in their power, in the work of development.

It was idle to expect anything material to develop from Sir Edward Watkin's offer at the South-Eastern Railway shareholders' meeting in 1891, unless some concrete action followed. Surely, if steps had been taken to form a company under the *ægis* of their chairman, such a large and wealthy body could and would, have subscribed the required capital. At a much later date, when the apathetic attitude of the directors was questioned, the explanation was given that the Railway Company was precluded from using its funds for any such purpose. Still, one would have thought that amongst the shareholders themselves there would have been some enterprising spirits to have taken the matter in hand.

It seems to be that their attitude was identical with that of the yokel at his first visit to the Zoo, who, on being brought face to face with the hippopotamus, could only gape and exclaim, "I don't believe it!"

However, be the explanation what it may, the fact remains that no move was made, and for nearly six years nothing was done towards following up the results of the Brady Boring. The comparison between our inertia and the energy displayed by the French in precisely similar circumstances, is not flattering to our *amour propre*, especially as we have always prided ourselves upon being a pre-eminently practical nation.

1826—1896.

We have thus taken a bird's-eye view of the 70 years between Buckland and Conybeare's recognition of the physical similarity of the Somersetshire coals with those of the Department du Nord, and the formation of a company to exploit an intermediate and newly-discovered Coalfield.

The development of this field has been hampered by many retarding influences—physical, financial and personal—what little of its history is known has reached the public in more or less garbled versions, controversially, from biassed sources. Hence it is my aim, though my record must necessarily be condensed, to give a "round unvarnish'd tale," in which I shall "nothing extenuate, nor set down aught in malice," of the 22 years that have elapsed since the diamond-studded tool of the borer gave place to the more prosaic pick and shovel of the sinker.

Part II.—Development.

CHAPTER IV.

Kent Coalfields Syndicate, Limited. Colliery and General Contract Company, Limited. Mid-Kent Coal Syndicate, Limited. Kent Coal Finance and Development Company, Limited. Kent Coal Exploration Company, Limited.

"We were the first that ever burst into that silent sea."
—COLERIDGE.

The first company formed for the purpose of establishing a working colliery was the

KENT COALFIELDS SYNDICATE, LTD.

which was registered in March, 1896, with a capital of £200,000 in shares of £1 each. The list of directors comprised the following:—G. P. Simpson, Esq., F.R.G.S. (managing director), F. Brady, Esq., M.Inst.C.E., P. S. M. Arbuthnot, Esq., R. Berens, Esq., Sir H. B. Robertson, G. F. Fry, Esq., F. Pitts, Esq.

This Syndicate was formed to take over the rights of the Channel Tunnel Company, Limited, in the Shakespeare Cliff works, including the Brady Boring, together with certain freeholds and mineral options. There was no public issue of capital, the bulk of which was raised, from time to time, as the result of Stock Exchange operations. When troubles arose, and shares fell, some brokers who ran speculative accounts undoubtedly got their fingers burnt; and the Syndicate's name was not as lavender in the purlieus of Throgmorton Street. On the other hand, the tremendous traffic in these shares must have yielded a very large amount in commissions to the market as a whole. I have seen some of the accounts! Just picture the trail of golden guineas that followed in the wake of dealings which in one period of only seven months approximated to £2,000,000! The Syndicate may have had a meteoric career, but the friction of its passage through the atmosphere of the Stock Exchange certainly engendered a golden shower in that quarter, at any rate.

Before reaching its latest re-incarnation in the form of the Channel Steel Company, Limited, of to-day, the Syndicate underwent several metamorphoses; these, within reasonable limits, I propose to follow in some detail. It is a curious anomaly that the site of the first boring to verify Godwin-Austen's much-discussed theory of *coal* deposits, should, by the whirligig of time, have become transformed into a mine for working the *iron* deposits that did not enter into his calculations.

The first of a long series of companies formed by Mr. Arthur Burr for the exploitation of coal in Kent, the misfortunes which dogged the career, not only of the Syndicate in question but of many of its successors, created such a prejudice against the entire coalfield that it is particularly desirable to set out the salient facts concerning all these companies.

The Kent coalfield warrants neither the fantastic claims put forward by optimists, who cannot or will not look facts in the face, nor the ill-judged and generally misinformed criticisms that have been so liberally directed against it. It is a genuine commercial proposition, and had the field been located in the neighbourhood of Timbuctoo or the coast of the Spanish Main instead of at their front doors, so to speak, it would not have been so neglected by our industrial magnates.

That the operations of the Kent Coalfields Syndicate were closely associated with, and to a large extent dependent upon, Stock Exchange dealings in its shares, the impartial historian has to maintain. Those responsible for the financial side of the undertaking must accept, therefore, their just proportion of the blame for the undoubtedly heavy losses sustained by the shareholders.

On the other hand, I see no reason why the Syndicate's scientific advisers should not likewise carry their share of the responsibility. No one—save in exceptional circumstances which do not arise in this connection—dreams of impugning the good faith of professional men who, by their mistaken calculations, cause investors to lose their money. When, however, the time comes for paying the piper, they are not even asked to join in the reckoning; it is only those responsible for the finances who have to stand the racket!

I have stated, and I maintain, that the Syndicate never was properly financed; but even so it would, I believe, have won through, had the experts, upon whom it relied, been less optimistic.

After completing the boring Mr. Brady consulted Mr. McMurtrie, of the Radstock Collieries, Mr. P. S. Reid, of Radstock, Mr. Emerson Bainbridge, M.P., and Monsieur Victor Watteyne, chief engineer of the Mons Colliery. These gentlemen's reports were published by Mr. Brady; their estimates for establishing a colliery with one shaft equipped for coal-winding ranged from £36,000 to £50,000, the latter sum being stated to include "working capital to go on with afterwards."

There has been spent on the works to date just on £1,000,000! And no working colliery has been established!

Water was the "rock" upon which the undertaking was wrecked—"honest water," which, according to Shakespeare, "ne'er left man i' the mire"! Nevertheless, in 1896, Messrs. F. Brady, M.Inst.C.E., G. P. Simpson, F.R.G.S., and Nath. R. Griffith, F.G.S., Assoc. R.S.M., who were respectively director, managing director, and consulting engineer of the Syndicate, in a Paper entitled "The Kent Coalfield," before the North of England Institute of Mining Engineers, dealing with the Brady boring, stated that:—

> "The secondary strata passed through before reaching the Coal Measures, gave no indications of the presence of water in sufficient volume to cause *serious difficulties* in sinking. (The italics are mine.) The impermeable Grey Chalk and the Gault below it appear to shut out the sea effectually from the lower beds; the clays as a rule were found to be dry, and the sands solid. The worst ground was met with at a short distance below the Wealden Beds."

I confess to a sense of amazement that immunity from water difficulties should have been so confidently taken for granted, even to the extent of undertaking the sinking without providing any pumping appliances whatever; especially when it was known to everyone concerned that the Lower Greensands outcropped only a short distance from the Pits.

No. 1 Pit (the Brady) was commenced in June, 1896, and was down to 366 ft. in the following October, when, on the 16th of that month, there was a sudden inrush of water, which brought sinking operations to a standstill. Notwithstanding this experience, No. 2 Pit (the Simpson) was started, also without pumps, in November, 1896, and had reached approximately the same depth (303 ft.) by March, 1897.

History repeated itself; there was another inrush of water, which rose so rapidly in the shaft that, despite the utmost efforts of those on the surface, only six out of the fourteen men who were working in the pit-bottom, were rescued.

Mr. John Gerrard, then H.M. Inspector of Mines, made some justifiably scathing comments on this second occurrence, stating in his Report that:—

> "Undoubtedly these lives might have been saved, and the progress of the work greatly developed, had it been foreseen that pumping appliances would be required. Further, it would have been to the distinct advantage of all concerned had some of the energy which had been displayed in Stock Exchange developments been devoted to the establishment of fitting plant, after the need for the same was so clearly demonstrated in October, 1896."

Mr. Whitaker, in his "Water Supply of Kent" (1908), also comments on this lack of pumps:—

> "It is strange (he says) that when dealing with such a formation as the Lower Greensand, no pump had been provided, but apparently the opinion of a geologist had not been taken, or, at all events, not been acted upon."

There is no gainsaying the strangeness of the lack of pumping plant, but there was no lack of expert opinion, given *and* taken! Putting aside the regrettable loss of life, there is a considerable amount of scientific interest attaching to the second influx of water.

In the course of the coroner's inquiry the evidence pointed to the Brady Borehole as being the primary cause of the disaster. The jury adopted the view that the inrush of water came, in the first instance, from the borehole, and that thereupon the water from the Brady Pit sought its level by entering the Simpson Pit—the bottom of which it burst up—rising rapidly 80 ft. in the shaft. The manager stated in evidence that the water coming up the borehole was so charged with firedamp that it lighted repeatedly upon the flame of a candle being brought near to it. In his opinion the water came from a depth of at least 1,200 ft.

Mr. John Gerrard, in his report of 1898, stated that:—

"Explorations have proved, since the accident, that the water came from two sources, one supply being cold, fresh water, having a temperature of 58 deg. Fah. This is probably Lower Greensand water. The other source was from the borehole. This has a temperature of 80 deg. Fah."

So that, whilst the high temperature of the borehole water presupposes that it came from a considerable depth, its salt content, which analysis shows to be no less than 450 grains (of chlorine as chlorides) to the gallon, would suggest some communication with the sea.

The presence of firedamp, in conjunction with the high temperature and extreme saltness of the water in question, has presented a problem which has never been satisfactorily explained.

Before leaving this question I might, however, quote the opinion of the eminent French engineer, Monsieur A. Fonville, who reported on the coalfield generally in 1912. He says:—

"The presence of water is due to the water level of the Greensands, which crop out under the sea, near the site chosen for the works. This porous bed of Greensands is, as we have shown, an open mouth under the sea. That is why, when passed through in pits situated so near the absorption area, it is almost impossible to avoid violent inrushes of water. The failure at Dover is due to imprudence in sinking on the foreshore at the very foot of the Cliff, in the neighbourhood of this water-bearing bed."

Incidentally I might state here that the sinking was being done by the

Colliery & General Contract Company, Limited,
in which, however, the public was never materially interested. This Company was co-existent with, and auxiliary to, the Kent Coalfields Syndicate, the two of them being very much interlocked, and their financing of a decidedly co-operative character—rather more than less dependent upon the Stock Exchange demand for the Syndicate's shares.

1897.

The immediate difficulties caused by the two inrushes of water already described having been surmounted, sinking was resumed; but, probably because the directors realised by now that very much larger funds would be needed to take the Pits into the coal, a little financial jugglery was resorted to. The Syndicate's shares had attained a premium that it was found difficult to maintain. Anyone having Stock Exchange experience will appreciate that it requires a long purse to hold 200,000 £1 shares at £6, and over, with no tangible results in sight to justify the high figure.

The obvious solution was to split the shares and capitalise the premium; hence a reconstruction was decided upon. The new Company was to take over the sinking, and the Colliery & General Contract Company was to be liquidated.

Before, however, the Kent Coalfields Syndicate gave up the ghost, and while its shares still stood at a high premium (from £4 to £5), other companies were launched in the same interest. Thus in March, 1897, there was registered an unimportant Syndicate entitled

The Mid-Kent Coal Syndicate, Limited.

This was quite small fry, formed for the specific object of putting down a boring at Penshurst, on the estate of Lord de L'Isle and Dudley, at a site selected by Prof. Boyd Dawkins. No public interest attaches to its proceedings. The borehole did nothing more than prove a negative, and the work was abandoned when it became evident that there was no possibility of reaching the Coal Measures at any reasonable depth, if at all. The strata passed through were: Wealden Purbeck beds, 1,114 ft.;

Portlandian, 116 ft.; Kimmeridgian, black or dark shales, 636 ft.; total, 1,866 ft.

In June of the same year a more ambitious Company came into being, in the form of

THE KENT COAL, FINANCE, & DEVELOPMENT COMPANY, LIMITED.

having for its principal object the purchase and development of the Broome Park Estate, afterwards to acquire more than passing interest as the seat of Lord Kitchener. No material benefit to the coalfield resulted from this Company's operations, as complications regarding the title prevented the completion of the purchase, and, after a short and certainly inglorious career, it faded out of existence.

The most important of the companies formed in 1897 in connection with the Kent Coal enterprise, and that which missed success only by a hair's breadth, was registered in April of that year under the title of

THE KENT COAL EXPLORATION COMPANY, LIMITED.

Having regard to the extent of its legitimate boring operations, and the valuable scientific data that resulted from them, I think no apology is needed for dealing with this Company's affairs somewhat lengthily; more especially in view of the litigation that marked its closing days.

Capital.—£250,000 in 225,000 £1 ordinary shares, and 25,000 £1 deferred shares; the latter being allotted to the promoters credited as fully paid.

Directors.—The Rt. Hon. the Earl de la Warr; the Rt. Hon. the Lord de L'Isle and Dudley; J. Browne-Martin, Esq. (Deputy Chairman of the Westminster Trust, Limited); G. P. Simpson, Esq., M.E., F.G.S. (managing director of Kent Coalfields Syndicate, Limited); George Wreford, Esq. (late Senior Official Receiver, Shortlands, Kent).

Managing Director.—W. J. Cousins, Esq. (managing director of the Colliery & General Contract Company, Limited).

Geological Adviser.—Professor W. Boyd Dawkins, F.G.S.

Consulting Engineer.—Nath. R. Griffith, Esq., F.G.S., A.R.S.M.

Other names well known in City circles also figured on the prospectus, such as: Messrs. Brown, Janson & Co. (bankers); Messrs. Smith & Pitts (brokers); Messrs. Wilson, Bristows & Carpmael (solicitors); Messrs. Chatteris, Nichols & Co. (auditors).

The prospectus stated that: "This Company will employ its capital in undertaking the exploration for minerals, and especially coal and iron, throughout the County of Kent and elsewhere in the south of England, and it is believed that there is both legitimate and profitable scope for such enterprise." That the belief expressed in the last two lines was fully justified later events have, of course, clearly proved. The fact that the Company ultimately came to grief was primarily due to its having followed after false gods—geologically speaking.

Had the sites for the boreholes, which it put down, been more judiciously selected, the anticipated success would have been realised, and the subsequent history of Kent Coal would have assumed a very different character. Professor Boyd Dawkins, in his report which accompanied the prospectus, stated:—

"The commercial interests are so great that one success in many borings is likely to be a mine of wealth to those engaged in the enterprise. There is every reason to expect success from borings judiciously planned."

It was the Company's misfortune that events were to show that the borings were *not* "judiciously planned." Professor Boyd Dawkins' advice on this point was as follows:—

"The question arises here as to whether the Coal Measures may be expected to occur in Kent at a depth at which mining can be carried out at a profit. At Dover they are 1,204 ft. below the surface, and, in my opinion, they lie buried to the *west* of Dover at about 1,100 ft. to 1,200 ft. Most of the important coalfields of Britain are worked to a depth of from 2,000 ft. to 3,000 ft., and in Belgium to a depth of from 3,000 ft. to 4,000 ft. Year by year, as the means of ventilation are improved, they are being pushed to greater depths. The Kentish Coal Measures are well within the workable limits."

The important point to note is the opinion expressed as to the *westward* trend of the Coal Measures, an opinion held also by Mr. Brady, who, in a letter dated April 22, 1897, which was published as a postscript to the prospectus, stated emphatically that:—

> "As engineer to the Channel Tunnel Company, and responsible for the selection of the boring by means of which the Dover Coalfield was discovered, I am strongly of the opinion that the field in question is likely to extend to the westward, as stated in my Paper on the 'Dover Coal,' dated June, 1892, and that its lateral extension north and south should be determined by further explorations."

The Company accordingly set to work at once, and put down the following boreholes, on sites selected by Prof. Boyd Dawkins (except that at Pluckley), with the results as given below:—

Ottinge.—Begun May, 1898; finished October, 1899, leaving off in the Kimmeridgian, 108 ft. of which it had penetrated at 836 ft.

Hothfield.—Begun July, 1898; finished October, 1899, leaving off in the Portlandian at 809 ft.

Pluckley.—Begun by the Kent Coalfields Syndicate (on Etheridge's advice) and continued by the Exploration Company. After penetrating 775 ft. of Kimmeridge Clay, left off in it at 1,699 ft.

Old Soar.—Begun August, 1898; finished October, 1899, leaving off in the Wealden at 858 ft.

The total thickness of unproductive borings thus amounted to:—Ottinge, 836 ft.; Hothfield, 809 ft.; Pluckley, 1,699 ft.; Old Soar, 858 ft.; total, 4,202 ft.

Prof. Boyd Dawkins selected another site at which he approached the district favoured by Godwin-Austen and Prestwich. It was here that the Exploration Company came so near to achieving a commercial success as to justify my previous remark, that it was missed by a hair's breadth. This boring was known as

Ropersole.—Begun in 1897; finished 1899. Boring started at 400 ft. O.D., struck the Coal Measures at 1,581 ft., penetrated them to the extent of 548 ft., finally leaving off in them after meeting with some thin bands of coal, and one small seam of 1 ft. 3 in. (2,065 ft.) at 2,129 ft.

In the light of after events there is no doubt that had it been possible to continue this boring, substantial and valuable seams would have been reached at workable depths.

It will be noticed that these borings all terminated at practically the same time. This was when, as the result of more water troubles at Shakespeare Cliff, there was a slump in all the shares. The various Kent Coal Companies found themselves jointly and severally in difficulties, very largely owing to their interdependent, not to say involved, system of finance. The Exploration Company, however, did explore. Therefore it was somewhat extraordinary that, while it was in course of liquidation, a disgruntled shareholder should have brought an action, in the Company's name, against everybody concerned in its promotion and management. The statement of claim contained charges of conspiracy to defraud, and as many other kindred offences as the wit of counsel could devise. After a hearing extending over seven days the plaintiff's counsel threw up the sponge. The presiding judge, in giving judgment for the defendants, was not, I think, going beyond the obvious in saying:—

> "I am satisfied that there was a *bona fide* scheme for the discovering and winning of this coal in Kent."

There certainly was a *bona fide* scheme for discovering the coal; and had the prescience as to the selection of the sites been as great as the recognition of the fact that the fortunes of the Company depended upon these being "judiciously planned," I might have had a very different story to relate. But, to quote the late Colonel Malleson, "If our foresight was as good as our hindsight, our sight would be a d——d sight better than it is!"

CHAPTER V.

1897. Kent Collieries Corporation, Limited. 1899-1905. Consolidated Kent Collieries Corporation, Limited. French Engineers Report on Dover Colliery. Dissensions amongst Directors. Rival Re-construction Schemes. French v. *British.*

"The quarrel is a very pretty quarrel as it stands; we should only spoil it by trying to explain it."

—THE RIVALS.

I must now return to the affairs of the original Kent Coalfields Syndicate, and chronicle its re-organisation in the form of the

KENT COLLIERIES CORPORATION, LIMITED,

(Registered in October, 1897.)

Capital.—£1,500,000, in shares of £1 each, of which 1,285,072 were issued. Also £100,000 in debentures.

Directors.—Sir Owen Slacke, Sir Miles Fenton, Messrs. R. Berens, F. Brady, G. F. Fry, J. Browne Martin, F. Pitts, E. C. Robson Roose, M.D., and G. P. Simpson (managing director).

The new company took over the following assets from the Kent Coalfields Syndicate, Limited:—About 681 acres, freehold, adjacent to the pits. The foreshore between Dover and the municipal boundary of Folkestone. Agreements in respect of 13,000 acres inland. Mineral rights two miles seaward, estimated at 6,000 acres. The collieries in course of construction. £4,000 in cash, and £30,000 in securities. The birth of the company, however, was attended by much travail, for at this most inopportune moment there was a slump in the Vendor Syndicate's shares, owing to the action of a leading firm of brokers in suddenly demanding that delivery should be taken of a large block they were carrying on a speculative account. There was quite a sensational fifteen minutes in the market while the shares were being hammered down from over £6 to £3. I know of one man who paid £20,000 in differences on that settlement!

By varying the terms of the purchase agreement the Kent Collieries Corporation managed to go to allotment and assume an entity; but it was badly handicapped from the start, like an infant suffering from malnutrition. It never, in fact, grew to man's estate. At the very outset of its career misfortune overtook it, for in November, 1897, when the shafts were down to 500 ft., there was another inrush of water, with the accompaniment of much silt from the Hastings Beds. This resulted in the abandonment of No. 1 Pit, to replace which No. 3 was started, immediately on the site of the Brady Borehole.

As a further result of this accident there was a slump in the shares, which quickly fell from somewhere about par to 7s. or 8s., and thereafter steadily depreciated to a merely nominal quotation.

Besides its sinking programme the Corporation, upon the advice of Etheridge, who was a strong supporter of the theory of the westward trend of the coal basin, put down a boring at Brabourne, about fourteen miles from and south-west of Dover. The borehole terminated at 2,010 ft., having, up to that point, penetrated 88 ft. of Devonian.

This work, while yielding negative results to the company, has been of positive value to later explorers, and moreover, has proved of great interest to the scientific community. Mr. Lamplugh (of the Geological Survey), writing in 1911, states that:—

> "Though unprofitable in its commercial aspect, we regard this boring as being, from the scientific standpoint, the most important of the Kentish exploration."

I am afraid, nevertheless, that the shareholders were not sufficiently philanthropic properly to appreciate the fact that science was being enriched at their expense!

This boring at any rate settled the question as to the westward trend of the Coal Basin; and demonstrated the great thickening of the bad sinking ground comprised in the Folkestone, Sandgate and Hastings Beds, as compared with the Brady Section.

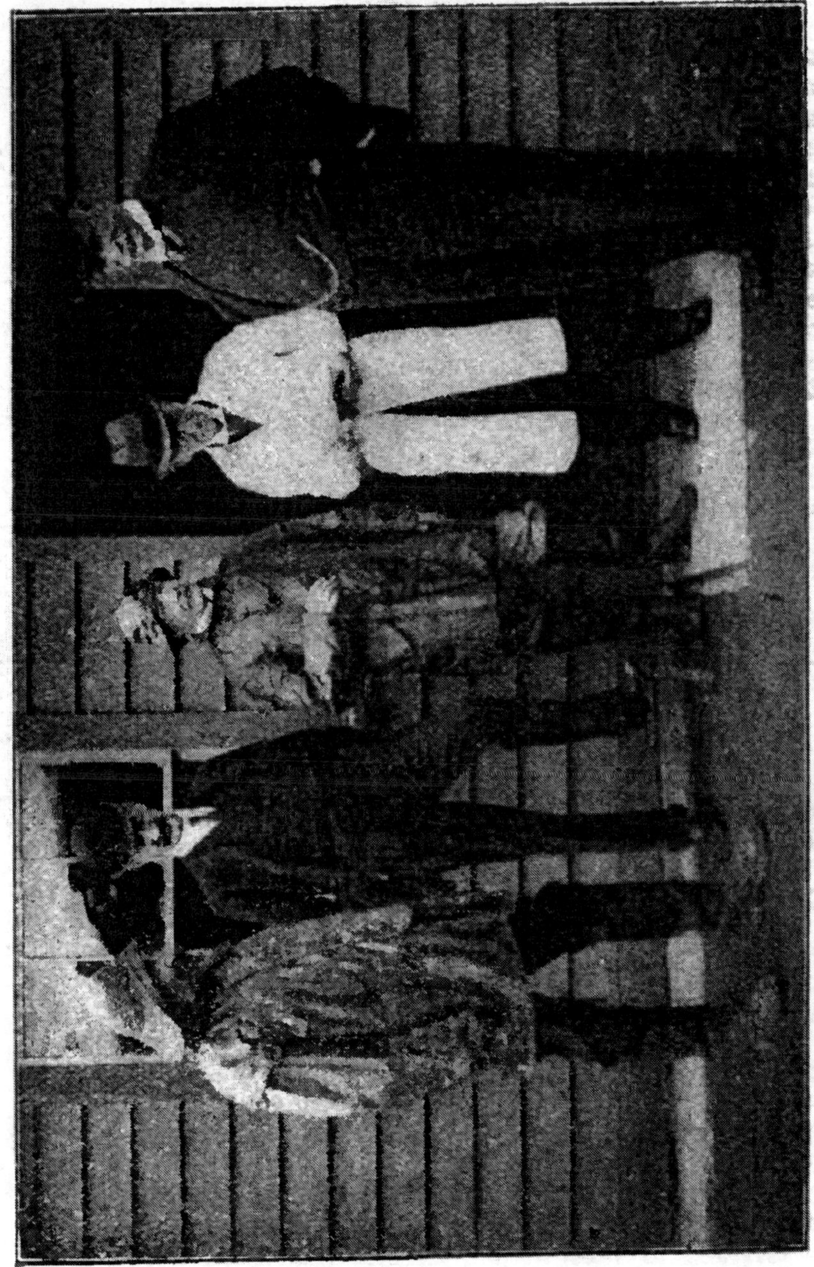

CONSOLIDATED KENT COLLIERIES CORPORATION, LIMITED, 1899.

Directors—from left to right—Mr. J. Y. MacAlister, Captain J. C. Tattersall Sir O. R. Slacke, C.B., Professor Etheridge (Geological Consultant), Mr James Sinclair

Another factor was making for the disintegration of the enterprise. For some reason, the genesis of which I will not seek to explain, the atmosphere of Kent coal, even in those early days, carried in it the germs of dissension. The directors of the various companies got to loggerheads with each other. They were disappointed, no doubt, that their labours had produced no concrete results; while the strain of trying to carry on with crippled finances probably put their nerves on edge. Be that as it may, it is certain that towards the middle of 1899 the whole structure was tottering to its fall. It was obvious that only a drastic reconstruction of the fabric could save it; and hence it was that on October 13, 1899—

THE CONSOLIDATED KENT COLLIERIES CORPORATION, LIMITED.

was registered to enact the part of Aaron's rod and swallow up:—The Kent Collieries Corporation, Limited, The Kent Coal Exploration, Limited, The Mid-Kent Coal Syndicate, Limited, The Kent Coal Finance & Development Company, Limited. By this means it was hoped to secure sufficient working capital to take the shafts into the coal.

A valuation of the above companies' assets was made by Messrs. C. L. Nicholls and Nath. R. Griffith, who appraised them at £1,065,395, made up as follows:—K.C. Corporation, £860,785; K.C. Exploration, £125,127; K.C. Finance, etc., £74,851; Mid-Kent Syndicate, £4,632.

The capital of the amalgamated company was £1,250,000, of which 1,211,824 shares of £1 each, credited with 17s. 7d. per share paid, were to be issued. The 2s. 5d. per share assessment, in the event of all the shares being taken, would produce £142,000 of fresh capital. There were also £150,000 of 6 per cent. debentures created.

Directors.—Sir Owen R. Slacke, C.B. (President); Mr. Florence O'Driscoll (Vice-President); Major H. E. Dering, Mr. John MacAlister, Mr. James Sinclair, Captain J. C. Tattersall, and Monsieur Jean Leroy. The directors soon found themselves face to face with difficulties in connection with the liabilities of the old companies, which at times seemed insuperable. Herculean efforts and admittedly unorthodox methods were necessary

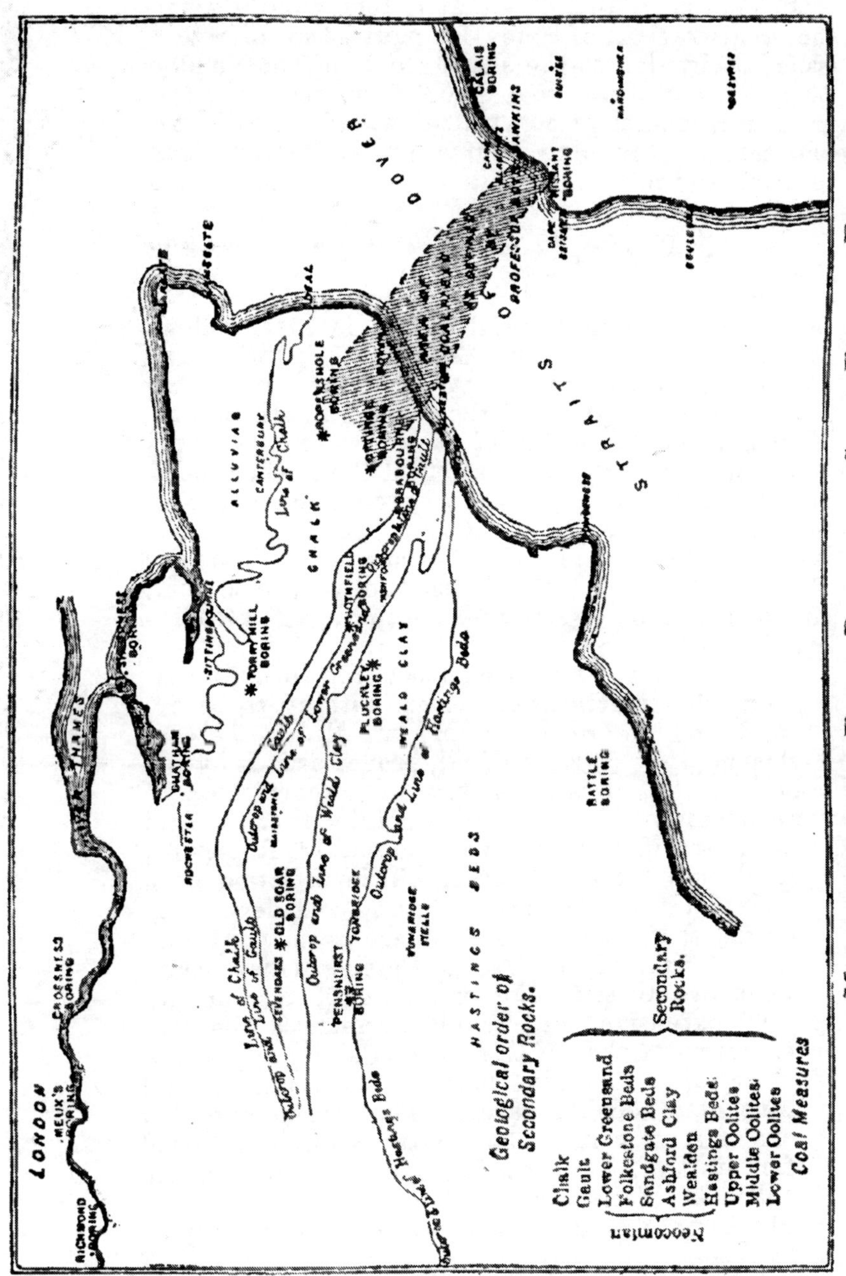

MAP SHOWING THE EARLY BORINGS IN SOUTH-EASTERN ENGLAND.

before any justification could be found for going to allotment.

On February 16, 1900—that is four months after the registration of the Company—the directors issued a circular to the shareholders of the Vendor Companies stating that 700,000 shares was the minimum subscription which would justify an allotment. In due course this minimum was secured, and letters of allotment were posted in the middle of March.

I do not propose to weary my readers with the innumerable incidents, mostly of a financial character, which clouded the early years of this Company. The most notable fact is that, following upon reports on the Shakespeare Cliff works and the coalfield generally, by Monsieur Victor Fumat (chief engineer of the Ostricourt Mines) and Monsieur Fontaine (chief engineer of the Courrières Mines) at the instigation of the French member of the board, a number of prominent men connected with the Pas de Calais Coalfield became largely interested in the Corporation. Monsieur Fumat's Report is voluminous and very technical, so I will content myself with quoting his final paragraphs:—

"At Dover, as at Ropersole, the formation is good; the stratification leaves nothing to be desired, and we are irresistibly impelled to the conclusion that this coalfield, proved as it is by two borings at a distance of six miles apart, must be an extensive one. We are of opinion that the thin inter-stratified seams which occur at Ropersole, similar to those at Dover, will be followed by a series of rich productive seams, considering, as we do, that this Dover Coalfield is the continuation of that of the Pas de Calais. Our conclusions are these:—The existence of a coalfield, rich, extensive, and regular, which is the continuation of that of the Pas de Calais, appears to us certain. It must therefore be acquired. (Il faut donc s'en emparer.) The works executed are of great value. The shafts are well equipped for sinking, but not for the extraction which will take place later on."

Monsieur Fontaine in the course of his report stated:—

"Having regard to the extent of the workable area, the Dover Collieries will last for a century upon what has been proved by the boring, calculating upon an annual output of a million tons. But it is very probable that the coal-bearing ground at Dover does not cease at the depth of 708 metres 47 cm., and that below this the basin will be found to continue in depth, with other seams of coal. Further, having regard to the fossils found in the bore, the classification of the coals, their analyses and volatile contents, I am of opinion that the seams which have been met belong to the Middle Coal Measures, and lie at the base of the series of seams at Radstock in Somersetshire.

"Another element of wealth to the Corporation is the presence in the property of an ore containing from 32 per cent. to 40 per cent. of iron, and a fireclay of excellent quality, capable of exploitation, and sometimes selling better than coal.

"To sum up, the mines of Dover have a great future, and will in due course of events rival the most successful undertakings of the Pas de Calais, if the sinking of the pits be directed with prudence by men who are competent and have knowledge and experience of the difficulties which are met with in similar works."

By way of comment on the concluding paragraph above, my own opinion is that had the proviso set out by Monsieur Fontaine with regard to the sinking of the pits been fulfilled, the successful future he prognosticated would have been realised, at any rate to a very large extent. I shall have occasion to return to the subject later on, when I will show that the French element never had that freedom of action, nor that amount of control, which their own records in the Pas de Calais should have ensured them.

Further, I am convinced that had they possessed sufficient faith in the English administration they would have found whatever money was necessary for the scientific and efficient prosecution of the sinking, in order that the prospects held out to them by their own experts might have been realised.

There is another point with respect to the above Reports that I should like to deal with: that is as to the connection between the Pas de Calais and the Kent Coalfields. It will be noted that both Messieurs Fumat and Fontaine were satisfied as to the continuity of the two basins; yet, strangely enough, the only authority I have encountered who questioned this was another celebrated French engineer, Monsieur Breton, whose practical experience in Kent was in connection with the Ellinge Boring.

The consensus of expert opinion undoubtedly favours the theory of a continuity extending back to Westphalia.

Dr. P. Krusch, who investigated the Kent Coalfield in 1912, on behalf of the promoters of the Anglo-Westphalian Syndicate (of which I shall have something to say later), stated:—

> "In 1856, more than thirty years before the discovery of coal in Kent, Godwin-Austen gave it as his opinion that there was an enormous Continental coal-trough stretching along a line through Westphalia, Belgium, the North of France, South and West of England and Wales. This opinion was further confirmed by many later explorers and is that prevailing to-day. Breton, on the contrary, held the opinion that the Kent Coalfield has no connection with the North of France. The discussion of the question as to which opinion is rightly held, is to-day, with the result of much investigation at our disposal, of much greater interest than ever. . . . We may presume that between the western boundary of the coalfield on the Dutch frontier and Kent there exists a rather close connection, although affected sometimes by interruptions, faults and denudations. We find, therefore, a practically uninterrupted stretch of rich Coal Measures from the Munster basin and Aix la Chapelle as far as Kent, separated by the old massive Palæozoic rocks of Brussels, frequently broken up and running north and south, which meet in the east in the Munster basin and in the west in Kent."

1901.

The French support, which I have mentioned, enabled the Corporation to make some substantial progress with the sinking of No. 2 Pit, which, standing at 611 ft. in October, 1900, had reached a depth of 1,100 ft. by May, 1901. With less than 100 ft. to go to the first seam of coal, it is not surprising that the management considered all was over, bar shouting! Hence it was a fearful blow to their expectations when, at this juncture, another totally unforeseen accident dashed their hopes to the ground.

Owing to the breaking of a clutch a long length of heavy steel rope went clattering down the shaft, smashing the delivery pipes of the pumping plant in its progress, and thus causing the pit to become flooded once more.

It took four months, and a lot of money, to unwater the shaft; and so depleted were the Company's resources that it was decided to reach and prove the coal by means of a 10-in. borehole, which was started by the Calyx Drill Company from the bottom of the pit.

The first seam, 2 ft. thick, was penetrated on October 3rd at a depth of 1,188 ft. 7 in., and after going through an 18-in. parting the second seam, 1 ft. 10 in. in thickness, was cut on the following day, thus giving 3 ft. 10 in. of coal against the 2 ft. 6 in. shown in the Brady section.

In deciding to make this boring the directors were influenced by the not unnatural thought that practical confirmation of the Brady section would enable them to raise the money for sinking the shaft into the seam. They were disappointed in this expectation, for before the end of the month the shares were almost unsaleable at 2s. 6d., and their troubles closed rapidly around them.

Such an unlooked-for sequel was partly due to the fact that the samples of coal from the boring were not of very high quality, owing to the large percentage of ash; not a matter for surprise in view of the seam being situated so near the top of the Coal Measures. On this point I might quote from a report by Etheridge to the directors at a later date, when he stated:—

> "The fragmentary condition of the coal in this 2 ft. 6 in. seam is, or rather was, entirely due to the denuding influence of the succeeding secondary or Jurassic series, of which the Lias is the lowest known in this section and was the immediate cause of the removal of the Coal Measures by denudation or planing down the uppermost members or beds of coal series to

1,157 ft., thus producing the present fragmentary condition of the 2 ft. 6 in. coal. Again, it must be understood that the Permian and Triassic Rocks, usually of great thickness, were either never deposited or developed in this immediate area, or if ever deposited were denuded before the deposition of the Lias; the bases of the Jurassic and Cretaceous series, 1,160 ft. thick, were accumulated under slow depression over the extensive area of the then great and rich coalfields, now well known to occur, probably 3,000 ft. thick, through the extensive East and West range of the great and productive coalfields of Northern France, Belgium and Germany."

A factor, even greater than the poorness of the seam, was the Press campaign that was launched against the enterprise. The Company, at this most critical juncture, again came under the lash of the envenomed pens of certain journalists. Notwithstanding the fact that the coal seam had been bored through in the presence of a representative of "The Times," who spent the whole day in the bottom of the shaft (see "The Times," October 4, 1901), it was insinuated by a leading London newspaper that the published results were fictitious, and that, in fact, the borehole had been "salted."

Undoubtedly the position was acute—the liabilities of the amalgamating companies had not been discharged, and the works were in the hands of the Receiver for the debenture-holders, who, in November, was threatening to sell.

The microbe of dissension, dormant while things were going fairly well, again became active, and vigorous attacks were made on the directors by a certain section of the shareholders.

The board called an extraordinary general meeting in December, and submitted a scheme of reconstruction. This was not acceptable, and the meeting appointed a joint committee, representing English and French interests, to confer with the directors; the meeting meanwhile to stand adjourned.

1902.

On January 27, 1902, the adjourned meeting took place, when the French group brought forward another scheme; this was duly carried, and the board unanimously decided to resign.

Under the scheme in question reconstruction was avoided. The capital was increased by the creation of 1,250,000 shares of 5s. each, which were entitled to all the profits until they had received 10s. per share, after which the profits were to be divisible equally between these new shares and the original capital. This arrangement was confirmed by the shareholders on February 11, 1902, and the new board was constituted thus:—Monsieur Jean Leroy (President), Mr. W. J. Cousins and Monsieur Réné Fonrobert (Vice-Presidents), Mr. James O'Connell, Mr. W. J. Horner, and Monsieur Maurice André Denizot.

Presumably the shareholders were becoming sick to death of these successive demands for more money, for it was not until April 7 that the first batch of allotment letters was posted, and these represented only 789,129 shares.

It is evident that tho directors themselves realised that they were setting out with insufficient funds, for in a circular to the shareholders, dated April 9, they stated:—

> "The debentures already placed (mainly in settlement of claims) amount to about £70,000, leaving some £80,000 debentures to be subscribed. As you are probably aware, the total claims against this Corporation and the amalgamated companies, including those arising on the debenture issue, amounted, on our taking office in February last, to over £190,000. This total we hope to reduce somewhat as to details, but the greater part will have to be dealt with to clear the assets of this Corporation and the properties to which it is entitled. It is evident that, in face of these extensive liabilities, the subscriptions for 800,000 shares of 5s. each would be entirely inadequate if sufficient working capital is to be provided. Therefore we have determined to offer to the shareholders the £80,000 of debentures not already placed, on terms so advantageous as, in our opinion, will preclude the possibility of their not being wholly applied for."

The faith of the board was greater, however, than that of the shareholders, and only a small proportion of the debentures was taken up.

Nothing daunted, and filled with the optimism of the immortal Micawber, the directors decided to go ahead and trust to luck. Really it was the only possible course to pursue, unless the shareholders' interests were to be entirely wiped out and the property abandoned to the debenture-holders. The question of getting the Pits through the water-bearing zones was tackled seriously, and, upon the advice of Messieurs Doise and Verwilghen, it was decided to adopt the Kind-Chaudron system of sinking.

1903.

It was not until the middle of 1903 that this new process of sinking got to work; no less than 21 months having elapsed since any sinking had been done. By October, however, No. 2 Pit had been taken 120 ft. into the Coal Measures. No. 3 Pit was standing at this date at 627 ft. Thus it will be seen that it had taken seven years to get one of the original shafts, started by the Kent Coalfields Syndicate in 1896, into the Coal Measures!

This shaft, however, was even yet in the embryo stage, having been sunk only 14 ft. in diameter by the small Trépan (or cutting tool), and was in process of enlargement to 18 ft. by means of the Great Trépan—a tool weighing no less than 27 tons.

On December 11, in the report accompanying the accounts to September 30, the directors again ventured into the regions of prophecy, stating that—

"A few weeks' work will complete the sinking of the Great Trépan, and we shall then commence operations for the insertion of the tubbing in the Pit. The successful carrying out of this will only leave about 90 ft. of sinking to reach the first seam of coal."

1904.

The weeks stretched out into months, and it was not until July 9, 1904, that they were in a position to issue a circular to shareholders announcing the completion of the above work, and stating that—

"Allowing one and a half months for the removal of the water and the taking out of the false bottom, the whole of these operations should be completed in November next, leaving only 90 ft. of dry sinking to reach the coal seam at 1,273 ft. Money will, of course, be required to carry us down to the workable coal, but a proposal for utilising the corporation's available resources is now under consideration, which the directors feel sure will meet with the hearty approval and support of the shareholders."

We are now rapidly approaching the last stage of the Corporation's existence, which was clouded with the same acute financial crises as those former ones which we have so briefly traversed. Dissensions arose between the French members of the board and their English colleagues. The microbe again!

I have already stated that the French element was denied its legitimate rights, both financial and technical; with the remembrance of the facts in my mind, I must say that I fully sympathise with the protest made by Monsieur Leroy.

At the outset Monsieur Leroy received his appointment of chairman at the hands of the shareholders, but in April of 1903 Sir Owen Slacke (chairman of the old board) rejoined the board in the anomalous position of English chairman. The situation became so acute that Monsieur Leroy felt compelled to bring the issue before the shareholders, which he did in a circular dated September 24. This is too lengthy to reproduce *in extenso*, but I think it desirable to quote freely from it in support of my previously expressed conviction that the French element—to speak plainly—was not treated fairly:—

> "The respect which I owe to myself, and the confidence which the shareholders were good enough to repose in me in electing me as chairman of the board, make it a duty on my part to bring to your knowledge certain facts of a particularly grave nature, which special considerations instigated by the fear of damaging the final success of our enterprise have compelled me up to now to keep to myself.
>
> "The divergence of views which have for long divided my colleagues and myself, on the interpretation of our reciprocal rôles and our duties as directors of the Company is so radical that I

consider myself at last obliged to refer to you and to ask what your views on the matter are, and to beg of you to decide yourselves which courses of conduct possess your approbation.

"I now protest against my gradual systematic exclusion from the affairs and plans of the Corporation, and which exclusion is expressly contrary to the desire so formally expressed by the shareholders whose intentions have thus found themselves so outrageously violated.

"Important meetings have been held without even my being informed, and without any agenda of the business of the day being submitted to me, thus not permitting me to study the questions dealt with, and copies of the minutes of the meetings have been refused to me.

"Systematic and continued appeals have been made to the shareholders in the absence of any fixed financial and well organised plan, resulting in the complete destruction of the credit of the Corporation, whereas it would have been so easy to act otherwise. Our preference shares under a normal administration would never have fallen below par. I can even go as far as affirming that the great success of the Kind-Chaudron process would have established considerable premiums.

"The only faculty left to me has been that of visiting and following the works, but I must add that recently I had again vehemently to protest against the loose way in which purchases of the necessary cement for the works have been arranged, which cementing is necessary to assure a definite success of the Kind-Chaudron process.

"I also protest with all the force I can command against the abuses of power which, under cover of the clauses contained in the Articles of Association, has rendered illusory the rights attached to my position, which position was accepted by me at the request of the shareholders, and a fact which is absolutely amazing is that I am now informed that I occupy my position only by favour of the directors. I am informed, moreover, that I am deposed from the position of chairman to which you elected me, and am but an ordinary director, and am not entitled to notices of board meetings, and receive none.

"I considered it desirable to put off my protest, contenting myself with assuring to the best of my ability the success of the works in their integrity; now that the success on that side is certain, provided that our engineers are not interfered with, I break though my silence which weighed upon me for so long."

When the co-operation of engineers and financiers connected with the Pas de Calais was secured, it was hailed as the harbinger of salvation to the Corporation. So it might have proved if, later on, the French directors and engineers had not been thwarted in every possible manner.

It is not surprising that, in view of Monsieur Leroy's dignified protest, the French financial support was withheld, with the result that the money the board stated was necessary to take the shaft down to the coal was not forthcoming.

The few remaining months of the Corporation's existence were occupied in unedifying quarrels, which it would serve no useful purpose to recapitulate. The sinking was at a standstill, and the public was more than ever shy of a company which seemingly had an unending amount of laundry work—not of the cleanest description—with which, unfortunately, it was unable to deal in private. So the inevitable happened—the Corporation, like its several predecessors, came to an inglorious end, unwept, unhonoured and (hitherto) unsung!

CHAPTER VI.

1905-1917. *Kent Collieries, Limited. The "Daily Mail" recommends its Shares. Gambling in South-Eastern Railway Stocks. Coal raised at Shakespeare Cliff. A Financial Crisis. Directors come and go. The Press announces the End of Kent Coal. Channel Collieries Trust, Limited. The Channel Steel Company. Limited.*

> " . . . What may this mean,
> That thou, dead corse, again, in complete steel
> Revisit'st thus . . . ?"
>
> —HAMLET.

1905.

With the collapse of the Consolidated Kent Collieries Corporation the control passed into entirely new hands, and

KENT COLLIERIES, LIMITED,

came into possession of the Shakespeare Cliff Works.

The extinction of the Corporation carried with it the extinction of what was generally designated the "Burr" element. A roseate dawn showed on the horizon, giving promise that the sun of prosperity was about to shine on the enterprise. The public was assured that the new brooms were going to sweep the Augean Stable clean; that the delays in getting the Pits into the coal, attributable to past bad management, soon would be but memories of an unfortunate episode in the history of the enterprise; that the old methods of finance which had so frequently and, one must admit, justly, evoked much acrid criticisms, were to have no counterpart in the halcyon days now dawning; that, in fact, to use a music-hall colloquialism, everything in the garden was to be lovely. In such an atmosphere was born Kent Collieries, Limited.

> "See how the promises of new-born life
> Fade from the bright hope picture, one by one,"

The capital of the company, which was registered on February 22, 1905, was £400,000 in 1,600,000 shares of 5s. each.

Directors.—Sir Owen Slacke, Mr. J. M. Fells, Professor E. Hull, Mr. W. J. Horner, and Mr. G. W. Lancaster.

The old Corporation received, by way of purchase consideration, only 150,000 of the above-mentioned 5s. shares, fully paid, whereas the assets which it had acquired from its predecessors were valued, as I have already stated, at over £1,000,000, to which must be added the large amount of cash provided by the shareholders for further working capital. True, they were offered the privilege of finding more money, having been given the right to apply for one 5s. share, at pár, in respect of each of their old 5s. preference shares, and a further 5s. share by reason of every four of their £1 ordinary shares in the Corporation.

In April, 1905, Kent Collieries, Limited, made its first issue of 1,200,000 5s. shares, of which about one-half were underwritten at a commission of 10 per cent., and 1,053,749 were ultimately allotted.

The Share Guarantee Trust, Limited, was the Company's financial godfather at this time, and helped it along later, when in what seems in this connection the natural order of things, troubles arose. It continued to occupy this responsible position until about the middle of 1910, when it was relieved of its burdens by the Channel Collieries Trust, Limited, which company apparently came into existence with that philanthropic object in view. But I am anticipating.

1906—1907.

In the latter part of 1906 and early in 1907 the "Daily Mail's" financial editor took Kent Collieries, Limited, under his wing, and strongly advised the purchase of its shares; thus, on January 3, 1907—

"Few shares ever seemed to present better prospects for a profitable gamble."

Again, on the 5th of that month—

"If the company is producing coal within two months it will not have much difficulty in finding capital, especially as its shares are at a substantial premium. Shareholders should hold on, especially as influential people have been buying."

But Press tips and jockeys' tips are equally unreliable, as each generation of punters learns to its cost; and so we find in the same column, under date April 29—

"Kent Collieries remained at half-a-crown, being unaffected by the circular notifying the next call of capital, and explaining the circumstances which have retarded the commencement of the output of coal."

By September 27 the true position seems at last to have dawned on the writer; thus—

"An enormous amount of shaft-sinking has to be done before this enterprise can be regarded as on a commercial basis."

The new administration and management, in spite of the fanfare of trumpets that heralded their morn, and the puffs of the "Daily Mail," proved as little able to overcome the physical difficulties pertaining to the Dover sinking as were their numerous predecessors in office.

Misfortune continued to dog the steps of the enterprise; even a new electrical pumping installation apparently found the strong sea air of Dover too bracing for it, with the result that the pits once more became flooded—the fourth time in their history.

A law-suit against the manufacturers yielded damages to the extent of £1,100 only—a very inadequate solatium to the company.

The sinking, therefore, made no greater progress than under previous *régimes*, and once again a Kent coal company had to feel the black hand of finance gripping at its vitals, and yet another board of directors had to lament the inadequacy of its resources.

1908.

Consequently, in the report for the year ending May 31, 1908, there appeared a sentence which those patient and long-suffering shareholders who had been involved since the old Kent Coal Syndicate days, then eleven years past, must have recognised as an old familiar—"The financial position of the company has recently been a source of anxiety to your directors."

With a view to relieving themselves of this anxiety the directors proposed to convert the

546,000 unissued 5s. shares into 136,500 preference shares of £1 each, and at the same time to create an additional 163,500 of such shares, making 300,000 in all. These shares were to be entitled to a 10 per cent. preferential cumulative dividend, and to 80 per cent. of the remaining divisible profits. The board was also to be strengthened.

So once again the kaleidoscope was to show all the colours of the rainbow in their most entrancing forms!

The preference share scheme was duly passed by the shareholders, but evidently the course of true finance did not run smooth, for it was not until the end of November that a prospectus inviting subscriptions was issued. The board, as promised, was strengthened by the following gentlemen becoming members:—Mr. Joseph Shaw (chairman of the Powell Duffryn Steam Collieries, Limited) as chairman, Mr. John Glasbrook (of the Penrikyber Navigation Colliery), Mr. E. M. Hann (of the Atlantic Merthyr Collieries).

At this period No. 2 Shaft remained at the same depth as at November, 1907, viz., 1,632 ft. Similarly, No. 3 Shaft, which was at 670 ft. at that date, had been sunk only a further 4 ft. Sinking had been suspended for some months, and the pits were full of water.

1909.

The new directors did not remain in office long, the early part of 1909 witnessing their abrupt retirement; but not before they had met the shareholders in general meeting, on January 20, when Mr. Shaw is reported to have said:—

> "You will be first in the field in a new district where you are far away from other sources of supply."

Matters were not going smoothly with the preference share issue, however, and it seems to have suddenly dawned on the new members of the board that they were becoming enmeshed in a tangled web of finance. They promptly cut themselves loose!

The situation which had arisen was not unamusing to the disinterested onlooker. While the board was engaged in counting up the proceeds of the preference share issue, the apparently solid ground beneath their feet proved to be badly mined: the explosive was provided by the debenture-holders, who laid claim to the cash by reason of their interest being six months overdue. In order to avoid this legalised looting, if I may change my metaphor, the directors returned the money to the subscribers, all parties then being "as you were"—save that the strengthened board had shed some of its component parts.

A certain section of the Press evidently took an extremely pessimistic view of the company's troubles, and of the future of the field generally. Being either unacquainted with, or purposely ignoring, other developments of a strikingly important character, they prematurely lamented the collapse of the whole Kent coal enterprise. I give the two following characteristic extracts:—

The "Financier and Bullionist," February 17, 1909, wrote:—

"While on the subject of rubbish, I may mention that Kent Collieries to-day experienced their final spasm, dropping from 1s. 6d. to the nominal price of 3d., on a report that the new board of Welsh experts, of whom some hope had been formed, have suddenly resigned, that the recently subscribed money is being returned, and that the debenture-holders are about to foreclose. Thus ends the lamentable history of the attempt to convert the Garden of England into a second Black Country. There are still, it is true, a few minor concerns engaged in shaft-sinking and the output of talk, but my chance of warming myself at my own fireside with the rays produced by Kent coal are, I fear, very remote."

"Daily Mail," February 20, 1909:—

"To whatever decision the largest debenture-holders and shareholders of Kent Collieries, Limited, may come at the meeting they are to hold, the enterprise must unfortunately now be regarded as something less than a forlorn hope. It has been given a fair trial by the present company—the first time in its history that Kent coal has been given a fair trial. The three practical men from the South Wales collieries have resigned, however, after their brief subscribed in the recent attempt to issue preference shares has been returned. Of all the Kent coal companies in existence, Kent Collieries, Limited, seemed the only one to have any chance of success, and now that it has fallen there seems more reason than ever to stand clear of the others. By good authorities the Kent coal experiment is now regarded as unsuccessfully completed."

For six winters past in front of a blazing fire of coal from a Kentish colliery I have re-read that last sentence with an unholy joy!

1910.

It was not until about the middle of 1910 that the difficulties with the debenture-holders were removed, Mr. Horner becoming trustee for them and ceasing to be a director. The board was yet again remodelled, the following gentlemen joining it:—Mr. John Morison, M.I.C.E. (consulting engineer), Newcastle-on-Tyne; Mr. William Armstrong (of Messrs. Wm. Armstrong & Sons, advisory mining engineers), Newcastle-on-Tyne. Here it was that the

CHANNEL COLLIERIES TRUST, LIMITED.

came on the scene, being registered with a capital of £750,000 for the purpose of acquiring

> "From the Share Guarantee Trust, Limited, the benefit of certain agreements with the Kent Collieries, Limited, and of negotiations with various coalowners in Kent, to provide capital for the said Collieries Company, and to acquire interests in coal-bearing areas in Kent."

With the coming of this company certain names well known in the iron and steel industry became associated with Kent, as will be seen from the following list of its directors:—Sir Hugh Bell, Bart., J.P. (chairman), Sir J. E. Johnson-Ferguson, Bart., J.P., Mr. A. J. Dorman (of Dorman, Long & Company), Mr. R. T. Smith, Mr. R. Grant, Junr., Mr. F. H. Hamilton, and Mr. F. Stobart, D.L., J.P. It was mainly owing to the new blood thus infused into the enterprise that, later on, practical steps were taken towards exploring and developing the iron ore deposits, so long neglected. This work is likely to have far-reaching results, inasmuch as it will lead to the establishment of smelting works on a large scale in the vicinity of Dover.

The first action of the Channel Collieries Trust, Limited, was to guarantee £140,000 of the £300,000 of preference shares which Kent Collieries, Limited, again offered for subscription; and this time nothing intervened to prevent an allotment!

1912.

Although the sinking at Shakespeare Cliff continued to be somewhat intermittent, and while it is almost a misuse of words to speak of its "progress," yet by April, 1912, one of the shafts (No. 2), which had been commenced so lightheartedly in 1896, on the statements of the engineers that no water difficulties need be anticipated, was down to 1.632 ft. No. 1 shaft had long since been abandoned, and No. 3, started in 1898 to replace it, was sunk to 1,008 ft.

At this juncture yet another shuffling of directors took place; Professor Hull retired, and Mr. J. S. P. Samborne (of the Canadian Agency) and Mr. E. T. McCarthy (consulting engineer to the Spassky Copper Company, Limited) became members of the board.

Notwithstanding that the second shaft, without which a colliery is not a colliery, had not even reached the Coal Measures, much less a coal seam—a flamboyant full-page illustrated puff, with a very minute "Advt." at foot thereof, appeared in "The Times" of April 24. In the light of later events this makes really funny reading. The headlines to this compilation of "tosh"—no other word is adequate—were these:—

First Commercial Deliveries of Kent Coal.

"Miners are now taking coal from the First Veins, and more men are being added as fast as extensions of workings make room for them. The vast wealth of Kent's great coalfields enters on the era of commercial development."

In the letterpress the public was informed that—

"The fact that men of such well-known conservative attitude in finance have associated themselves with the future of the Kent Collieries Company is in itself the best possible proof that

Kent coal has passed the stage of uncertainty or mere hope, and is now to take its place among the other business certainties of coal-mining in England."

Further, that—

"A year from now the existing pits will be producing coal at the rate of 150,000 tons a year, estimated conservatively by the mine managers, men of long successful experience in other coalfields, who are now in charge of the work."

[The expression "at the rate of" reminds me that when I was a youngster, in far-away Melbourne, my boon companions and I after a gay evening, used to reckon that we had been living "at the rate of" £20,000 a year! No doubt we had—for an hour or two!]

The small quantity of coal then being raised was got from the 1 ft. 10 in. seam at 1,200 ft.; so that the second shaft had still to be sunk a further 265 ft. before production on a commercial scale would be possible, even from this small upper seam.

Although "The Times" published this advertisement, those who paid the bill must have been deeply chagrined at the article which appeared in the next day's issue under the heading, "The Finance of Kent Coal." The writer of it apparently knew more about practical mining than the "men of long successful experience in other coalfields" who figured in the advertisement. Amongst quite a number of other pungent things he wrote :—

"In addition to the necessity of regarding the present hopes in the light of past disappointments, it must be noted that according to the published plans showing the present stage of operations at the mine, there is no connection between the two shafts. Although some coal would, of course, have to be raised in the course of further sinking and making the necessary galleries, it is, of course, impossible to suppose that coal can be produced upon what is really a commercial scale until the mine is in a much more complete state. That entails the overcoming of more water difficulty, which, with bad finance, seems to have been the bug-bear of what, by courtesy, may be called the Kent coal industry."

The cynic might be tempted to seek some connection between the puffing advertisement in "The Times" and the movements of Southern railway stocks about this period, as instance the following quotations:—

January 29, 1912.

Dover "A," $55\frac{3}{8}$ ... Chatham Ordinary, $17\frac{5}{8}$

Mid-April Settlement.

Dover "A," $57\frac{3}{4}$ ... Chatham Ordinary, $19\frac{3}{8}$

April 23, 1912.

Dover "A," $71\frac{3}{8}$ ... Chatham Ordinary, $23\frac{7}{8}$

whilst the morning that the advertisement appeared, being Contango day, the prices were put up to—

Dover "A," 73 ... Chatham Ordinary, $24\frac{5}{8}$

No doubt some of those speculators who got landed at the top prices paid their differences on "The Times" Book System of instalments!

On May 30 we find Satan rebuking Sin, for "The Times" published this homily:—

> "At least half a dozen markets have during the past six months been rigged systematically on various pretexts. Up to a certain point these manipulators appeared to be very successful. . . . . . . The effect of such operations on the Stock Exchange as a whole is, in the view of prudent members, very questionable. They certainly tempted many people, jobbers, brokers and clients, to speculate beyond their means, and if the few who got in early made large profits, the many who came in at the end have made enormous losses . . . . . . capital has been diverted from markets where it was usually employed into inflated securities, where it will be a continual anxiety for some time to come."

The result of the loudly proclaimed, but immature, entry on the producing stage was the despatch, on April 30, 1912, of twelve 10-ton wagons of coal to various works for testing purposes. That is the only real consignment of coal that has ever been made from Shakespeare Cliff!

1912—1914.

Coal-winding continued for a limited period and on a very limited scale, the quantity raised being at no time sufficient even for colliery requirements. Supplies were obtained from another colliery on

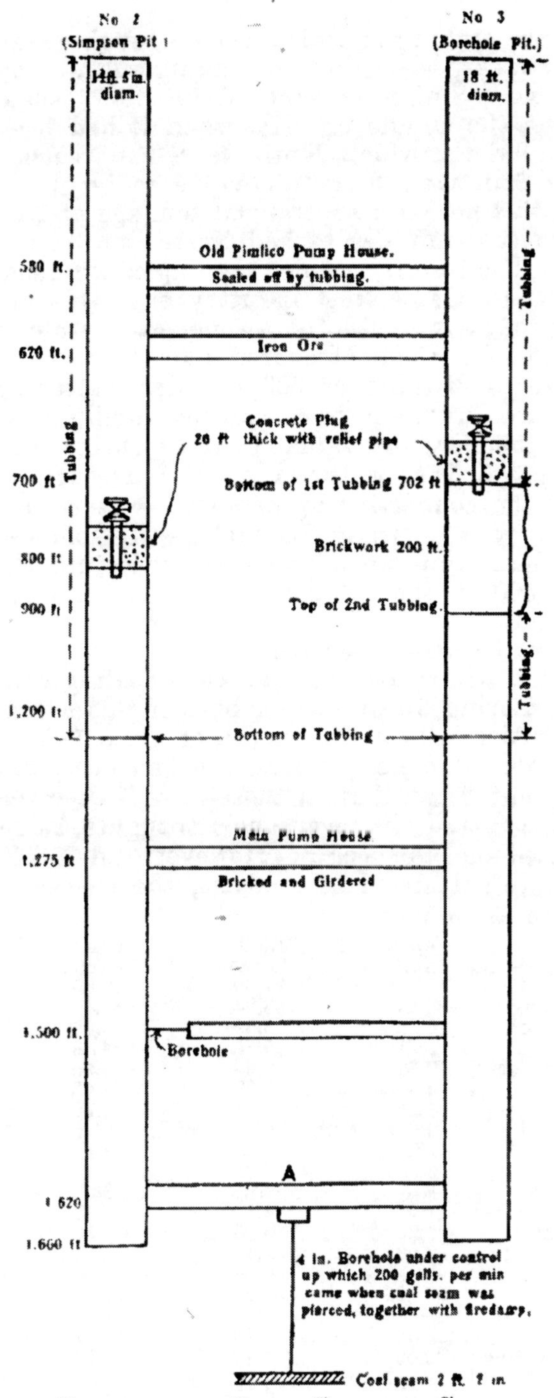

SHAKESPEARE CLIFF COLLIERY SHAFTS.

the field, the sinking of which was not even begun when the Shakespeare Cliff undertaking was already 12 years old. Sinking proceeded in No. 3 shaft until about the middle of 1914, when it had been taken to 1,632 ft., which depth No. 2 had reached in 1911. Still the colliery was not a colliery!

During this period a substantial tonnage of iron ore was raised and despatched North for testing purposes. The results satisfied the important members of the iron and steel industry that this ore could be profitably worked on a commercial scale.

Although the Coal Measures had been sunk through for a distance of 500 ft., demonstrating the existence—under normal working conditions—of several commercially valuable seams, success was not in sight. The water—the ever-present reminder of the connecting-up of all the water-bearing strata by the Brady Borehole—still followed the workings; while an advance borehole into the seam at 1,800 ft. showed that there was yet more water ahead.

Hence, exit Coal—enter Iron.

My readers will remember that when dealing with the Brady Boring, in an earlier part of this narrative, I mentioned that at a depth of about 600 ft. a considerable thickness of iron ore had been met with. I pointed out that in those days it received only passing attention, everyone's thoughts being concentrated on the coal. However, in 1899, samples were submitted to analysis, the results of which were as under:—

	Upper 6 feet.	Middle 2 feet.	Lower 4 feet.
Silica	15.10	11.00	12.00
Peroxide of iron .	38 54	55.24	47.83
Protoxide of iron .	6 56	3.59	8.39
Alumina . .	5 71	5.75	4.88
Oxide of manganese	0.30	0.30	0.20
Lime	9 94	5.23	4.42
Magnesia .	1.55	1.14	1.76
Phosphoric acid ..	0.97=0 42P.	1 37=0 59P.	1.03=0.45P
Arsenic acid .. .	Nil	Nil	Nil
Sulphur .. .	0.084	0.063	0.16
Oxide of copper .	Nil	Nil	Nil
Carbonic acid ..	11.43	4.10	8.48
Combined water .	7.22	9.90	8.38
Moisture	2.08	2.18	1 77
	99.484	99 863	99.30
Metallic iron ..	32.08	41.46	40.01
Loss on calcination..	20.00	15.78	17.70
Metallic iron in calcined ore	40 10	9.23	48.01

Thirteen years later—in 1912—Dr. P. Krusch (director of a Geological Department at Berlin), whose name I have already mentioned in connection with the Anglo-Westphalian Syndicate, wrote as follows concerning the iron ore of East Kent:—

> "Iron ore was first discovered in the Dover boring. It caused a good deal of excitement at the time, but later, however, faded into oblivion. In the Tilmanstone shaft it can be seen more closely in greater cross-section. It occurs chiefly in the Corallian series, and has, to all appearance, a varying thickness up to several metres. Further towards the north the ore is also found in the Jurassic Beds, *i.e.*, the Oxford Clay. The ore is Oolitic, and contains ferro-carbonate with approximately 20 per cent. lime and many minute particles of magnetite. The metallic iron varies between 29.55 per cent. and 33 per cent., with 0.72 per cent. phosphorus. After calcination it yields 43 per cent. iron. Of great importance is the fact that the ore is self-fluxing. The profitable pig-iron obtained from this ore contains about 2 per cent. phosphorus. Those who are acquainted with the deep borings at Niederrhein, in the district of Gegend, will remember that Oolitic iron-ore beds are also found there in the Jurassic. They lie, according to the late District Geologist, Dr. Gottfried Muller, in a deeper horizon (Upper Lias), and are not connected with the Kentish iron ore."

It was, of course, the existence of the ore that attracted the attention of certain ironmasters; and after their advent on the board of the Channel Collieries Trust, systematic borings were made in the neighbourhood of the pits, and coastwise towards Folkestone. The results were highly satisfactory, and proved that the quantity of easily accessible ore was practically inexhaustible. Salvation was therefore sought in this direction, and it was decided to raise sufficient ore for a test on a commercial scale at some established smelting works.

The results were evidently satisfactory, for it is practically certain that no further attempt will be made to raise coal from the Shakespeare Cliff Pits, which to-day are no longer in the possession of a company having even the words "coal" or "colliery" as part of its title.

The accompanying plan (*see* page 74) shows the present position of the pits, with cement plugs in each sealing off the lower water, thus rendering possible the working of the iron ore deposits with a minimum of pumping.

1917.

Before finally parting with Kent Collieries, Limited, the following statistical information may be given :—

Kent Coalfields Syndicate existed for 1 year 7 months.

Kent Collieries Corporation existed for 1 year 8 months.

Consolidated Kent Collieries Corporation existed for 6 years.

Kent Collieries, Limited, existed for 12 years.

During varying periods of the eventful careers of the above companies the following gentlemen have acted as directors :—Messrs. P. S. M. Arbuthnot, R. Berens, Sir H. B. Robertson, Messrs. G. F. Fry, F. Pitts, G. P. Simpson, Sir Owen R. Slacke, C.B., Sir Miles Fenton, Messrs. F. Brady, J. Browne-Martin, E. C. Robson Roose, M.D., J. M. Fells, Professor Edward Hull, Messrs. W. J. Horner, G. W. Lancaster, W. J. Cousins, Sir Henry E. Dering, Professor W. Galloway, Messrs. J. O'Connell, John Morison, Joseph Shaw, William Armstrong, J. S. P. Samborne, E. T. McCarthy, E. M. Hann, John Glasbrook, Florence O'Driscoll, Captain Tattersall, Jean Leroy, Maurice A. Denizot, J. Y. MacAlister, James Sinclair, S. Hare, J. J. Prest, and J. A. Selway. With apologies to any others whose names I may have omitted.

The Last Phase.

CHANNEL STEEL COMPANY, LIMITED.

Registered on September 26, 1917, by Messrs. Bristows, Cooke & Carpmael (who, my readers will recall, were solicitors to the long-vanished Kent Coal Exploration Company).

Capital.—£750,000, in 600,000 preferred ordinary shares of £1 each, and 3,000,000 deferred shares of 1s. each. The former to be entitled to a fixed non-cumulative dividend of 10 per cent. per annum, and to participate, *pari passu*, with the remaining distributable profits in each year until 1926; after which date both classes of shares are to rank *pari passu*.

Directors.—Sir Hugh Bell, Bart., Northallerton, ironmaster; Mr. A. J. Dorman, Nunthorpe, Yorkshire, ironmaster; Mr. R. Grant, Junr., Lombard Street; Sir J. E. Johnson-Ferguson, Bart.; Mr. F. Stobart, and Mr. J. M. Fells.

The objects for which the company was formed were, *inter alia*, "To take over the undertaking and all or part of the business of the Kent Collieries, Limited, and the Channel Collieries Trust, Limited, in accordance with an amalgamation scheme approved by them respectively."

In addition to the properties comprised in the assets of the above companies, the Channel Steel Company has since acquired a substantial interest in the Betteshanger Boring Syndicate's minerals. It is from this source that, ultimately, fuel for its smelting works will be drawn.

1918.

The second ordinary general meeting of the company was held on December 27th, 1918, Sir Hugh Bell, Bart, C.B., in the chair. The accounts to September 30th, 1918, were adopted, but as they deal almost entirely with matters arising out of the liquidation of the vendor companies they call for no comment.

Owing to the exigencies of the war nothing has yet been done of a development character, though the Chairman stated that the matter was having careful consideration, and added that he believed there was a great future for the Kent Coalfield.

The official statement regarding the proposed smelting works is worthy of permanent record, because this was the first company meeting in the history of the Coalfield at which the development or the iron ore deposits was given precedence over that of the coal seams. Therefore, my readers cannot fail to be interested in the following extracts from the Chairman s speech :—

"There is an important bed of ironstone in the County of Kent with which we are well acquainted. We hope to work it and produce steel from it. It is of a character which in all probability will smelt satisfactorily. It will produce iron not very greatly differing in quality from that of the North-East Coast. In order to convert the pig-iron thus made it will be necessary to use a certain quantity of pure imported ores. Therefore, so far the production of iron or steel in Kent will depend upon imported ores. That is the case with almost all the steel made in Great Britain, except the steel made in the Counties of Cumberland and Westmorland. It is true of all the other steel made in England—pure ore is imported for the purpose of being used as a reducing agent in the smelting furnaces. There are important deposits of iron in the north-west of France, but there is no convenient fuel for their smelting. It is not improbable that an interchange of these two commodities should take place between the two countries, and that Great Britain should furnish the fuel to make steel in the north-west of France and that France should furnish the ore to make steel in Great Britain.''

* * * *

Thus have we lightly skimmed over the history of the endeavour to plant a colliery at the foot of that "dread summit" where ". . . . . . the murmuring surge, that on th' unnumber'd idle pebbles chafes," to-day beats itself to spray against the wall that now forbids the sea access to the spot where poor blinded Gloster believed he "perpendicularly fell." There is little of poetry about that spot to-day; though in a certain sense "romance" is not entirely unassociated with it.

My endeavour has been to give a clear and connected story, omitting many accessory details which would only confuse, unless dealt with at unwarrantable length. My amanuensis, who knows a good deal of these happenings, tells me that I have left out the tit-bits—but this is no place for personal "reminiscences," and tit-bits might not appeal to my publishers!

Through the thick forest and tangled undergrowth I have sought to blaze a trail that all can follow; but I ask myself, is it to be wondered at that the public became hopelessly befogged regarding Kent coal affairs?

THE GENERAL MEETING OF KENT COLLIERIES, LIMITED, WAS HELD LAST TUESDAY.

The Chairman:—Gentlemen, as Director, and great grandson of one of the original shareholders, I have pleasure in calling your attention to this piece of coal, which represents nearly three centuries of patient endeavour. Owing to the fact of the world's supply of coal having become exhausted nearly a century ago, this specimen is well-nigh priceless, and will amply repay, etc,, etc , etc.

The celebrated maze at Hampton Court is an open road compared with the labyrinthine intricacies that those must travel who would find their way about the past involutions of the Shakespeare Cliff undertaking.

They may have been all very clear to the shareholders, though I doubt it; there was no lack of guide books for them; paper was cheap in those days, and prospectuses, progress reports with appeals for more money, amalgamation proposals, reconstruction literature, share issues of every imaginable variety, liquidators' accounts, circulars of attack and counter-attack when the microbe set contending factions on the war-path, were theirs in abundance. In fact, the only other form possible in which paper relating to the companies' affairs could have reached the long-suffering shareholders, would have been in the shape of dividend warrants. These they never saw!

CHAPTER VII.

Dover Coalfield Extension, Limited. An offshoot from Kent Collieries. The Ellinge Boring. Lack of Funds. No lack of internal dissensions. Collapse of the Company. Kent Coal Concessions, Limited, registered by Mr. Burr on April 19, 1904.

"Oh, that a man might know the end of this day's business ere it come."

—JULIUS CÆSAR.

Having thus followed in some detail up to the present date the history of the many attempts to found a colliery at Shakespeare Cliff, and having finally, after many vicissitudes, handed over the goods and chattels of Kent Collieries, Limited, into the safe-keeping of the Channel Steel Company, Limited, it is time that I resumed my story.

One thing was quite certain—that the coalfield was not confined within the limits of the areas attaching to the Shakespeare Cliff Pits, and although the borings at Brabourne and Ottinge had not proved successful, this did not daunt other explorers. We will therefore return to our chronological sequence and continue to record the development of the coalfield in general, the embryo of which had been unearthed by the Brady Boring.

Some years before Kent Collieries, Limited, ended its hectic career a certain section of the original personnel, headed by Mr. Arthur Burr, severed their connection with Shakespeare Cliff. Their programme was to carve out another portion of the field, and for this purpose in

1901.

they embodied themselves under the title of—

THE DOVER COALFIELD EXTENSION, LIMITED.

The capital of this company was only £25,000, and its aims were on a commensurably moderate scale. It was responsible for one additional abortive boring, viz., that at Ellinge; and in due course, after some of the apparently inevitable quarrels within its body-politic, it went into compulsory liquidation in 1903.

The Ellinge bore was abortive in the sense that no coal seams were discovered; it was situated about five miles from Dover, a little north of west from Shakespeare Cliff, and ended at a depth of 1,805 ft. after penetrating 119 ft. of unproductive Coal Measures. It is certain, though, that had the work (which came to an untimely end owing to lack of funds) been continued, some seams would have been met with. Later explorations, however, lead to the belief that nothing of a substantial nature can be looked for in this direction.

The Ellinge Boring.

(466 O.D.)

Details of strata as given by Monsieur Ludovic Breton, under whose supervision the work was done :—

	Ft.	in.
Upper chalk	220	0
Middle chalk	117	8
Lower chalk	220	0
Glauconitic marl	16	5
Gault	164	0
Lower greensand	47	7
Atherfield clay	19	8
Wealden	62	0
Purbeck	66	11
Kimmeridgian	150	8
Corallian	201	0
Oxfordian	185	3
Bathonian	99	7
Bajocian	54	1
Lias...	54	1
Coal measures	—	

Tho Coal Measures were struck at 1,686 ft. from the surface, and consisted of Binds and characteristic Coal Measure sandstones.

One cannot help remarking on the extraordinary blindness, or obtuseness, of those responsible for the long series of borings so far to the west of the Dover-Canterbury road, although it is true that some of the eminent geologists of the middle of last century indicated that trials might profitably be made in the Wealds of Kent and Sussex still farther west.

Compared with modern systems of boring, those available at that period were decidedly inefficient; this fact doubtless was a contributing cause in their recommendation that boring sites should be at points where the over-lying chalk formation had been denuded either wholly or in part. It was never anticipated that the Wealden deposits were of such great thickness as recent borings have demonstrated.

Houldsworth, who wrote in 1866, propounded the query, "Does coal exist near London?" and referred to the important consideration which a skilful and judicious selection of sites for coal trials involves. He added: "For any first attempts of this kind localities situated clear of the Cretaceous and Tertiary beds are obviously the most eligible." And further that: "The position of the Wealden beds immediately below the Cretaceous System, and their comparative nearness to the Pas de Calais, where the chalk is superincumbent on the Coal Measures, invests any well-chosen locality of the Wealden tract for a coal trial with a pre-eminence which admits of no dispute." That is all very well, having regard to the known geological facts of Houldsworth's day; but when the bore-holes to which I am referring were inaugurated the negative result of the original Sub-Wealden boring was a matter of history.

The Brabourne boring, 13¾ miles west 10 deg. north of Dover, also had demonstrated in 1898 the non-existence of Coal Measures at that point.

Godwin-Austen's recommendation of a site in the vicinity of Canterbury still remained to be put to the test; it was, in fact, entirely ignored, while successive borings far to the west of the Dover-Canterbury road followed one another registering an unbroken series of failures of a greater or lesser degree. The only possible explanation is that the opinions of three modern engineers, supported as they were by Professors Boyd Dawkins and Etheridge, carried more weight than the scientific deductions of eminent geologists of a former day. In support of this contention I quote the following extract from a Paper by Messrs. F. Brady, G. P. Simpson and Nath. Griffith, with whose names my readers are already familiar, given before the North of England Institute of Mining and Mechanical Engineers, at Wigan on July 14, 1896:—

"As we have now the evidence of numerous borings to prove the existence of a range of rocks older than the Carboniferous running east and west underneath London, and also know that the horizontal character of the seams found at Dover, together with the clean, bright, and uniform quality of the coal, indicate a central position in the coal-basin, it will be tolerably safe to assume that future explorations should follow a direct westerly course from Dover towards Bristol; as shown by a dotted line on the accompanying map."

The map referred to shows a line running parallel with, and a little to the north of, the South-Eastern Railway from Folkestone to Tonbridge, and on by Guildford and Basingstoke to Bath. It was in the direction thus indicated that the unsuccessful borings at Hothfield, Penshurst, Pluckley, Ottinge, and Old Soar were made; as well as that already mentioned put down later by the Dover Coalfield Extension Company, at Ellinge.

I must confess that I do not appreciate the reasoning which led Boyd Dawkins to select some of the sites, for, in his evidence before the Royal Commission on Coal Supplies, in 1903, he stated that he attached great importance to the fact that the Dover site was not more than six miles south of the Lydden tunnel, on the South-Eastern line, during the making of which about 4 cwt. of bituminous material had been found imbedded in the chalk, which, according to Godwin-Austen, had been derived from the Coal Measures below. He further emphasised this point in a foot-note to his evidence (see Final Report Vol. X. p. 28) in which he said: "I might mention that again and again in connection with the Coal Measures, say of Lancashire and the adjacent parts, I have had occasion to meet with similar accumulations of bituminous material in fissures and so on, in the rocks; so that really the significance of this was, to my mind, very great." It is therefore difficult to understand why, after the significance of this geological pointer had been confirmed by the Brady boring, Boyd Dawkins should have selected sites so far afield as Hothfield, Old Soar and Penshurst, which are respectively 13, 32 and 42 miles from the Lydden tunnel, and, of course, still further from Dover.

1904.

This year is to be noted as a most important landmark in the history of the enterprise, for in it the Dover Coalfield Extension Company, Limited, arose, Phœnix-like, from its ashes, and assumed the guise of the Kent Coal Concessions, Limited, which was the first Kent Coal Company to achieve a really practical success. A success which was sufficient to attract numerous competitors, even from Westphalia; a success which, whatever happens to the pioneers so far as their individual investments are concerned, cannot fail to enrich the nation with a coalfield that must prove an important factor in its industrial future.

Any record of the rise and progress of the Kent Coal enterprise would be incomplete without reference being made to the outstanding name of the man to whom more than any other the coalfield owes its existence—Mr. Arthur Burr.

This is not the place to deal in personalities; nor am I the person to act the part of Counsel, either for the defence or prosecution, in respect of the enmities Mr. Burr has aroused or the criticisms he has incurred. My object is to set forth the facts regarding the inception and development of the Coalfield. Personal issues form neither part nor parcel of my scheme; whether the man responsible for the position of the Field to-day were guilty of all the offences imputed to him, or were he as white as the driven snow, does not affect the following historical facts:—

(1) In 1855 Godwin-Austen suggested the possibility of a continuation of the Continental Coal Measures beneath the Channel and into the South of England.

(2) Not until forty years later, in circumstances already described, was this theory established.

(3) For five years after the proving of workable coal not a man appeared courageous enough to tackle the problem, and establish a working colliery.

(4) Failing the advent of such a man, or corporate body, the work was inaugurated by Mr. Arthur Burr.

(5) There is no palpable evidence that had Mr. Burr not stepped into the breach anyone else would have done so. The opportunity was open to

all, and indeed went begging—as I have shown. The successful boring at Shakespeare Cliff was under the *ægis* of the Chairman of such a power as the South-Eastern Railway Co., but the Directors sat down in front of their coal and did nothing. Instead of its urging them to high endeavour it seemed to have for them the basilisk eye which hypnotised them into a coma!

KENT COAL CONCESSIONS, LIMITED.

(Registered April 19. 1904.)

The Company was formed to purchase the assets and liabilities of the Dover Coalfield Extension, Limited, from its liquidator; and for the purpose of acquiring and developing mineral areas in Kent. The original capital was £50,000 in 48,500 ordinary and 1,500 deferred shares, all of £1 each, the former being entitled to receive out of the profits in each year a preferential dividend at the rate of 12 per cent. The remaining profits available belonging as to two-thirds to the holders of ordinary shares and one-third to holders of deferred shares. Of the ordinary shares 20,000 were set aside for the shareholders in the late Dover Coalfield Extension Company, and offered to them at 12s. 6d. paid. These were all ultimately absorbed in one quarter or another. The remaining 28,500 shares were offered for public subscription, but only 15,027 were then applied for and allotted. The 1,500 deferred shares were at the disposal of the promoters, and a certain number were allotted to the subscribers of the original issue.

The first directors were Mr. F. G. B. Wells and Monsieur Jean Leroy, who held office respectively until January and May, 1906; Monsieur Leroy's retirement being mainly due to his failure to introduce a substantial amount of French capital, as he had undertaken. The Board, as eventually constituted, was as follows:—

Mr. H. A. Johnston (Chairman), appointed October 20, 1904.

Sir Henry E. Dering, Bart., appointed February 7, 1905.

Mr. A. C. G. Hervey, appointed January 9, 1906.

Mr. H. S. Close, appointed June 26, 1906.

Mr. Arthur Burr (Managing Director), appointed October 23, 1906.

Other than Mr. Burr, none of these gentlemen had any responsibility with regard to the promotion and early transactions of the Company. The Prospectus stated :—

> " This Company has been formed to acquire (*inter alia*) ———— the properties, mining rights and options of the Dover Coalfield Extension, Limited, and, with additional working capital, to organise their development to the best advantage. Negotiations have been initiated and are progressing favourably for the acquisition of further options and leases over extensive and well situated areas within the Kent Coalfield as defined by Professor Boyd Dawkins. These options cover many thousands of acres adjoining those already secured, and add many hundreds of millions of tons of coal to the estimated quantity for exploitation."

An examination of the Company's prospective acquisitions had been made by Boyd Dawkins, who reported as follows :—

> " I beg to report that the areas over which your Company has acquired mineral options, as described in the plans furnished to me, are, in all human probability, within the area of the South-Eastern Coalfield. . . . I see no reason why the same sections and the same seams of coal as those at Dover should not be proved in your areas by experimental shafts or borings with a view to sites for collieries. The areas in question afford ample room for the establishment of many collieries, and are far more favourably situated than at Dover. In them the water in the strata above the Coal Measures is not likely to present engineering difficulty."

Here, again, we have a Kent Coal Company attempting an ambitious programme with only very limited resources; setting out, in fact, to do a man's work with a boy's tools, and further, be it noted, receiving the advice that no water difficulties need be anticipated. This lack of resources was admitted some years later by the Directors in a circular to the shareholders, from which I quote :

> " In carrying out our constructive programme with inherited liabilities and with inadequate or no substantial financial resources, the want of capital was chronic."

CHAPTER VIII.

The Sondage Syndicate, Limited. Its Genesis. No results, no Pay. A legitimate Gamble. The Waldershare Boring. First Coal Seam on Concessions' Area. The "Rockefeller" Seam. Successful results at Fredville.

"I have a kind of alacrity in sinking."
—MERRY WIVES.

The Concessions Board soon realised that the properties to be taken over from the liquidators of the Dover Coalfield Extension, Limited, were of little or no value, so no time was lost in completing the negotiations for the further areas referred to in the prospectus.

It was fortunate that the borings incidental to these acquisitions were not dependent upon the Company's meagre working capital, the money being provided by a small subsidiary company entitled

THE SONDAGE SYNDICATE, LIMITED.

which was registered in January, 1905, with a capital of £5,000 for that purpose—thus enabling the Concessions Company to increase its mineral acreage, in accordance with the pledges given to the first subscribers who furnished most of the original capital.

From some quarters, uninformed as to the early history of the Company, criticism has been levelled against the first Directors of the Concessions for handing over the exploratory work instead of undertaking it themselves. Therefore it is necessary to emphasise the fact that the Board had no option in the matter. Prior to the issue of the prospectus, advance application forms were sent out with a covering letter in which it was distinctly stated that Kent Coal Concessions would *not* itself sink shafts, or put down borings, which work would be undertaken by the various sub-companies. "Our capital," it was declared, "will be devoted to maintaining the options and enlarging them." This deliberately adopted policy was further brought home to Concessions shareholders in a circular letter issued by Mr. Burr, under date August 18, 1904, in which he stated that

"It was also adopted as a principle that the company itself would undertake no speculative or exploratory work, but that such would be carried out by a sub-company or companies to be promoted for that purpose. Upon these lines the company has proceeded."

At this date Mr. Burr had no official appointment under the company, but that this was no bar to his exercising a control over its policy may be gathered from his letter to Concessions shareholders, dated October 13, 1906, wherein he stated that "ever since the formation of the company I have acted as honorary managing director without remuneration."

Concessions made what was in reality a one-sided bargain, on the principle of "no results—no pay." The Sondage Syndicate risked the entire loss of its capital, not a negligible risk either in view of the many abortive borings of the past. Concessions shareholders were invited to join in the venture, the capital being offered to them preferentially. The application forms were accompanied by a circular in which it was stated that "It is hardly necessary to repeat that money invested in the Sondage Syndicate must be regarded in the light of a speculation and *liable to total loss.*"

A copy of the contract which Concessions had made in November, 1904, between itself, Arthur Burr, and a Trustee for the proposed Syndicate was also enclosed with the application forms. For reasons which will appear presently I reproduce some of its more important provisions, thus:—

"One of the principal objects to be set forth in the Memorandum of Association of the said Syndicate shall be to undertake boring or other engineering works for the purpose of finding and proving coal in the properties of Kent Coal Concessions, Limited."

. . . . . .

"The Syndicate, as soon as convenient, but not later than January, 1905, and as long thereafter as the parties of the second and third parts fulfil their obligations hereunder, undertake for and on behalf of the Kent Coal Concessions, Limited, the work of boring for and proving the coal area upon the properties of the Kent Coal Concessions, Limited."

"So long as the Syndicate and/or Arthur Burr fulfil their obligations aforesaid under the contract, no other person or corporation shall be employed by the Kent Coal Concessions, Limited, to bore for or prove coal upon their coal properties without the written consent of the Syndicate."

. . . . . .

"The sites upon which such borings shall be made shall be specified by the Kent Coal Concessions, Limited, but the Syndicate shall not be required to undertake more than one bore-hole in any one year."

. . . . . .

"The Syndicate shall undertake no work and enter into no contract on its own behalf other than work or works required by Kent Coal Concessions, Limited."

. . . . . .

"In the event of any boring proving a success as aforesaid, the Syndicate shall be entitled to be paid 100 per cent. cash as and by way of bonus upon the amount of its capital outlay thereon, together with the return of such outlay from the Kent Coal Concessions, Limited, and also 10 per cent. to be paid out of the nominal capital to be issued as fully paid of any company formed to work the minerals under the area proved by such boring (that is to say) to one-tenth of all cash or/and shares or/and debentures of whatever denomination or variety that may be issued by such company, or in the alternative to 10 per cent. of the prices in cash and/or shares that may be paid for any area upon any sale thereof by the Kent Coal Concessions, Limited, or upon the profits arising from any improved rent or royalty obtained, provided always that such percentage shall only be payable as and when received by the Kent Coal Concessions, Limited, and not otherwise."

. . . . . .

"In the event of the failure of any such boring the Syndicate shall bear solely the loss incurred by its capital outlay thereon, and the Kent Coal Concessions, Limited, shall not be liable to contribute thereto either directly or indirectly."

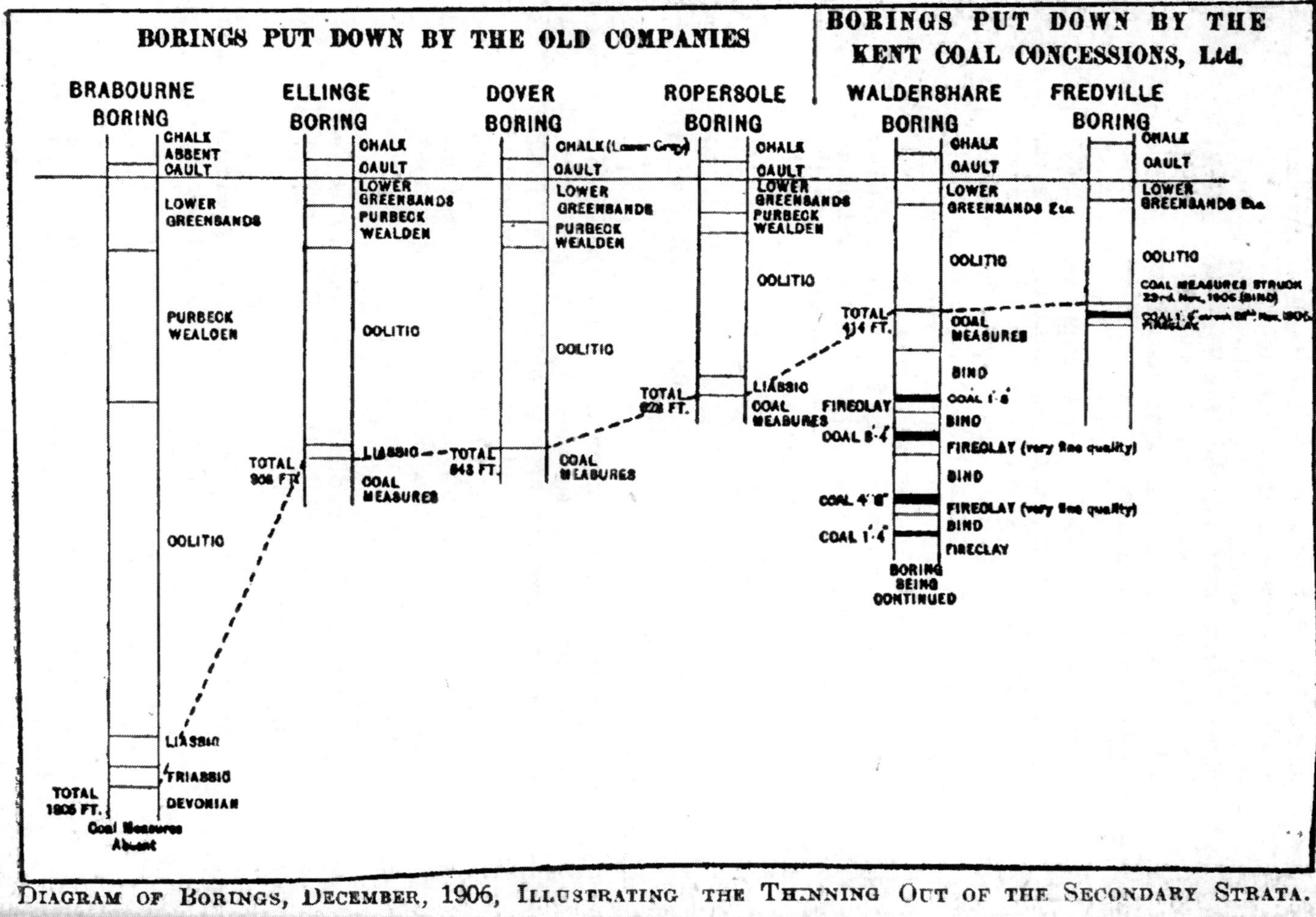

Diagram of Borings, December, 1906, Illustrating the Thinning Out of the Secondary Strata.

Under a supplementary agreement, dated September 13, 1905, it was provided that in any case in which Concessions should make a sale of any land without calling on the Sondage Syndicate to make a boring thereon, then the Syndicate in consideration of its waiving and releasing its rights of boring should be entitled to 10 per cent. of the net profits of such sale.

There was no board of directors, though a small committee of shareholders was supposed to have consultative powers; the sole control, however, was vested in Mr. Arthur Burr, as life manager, with Professor Boyd Dawkins as geological adviser.

The operations of the Syndicate, as is generally known, have proved phenomenally successful, and consequently the Concessions Company has now become its debtor to the extent of many thousands of pounds. Companies are said to differ from human beings inasmuch as they have no souls; but the Kent Coal Concessions Company is displaying the very human failing of not wanting to pay the piper, after having called the tune.

This is in marked contrast to the attitude of those Directors who were in office in 1906, as is shown by the following excerpts from a circular, dated November 30 of that year, issued to the shareholders over the signature of the then chairman of the company, thus :—

> "Your directors are of opinion that fresh capital to the extent of £50,000 should be authorised, of which £15,000 will be required for the contemplated Workmen's Dwellings Company, £15,000 for new borings and explorations, and to include a substantial payment to the Sondage Syndicate, this Company being already indebted to the Syndicate for boring in excess of its contract obligations to the extent of £12,000 and upwards."
>
> "Your Directors desire to record their appreciation of the enterprising and liberal spirit in which the Sondage Syndicate has interpreted such obligations."

But *autres temps autres moeurs*, and quite recently I have heard this Sondage Syndicate even stigmatised as a "parasite" upon the Kent Coal undertaking, as though such a contract as that concluded between it and the

Concessions Company were an unheard-of thing, with something sinister in its conception. Whereas it merely exemplifies the sporting element which in us is proverbial. I am sure that readers can multiply similar instances for themselves where money has been forthcoming for most adventurous schemes on the chance of "striking it rich."

An almost parallel example is to be found in the records of one of the most successful collieries in the Pas de Calais. The celebrated Courrières mine, to which I have referred before, came into existence as the result of a boring financed by the Société Bigo, to which were issued founders' shares in the Colliery Company in return for the services rendered. These shares were nominally of 1,000 francs each, carrying the right to 20 per cent. of the profits; and within a little over twenty years their market value had risen to 200,000 francs per share. Courrières paid up and looked pleasant!

The first boring under the contract was that of Waldershare adjoining the Park of that name—the seat of the Earl of Guilford. Professor Boyd Dawkins, who selected the site, stated that "Coal Measures are likely to be struck at this spot, either directly below or within a short distance of the bottom of the Gault."

The hole was started in January, 1905, by Messrs. A. C. Potter & Company, who carried it down to 1,409 ft.; at which point the work passed into the hands of Mr. John Thom, who bored down to 2,863 ft.

Although the Sondage Syndicate was not bound under the contract to undertake more than one boring in any one year, in June, 1905, Professor Boyd Dawkins selected a site for a second borehole, as to which he reported to the Concessions Company that it "will give information as to the presence of Coal Measures in the two large properties north of Waldershare, and probably render another boring unnecessary within their limits." He also stated that "a site for a third boring to test a property still further to the north is now under consideration." And his report concluded thus:—"Each boring will give fresh information that will indicate the best direction to extend the holding of the Company, if it be thought fit to do so."

When issuing this report of Boyd Dawkins to their shareholders the Concessions Directors stated, in a covering letter dated July 12, 1905, that—"It is not intended to make any actual start at the site chosen for the third boring until after the coal has been proved at Waldershare, but all preliminary arrangements are being made in preparation, so that there may be no loss of valuable time."

It was the readiness on the part of the Syndicate to go beyond its contract obligations that evoked from the Directors of Concessions their appreciation of "the enterprising and liberal spirit in which the Sondage Syndicate has interpreted its obligations," which I have already quoted.

This testimony to the services rendered by the "parasite" does not stand alone. The circulars issued by the Concessions Directors, during the exploratory period, bear constant witness to the fact that the Company's extended areas and enhanced prospects were directly attributable to the activities of the Sondage Syndicate; thus, for example:—

> "The cost of our borings varies according to the footage explored and the extent to which lining becomes necessary, but, as a rough estimate, from £500 to £1,000 per month must be provided. Thanks, however, to the systematic and exhaustive exploration of our vast acreage, we are securing, by means of these borings, exclusive knowledge of the coalfield that will repay their cost a thousand-fold."

There is also another direction in which the Concessions Company benefited by the Sondage borings, apart from proving the value of their existing properties, for as the borings progressed the value of Concessions shares appreciated. The Directors thus found it possible not only to increase their capital but to get it subscribed at a substantial premium.

For such a statement one might be called upon to give chapter and verse, than which nothing is easier. In an official circular to Concessions shareholders, of September 23, 1908, reporting the result of an issue of 40,000 10 per cent. cumulative preference shares, of which only 20,000 were subscribed, appears the following.

"It is not proposed to make any premature public issue of the remaining shares. For one reason *that results from at least two of our borings must in the near future justify a higher price of issue than £1 17s. 6d., and certainly attract more subscriptions.*" (The italics are mine.)

Upon the foregoing facts it must be conceded that by getting another company to put up the cash, and take the risk in respect of its borings, Concessions was enabled to acquire a much larger mineral acreage than its slender financial resources would otherwise have permitted. How attenuated these resources were is evidenced by the state of its banking account during the early part of its career, thus:—

June 30, 1904	... ...	£5	3s.	4d.,	Cr.
December 31, 1904	...	£67	8s.	10d.,	Cr.
June 30, 1905	... ...	£50	11s.	3d.,	Dr.
December 31, 1905	...	£20	7s.	5d.,	Dr.
June 30, 1906	... ...	£349	13s.	7d.,	Dr.

There are some 4,000 persons interested in these two companies, thus no apology should be necessary for having arrested the course of my narrative in order to deal at some length with the business relations of the Syndicate *vis a vis* Kent Coal Concessions. Unluckily for me, I have never owned a single Sondage share, hence, in dealing with these matters, I have been under no temptation to depart from my role of unbiassed historian, in which capacity I will now resume my record of the development of the Coalfield.

The first seam of coal proved in the Waldershare boring—the first of many seams on the areas of Kent Coal Concessions and its later allied Companies—was struck on September 19, 1906, at a depth of 1,818 ft. 7 in. It was only 1 ft. 8 in. in thickness, but as it was rightly estimated that the true trend of the coalfield had been located at last, it was named the "Welcome" Seam. This estimate was amply confirmed by the following further seams proved at this boring:—

September 27, 1906, 3 ft. 4 in. seam, the "Alexandra."

October 18, 1906, 4 ft. 6 in. seam, the "King Edward."

March 8, 1907, 5 ft. 2 in. seam, the "Rockefeller."

Nothing, of course, can deprive the Brady boring of its historic importance as being the first to determine the existence of coal in Kent. In all other respects, however, the Waldershare boring is entitled to precedence, for it not only disclosed thicker and more valuable seams, but evidenced the extension of the Coal Measures to the north-east under a greatly reduced covering of Secondary rocks, as is shown hereunder :—

General Section of the Waldershare Boring.

(335 Ft. O.D.)

	Ft.	
Chalk	813	
Gault	163	
Lower Greensand	70	
Wealden	42	
Oolites	301	
Lias	5	
		Ft.
Coal Measures		at 1,394

	Ft.	in.	
Coarse Sandstone full of pebbles of coal, some bind, clays and shales	376	6	
Hard grey bind	45	6	
"Welcome" Seam...	1	8	at 1,818
Fireclay	6	8	
Grey bind	52	9	
"Alexandra" Seam	3	4	at 1,878
Fireclay	5	10	
Grey bind	16	1	
"King Edward" Seam	4	6	at 1,904
Fireclay	2	3	
Grey bind	44	4	
"Watkin" Seam	1	4	at 1,955
Fireclay	5	0	
Sandstones and bind... ...	410	2	
"Rockefeller" Seam	5	2	at 2,372
Fireclay	2	6	
Blue bind	16	2	
Coal vein	0	4	
Fireclay	4	8	
Sandstone and bind	155	0	

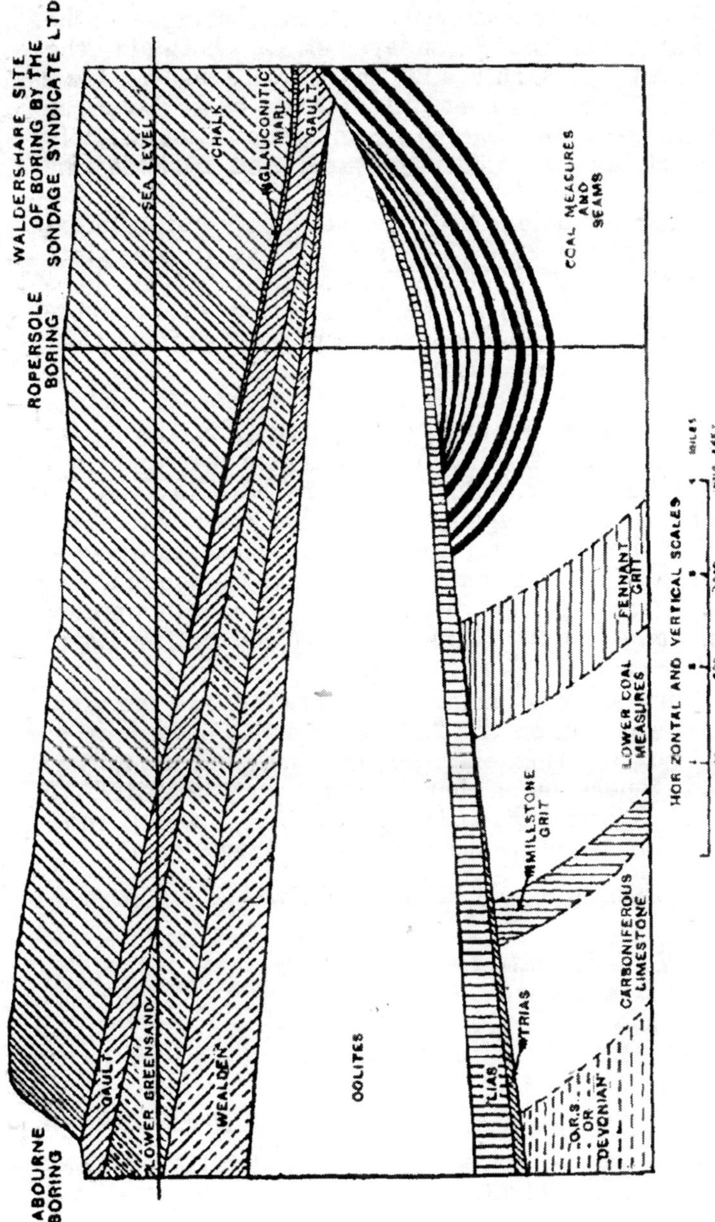

SECTION FROM BRABOURNE AND WALDERSHARE AS ASSUMED IN 1905.

At a depth of 2,555 ft. the hole was too reduced to permit of further boring.

The chief characteristics of this boring are the reduction of the Secondary strata between the base of the Gault and the Coal Measures from 842 ft., as at Dover, to 414 ft., and the great thicknesses of barren Sandstones immediately underlying the Coal Measures and between the "Watkin" and "Rockefeller" Seams. The first of these Sandstone beds was so thickly impregnated with coal particles as in some places to constitute almost a coal conglomerate—a silent but eloquent witness to the forces of Nature that in a remote epoch had denuded and scattered some of the then existing upper seams.

Although the Secondary strata showed such a substantial reduction as compared with the Brady Section, the thinning out was much less than had been hoped for. Boyd Dawkins had advised the Concessions Company that the Coal Measures might be looked for immediately below the Gault, and in 1905 that company issued the accompanying plan (*see* pags 98) which was based on this opinion and on Boyd Dawkins' evidence before the Royal Commission on Coal Supplies.

Further, this boring is remarkable for the seam that was named the "Rockefeller" on account of its amazing richness. The following is the analysis and report on a borehole sample submitted to Mr. George R. Hislop, F.C.S., M.S.C.Ind., F.R.S.S.A., of the Paisley Gas Works:—

Analysis (Sample Free from Foreign Matters).

	Per cent.
Volatile matters	40.23
Fixed carbon	52.66
Ash	1.90
Water	5.21
	100.00

Evaporative power in lbs. of water from and at 212 deg. F., 14.73.

Report.—The above results prove this to be an exceptionally valuable coal for gas-manufacturing purposes, and will yield approximately 13,000 cub. ft. of 23.5-candle gas.

At a later date Mr. Hislop furnished the following table of comparative centisimal values of this seam and nine of the leading gas coals in England:

Standard Coal value equal to unity, or	100.00
"Rockefeller" Seam—Kent	73.22
Abram Gas and Coking Coal—Lancashire	64.81
Blainscough Arley Gas Coal—Lancashire	60.81
Golborne Gas Coal—Lancashire	64.19
Hindley Field Long Arley Gas Coal—Lancashire	60.63
Princess Arley Gas Coal—Lancashire ...	59.74
Flocton Gas Coal—Staffordshire	60.80
Talk o' th' Hill Gas Coal—Staffordshire	59.90
Hardwick Cavendish Gas Coal—Derbyshire	64.59
Silkstone Best Gas Coal—Yorkshire ...	59.40

The proving of a 4-ft. 4-in. seam at the contemporary boring which was commenced by the Sondage Syndicate on August 8, 1905, at Fredville, three miles north-west of Waldershare, on the estate of Mr. H. Western Plumptre, made assurance double sure: It was named the "Beresford," after the late Mr. Beresford Wright, then chairman of the famous Butterley Company, who was largely interested in the coalfield. This seam is now being worked by Snowdown Colliery, Limited, and already some half a million tons of coal have been won from it.

Thus after many years the true trend of the South-Eastern Coalfield was definitely located, and the thinning-out of the Secondary rocks towards the north-east, already indicated in the earlier borings, was still further established—thus:—

Borings.	Secondary Rocks below the Gault. Ft.
Brabourne	1,899
Ellinge	939
Dover	842
Ropersole	627
Waldershare	414
Fredville	380

It is a far cry, both as regards distance and time, from the Sub-Wealden boring at Netherfield in 1872, *viâ* that at Shakespeare Cliff, and the many failures westward, to the successful results at Waldershare in 1906.

The failures that have had to be recorded must have occasioned the loss of large sums of money by a numerous body of shareholders; but the country was eventually enriched by a proven coalfield, whose then known boundaries have been enlarged from year to year by one successful boring after another. All, be it noted, to the east of the Dover-Canterbury road.

The theory of the "Western Front" proved inapplicable to Kent!

CHAPTER IX.

Upper Transition Series at Waldershare and Fredville. Estimates as to Coal-contents of the Basin. The Fonçage Syndicate. Goodnestone and Barfrestone Borings started. Several new Companies registered. The East Kent Colliery Company, Limited.

"One plows, another sows;
Who will reap no one knows."
—ANON.

The horizon of the seams at the Waldershare and Fredville borings has been referred to the Upper Transition Series by Professor Newell Arber, F.G.S., after an exhaustive examination of the fossil plants which he had made at the request of the Concessions Co. (See "Quarterly Journal" of the Geological Society, Vol. XV., pp. 21-40.)

This is, I believe, in conformity with Monsieur Zeiller's latest pronouncement regarding the Brady section, and determines the classification of the coals in these borings as identical with those of the richest zone of the Pas de Calais.

These seams are also considered to be the homotaxial equivalents of the undermentioned deposits in other British coalfields, thus:—

Coalfield.	*Series.*
North Staffordshire	Newcastle-under-Lyme. Etruria Marl. Blackband Group.
South Staffordshire	Hamstead Colliery, Great Barr, below 1,223 ft.
Denbighshire	Coedyratt. Ruabon Marls.
South Wales	Ardwick Series. Bradford Colliery, above the Four-Foot coal.
	Lower Pennant Grit.
Somerset	New Rock Vobster.

Prior to the discoveries at Waldershare and Fredville, the amount of coal in this new field was considered too problematical to warrant any credit being taken for it in the estimates of the nation's reserves, given in the Final Report of the Commission on Coal Supplies issued in 1905, as is shown by the following extracts:—

> "It will be understood that while the position of some concealed coalfields may be determined with approximate precision, others are more hypothetical. In some cases, as, for example, in Kent, the limits are so doubtful as to render an estimate impossible" (Part IX., page 3).
>
> "While it may be inferred that this Brabourne boring proves the limits of the Coal Measures in a south-westerly direction, their extent in other directions remains yet to be ascertained. In view of this fact, and that our knowledge of the coals is founded on two borings only, I find it impossible to make any estimate of the amount of coal likely to exist in Kent" (Part IX., page 16).

In their evidence before the Commission neither Boyd Dawkins nor Whitaker, while expressing belief in the potentialities of the Kentish Coalfield, would venture on any figures.

Events have marched since then, for in 1913 Dr. Aubrey Strahan, then Assistant-Director of the Geological Survey, estimated the contents of the coal basin at 2,000,000,000 tons; but his figures are largely exceeded by Mr. H. Stanley Jevons in his exhaustive work, "The British Coal Trade," published in 1915. Mr. Jevons puts the reserve of proved coal at 6,000,000,000 tons, with a probable further 3,600,000,000 tons, or 9,600,000,000 tons in all.

Personally, on the present available data, I should be satisfied to stand on Mr. Jevons' 6,000,000,000 tons; the later extensions of the field on which he based his supplementary figures are not so great as he reckoned, and in my opinion his "probable further 3,600,000,000 tons" should be disregarded.

It will have been observed that, although the Waldershare boring started in January, 1905, it was not until September 17 of the following year that the first seam was struck, at a depth of 1,818 ft.—an average rate of boring of only a fraction over 88 ft. per month.

Houldsworth's lament, in 1866, over the inadequacy of our boring systems in his day might well have been echoed by the explorers of 1905!

It would have been of inestimable value and benefit to the Concessions Company had its first boring been entrusted to such a firm as the Société Tréfor, of Brussels, which later on put down a bore at Maydensole to a depth of 3,760 ft. in exactly 12 months, or at the rate of 313 ft. per month! The first 900 ft. only were bored with the chisel.

The delay in getting definite results at Waldershare was responsible for the formation of another small subsidiary Company—the

FONÇAGE SYNDICATE, LIMITED.

registered April 18, 1906, with a capital of £5,000, which was subsequently raised to £20,000. This Syndicate undertook the preliminary surface works and some small amount of sinking at the sites of the present Guilford and Snowdown Collieries, and likewise in association with the Sondage Syndicate at that of Tilmanstone. It commenced work at the first-named prior to, and in anticipation of, the Waldershare bore reaching coal.

The Fonçage Syndicate concluded its activities in 1908, since when it has remained in a state of suspended animation awaiting the Happy Despatch.

I shall have no further occasion to refer to this Syndicate, therefore I take this opportunity of recording the fact that with a view to facilitating a settlement of its affairs, particularly those in which the Concessions Company is concerned, Mr. Arthur Burr, at the end of 1918, resigned his Life-Managership in favour of his son, Dr. Malcolm Burr, who in his turn likewise resigned in order that a Board of Directors might be appointed.

In consideration for giving up his right of succession, which was provided for under the Articles of Association, Dr. Burr received from the Syndicate £300 in cash and an assignment of £2,000, being part of a debt due to the Syndicate, which may or may not realise its face value.

At an Extraordinary General Meeting held on March 5, 1919, to confirm the necessary alterations to the Articles of Association, the following gentlemen were appointed Directors:—Mr. J. J. Clark, Mr. W. Egerton Martin, Sir Henry F. Woods, Mr. H. W. Marley.

The Syndicate holds the bulk of the Ordinary shares in Snowdown Colliery, Ltd., the value of which is very problematical, and it also has claims against Concessions Co. in respect of certain areas now in course of realisation. It is impossible to give any estimate as to what return shareholders are likely to get—they must "wait and see."

While the Waldershare boring operations were "furiously loitering," and calling forth anathemas from those who so anxiously awaited results, the Concessions Company, whose capital had been increased by £50,000 in July, 1906, greatly daring, pursued the bold policy which after events were so amply to justify.

Numerous options were acquired over extensive and well-situated mineral areas. As is usually the case, these options carried an obligation to bore; therefore, in December, 1906, the Sondage Syndicate started a boring, their third, on Mr. Fitzwalter Plumptre's property at Goodnestone, about four miles from, and almost due north of, Waldershare. This borehole was carried down to a depth of 2,906 ft., leaving off in November, 1910—in Coal-Measure binds, owing to the inability of the contractor to go any deeper.

Many valuable seams were proved, the principal of which were one of 8 ft. 8 in., one of 6 ft. 7 in., and two of 4 ft. 6 in.; their horizon is almost certainly that of the upper portion of the Middle Coal Measures, and analyses of the borehole samples show them to be high-grade steam coals, with volatiles ranging from 15.5 to 20 per cent. The time occupied in this boring was no less than three years and nine and a half months, an average monthly progress (if one may employ that word!) of only 64 ft.

1907.

In February, 1907, following upon the successful results at Waldershare and Fredville, the Concessions Company again increased its capital and made a public issue of £35,000 (part of £50,000 created) of 10 per cent. cumulative preference shares of £1 each, to the Prospectus of which Boyd Dawkins contributed the following memorandum :—

> " I beg to give you the summary of my previous reports as to the results of the borings at Waldershare and Fredville. They undoubtedly prove that a rich coalfield exists in the mineral area of the Company, which must be counted among the national assets of Great Britain. They prove further that it exists under physical and geological conditions that make it easy of access, as compared with Dover. How rich and how valuable it will turn out to be remains to be proved by further discoveries in these borings and in others now in progress that have not yet reached the Coal Measures."

Mr. G. H. Hollingworth, F.G.S., M.Inst.M.E., who had been appointed consulting engineer to the Company, also emphasised the great potential value of its areas—then estimated at 40 sq. miles. His report concluded thus :—

> " The Pas de Calais Coalfield, which has been opened up within the last 50 years under somewhat similar circumstances, has yielded enormous profits to those engaged in the coal industry under difficulties which are not existing in the Kent Coalfield, and there appears no reason to doubt that the working of the latter will yield fully as favourable results."

The Waldershare boring had further disclosed the existence of a valuable bed of fireclay underlying the 4-ft. 6-in. seam. Samples had been submitted to Mr. Ed. Wheldon, a well-known authority in North Wales, who advised the board that it had proved to be " of very exceptional quality equal to the best Staffordshire clays; in fact, I have never met with better and rarely such good fireclay in my 40 years' experience. With this clay you can make any class of stoneware and enamelled goods."

In November, 1907, the Sondage Syndicate started its fourth boring on behalf of the Concessions Company, at Barfrestone, about a mile and a half north-west of Waldershare, and the same distance south-east of Fredville, the results of which will be given in due course.

Earlier in the year, however, some important additions were made to the number of companies operating under the *ægis* of Kent Coal Concessions, Limited, which, by reason of its increasing progeny, became known as the Parent Company. These were:—

The East Kent Colliery Company, Limited, registered March 28.

South-Eastern Coalfield Extension, Limited, registered June 6.

Guilford Syndicate, Limited, registered August 2.

East Kent Contract and Financial Company, Limited, registered December 13.

Having enumerated the important events of the year 1907, I will now proceed to deal in detail with the history of the above Companies, the first on the list being—

THE EAST KENT COLLIERY COMPANY, LIMITED.

This company acquired through the medium of the Central Trust, Limited, which acted as vendors, the benefit of the Sondage and Fonçage Syndicates' agreements with Concessions, including the surface plant and equipment, and, of course, the Pit that had already been started by the two Syndicates and which was then down to 508 ft.

The original capital of the Company was £250,000, in 960,000 ordinary shares of 5s. each, and 200,000 vendors' shares of 1s. each. The former are entitled to a preferential dividend of 10 per cent. and one moiety of the remaining profits, while the vendors' shares are to receive the other moiety; 125,000 of these latter were allotted to the Parent Company as fully paid; similarly the Fonçage and Sondage Syndicates were allotted 50,000 and 25,000 respectively.

The directors were Mr. Arthur Burr, Mr. H. W. Marley and, later on, Mr. H. G. Gompertz. There was no public issue of the shares, the bulk of which were allotted fully paid to the Central Trust, Limited, which undertook to finance the sinking. The necessary funds were provided by the sale of the shares, which were peddled out at such prices as could be obtained. It was a long time before a par basis was established.

In November, 1907, there was, however, an issue to existing shareholders of the allied companies of 60,000 shares, the subscribers for which received from the vendors two fully-paid shares for every three shares applied for. In course of time there were other issues, and the capital was increased to £500,000; but even this amount did not suffice to keep the Company out of "Queer Street," and later on debentures had to be created that materially modified the rights of the shareholders. These financial matters will be dealt with presently; for the moment I will confine myself more particularly to the practical side of the undertaking.

Tilmanstone Colliery, as it is always called, is situated about a mile from the village of that name, and one and a half miles north of the Waldershare boring, alongside the Sandwich road. Until the advent of the East Kent Light Railway, in 1911, the nearest railway station was that of Shepherdswell on the South-Eastern and Chatham line some three miles distant. Lack of direct railway communication was a severe handicap during a great part of the constructional period, adding materially to the cost of the work and resulting in heavy claims from the local authorities for extraordinary traffic.

The foundation of the colliery may be said to have been laid by the Sondage Syndicate in August, 1906, when, owing to the intermittent progress of the Waldershare boring, the Concessions Company arranged that the Syndicate should start a 7-ft. exploratory shaft with a view to proving the minerals under the Tilmanstone area. The shaft had reached a depth of 270 ft. when the discovery of the good seams at Waldershare gave all the information that was considered necessary as regards the trend of the coal basin. It was decided therefore to enlarge it to 14 ft. diameter, and to proceed to sink to the coal.

The finances of the Syndicate, even when supplemented by those of Fonçage, permitted only of the installation of a pair of small-capacity second-hand winding engines, a circumstance which proved later on a serious handicap to the management.

At this period the sinking was in the hands of Mr. Maurice Griffith, son of Mr. Nath. R. Griffith, whose name has been mentioned in connection with the Dover Cliff works. Very little water was encountered in the chalk and was dealt with by an

Evans steam ram-pump, cylinder 38-in. bore, ram 14-in. diameter, stroke 3-ft., which was erected in an inset at 600 ft.

The progress through the chalk and gault was good, but a great mistake was made in sacrificing everything to speed. "Safety First" is equally as good a motto in sinking pits as in crossing streets. The shaft had been carried down to a depth of 913 ft.—almost to the base of the Gault—by the end of May, 1908, but had been left unbricked from 631 ft. Before the bricking of this unprotected section had been even commenced, the shaft sides in the gault showed a decided tendency to collapse, and chalk and débris had to be thrown into the pit to support them. This length consequently had to be re-sunk and bricked up in short stages, and it was not until the end of the year that the sinkers broke fresh ground. This was the first, but by no means the last nor the greatest, of the many set-backs experienced in connection with No. 1 Pit.

On November 19, 1907, the first sod of a second shaft, 18 ft. diameter, was turned, which was made the occasion of some ceremony, a large number of shareholders and others being invited to be present. Mr. Burr's little granddaughter, aged 3, after whom the pit was named the "Gabrielle," performed the actual rite of turning the sod. There were refreshments, speechifying, much mutual congratulation upon a further stage in the development of the colliery having been reached, and once more hope told a flattering tale! Not a soul present dreamed of the weary years of heart-breaking anxieties that were to elapse before the "Gabrielle" shaft, so happily inaugurated, was to be safely taken into the Coal Measures.

The annual report of the directors at a later date (June, 1910) admitted that this shaft had been started without sufficient capital even to pay for its winding engines, and that none of the other companies was in a position to help financially. Yet a second shaft, with a powerful equipment, was an absolute necessity, and without it sinking through the Lower Greensands would have been an impossibility.

Therefore, while financial purists may profess amazement at their unorthodoxy, the directors had to take their courage in both hands in the way they did, or it is certain that the works would have come to an untimely end, and the coalfield would have experienced another set-back that might well have proved disastrous. The only law governing the financing of this and other undertakings of the group was that of expediency—the money had to be found somehow. I have heard it suggested that criticism might well be tempered by the reflection that the end has justified the means.

Many and great were the difficulties that had to be surmounted before the Tilmanstone shafts reached the first seam of coal, each of which would demand a chapter to itself if the geological and engineering problems involved were to be dealt with *in extenso*. A brief but comprehensive summary of the sinking operations will suffice to show those of my readers who have followed the misfortunes of the Shakespeare Cliff works, how, and with what painful exactitude, history repeated itself.

During 1908 the "Gabrielle," to which I shall hereafter refer as No. 2 Pit, made fairly satisfactory progress, especially after the middle of July when the temporary winding engines with which it had been started were replaced by a pair built by Messrs. Martyn Bros., of Airdrie. These have two horizontal cylinders, 30-in. bore by 60-in. stroke, with a cylindrical drum 13 ft. diameter and 6 ft. 6 in. wide.

CHAPTER X.

East Kent Colliery, continued. Sinking through the Lower Greensands.

"To suffer wet damnation to run through 'em."
—OLD PLAY.

1909.

Sinking through the Lower Greensands.

When referring to the Lower Greensands it must be understood that this is a comprehensive term embracing several sub-divisions which, together with other sections of the Lower Cretaceous series, are sometimes styled, in geological parlance, "Neocomian." "Lower Greensand" is even at times a misnomer, for frequently the Clays predominate over the Sands; but however inappropriate, the name has received the authority of usage.

The Lower Greensands which are so much a feature of the Weald are sub-divided in descending order, thus:—

Folkestone Sands.
Sandgate Beds.
Hythe Beds.
Atherfield Clay.

The Hythe Beds, which are composed largely of loose sands, at times carrying considerable quantities of water, were not met with at Tilmanstone—a small matter for congratulation, perhaps, seeing that nearly every other known water-bearing stratum was! These Beds are all of marine origin, and were laid down under somewhat shallow water, as the Wealden clays and silts, which were deposited in fresh water under estuarine conditions, gradually subsided.

Overlying the Lower Greensand series is an interesting agglomerate known as the Mammilatus Bed by reason of its being largely composed of the remains of the ammonite *Acanthoceras Mammilatum.* It is a curious fact that traces of gold were detected in samples from this Bed in the Tilmanstone Pits; and, further, that a good-sized piece of

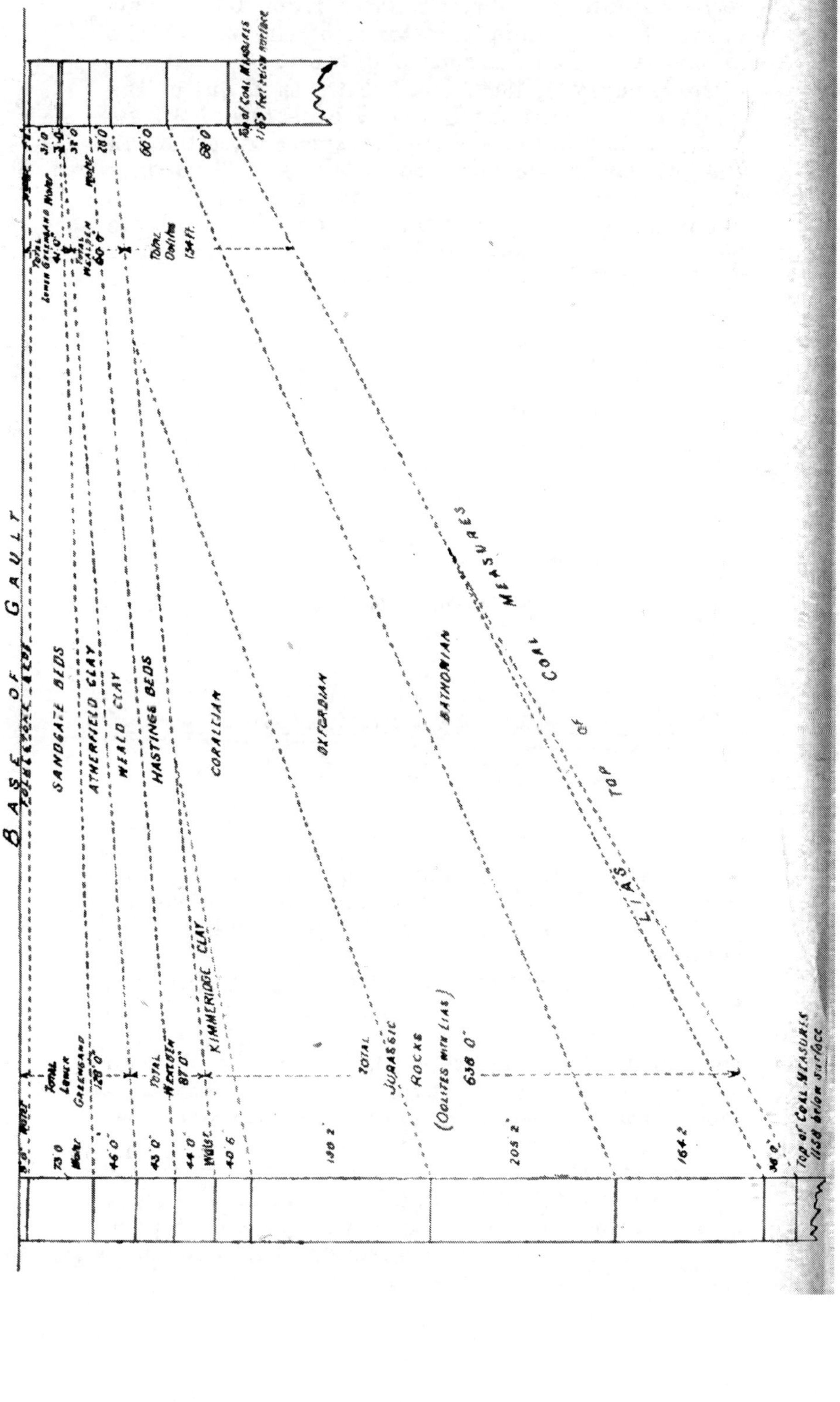

BASE OF GAULT
FOLKESTONE BEDS
SANDGATE BEDS
ATHERFIELD CLAY
WEALD CLAY
HASTINGS BEDS
KIMMERIDGE CLAY
CORALLIAN
OXFORDIAN
BATHONIAN
LIAS
TOP OF COAL MEASURES

73' 0" Water
46' 0"
43' 0"
44' 0" Water
40' 6"
130' 2"
205' 2"
164' 2"
36' 0"
Top of Coal Measures 1158 below surface

Total Lower Greensand 128' 0"
Total Wealden 87' 0"
Total Jurassic Rocks (Oolites with Lias) 638' 0"

31' 0"
32' 0"
28' 0"
66' 0"
68' 0"
Total Lower Greensand Water 41' 0"
Total Wealden Water 60' 0"
Total Oolites 134 ft.
Top of Coal Measures 1163 feet below surface

this rock has been found built into the old Fisher Gate at Sandwich, which dates from 1558. This is said to be a unique instance of the use of the Mammilatus Bed for such a purpose.

On January 5, 1909, No. 1 Pit passed out of the gault and entered the Lower Greensands at 942 ft. without meeting any water to speak of, either in the pit or in the advance borehole. Two days later, however, there was an influx, amounting to about 60 gallons per minute, from the Sandgate beds. The water-barrel dealt with this quite easily until the 14th of the month, when, owing

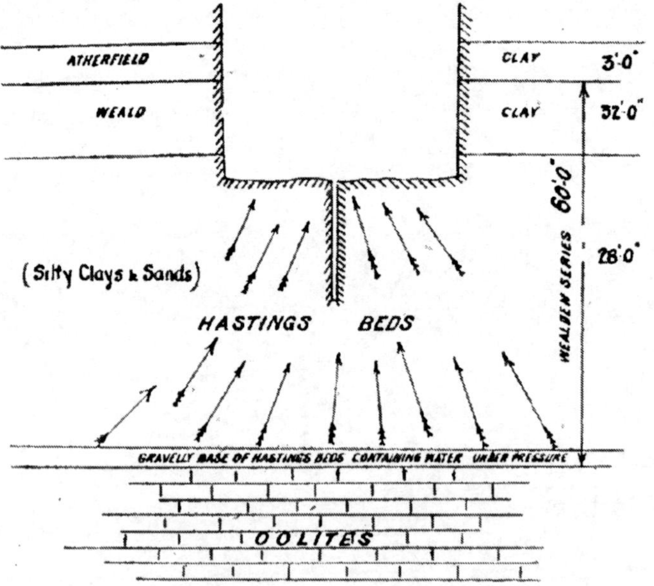

to an overwind, the hoppit dropped down the pit, damaging the sides, smashing the ventilating pipes, and, unfortunately, killing three of the sinkers.

Another suspension of sinking operations was thus rendered necessary until No. 2 Pit could be taken down to the same depth, in order that a connecting road might be made between the two shafts for ventilation purposes, and to enable its more powerful winding engines to relieve those at No. 1 of the water-winding.

The Greensands, however, were found to be dry when No. 2 reached them, all their water evidently being drained by No. 1, so it was decided to push further ahead before connecting the two pits

Sinking was suspended at 974 ft. and preparations were in progress for continuing No. 1 shaft to that depth when Dame Fortune again frowned on the enterprise.

Although the borehole from the bottom of No. 2 had given no indication of breakers ahead, yet the water was lying in wait, locked up in the gravelly base of the Hastings beds. Its pressure, which was estimated to be 300 lbs. to the sq. in., was too great for the covering strata, through which it gradually forced its way, gathering volume in its progress until it finally burst up the bottom of the shaft, as is shown in the small plan on page 113. The water, coming in at the rate of 1,000 gallons a minute, rose 16 ft. up the shaft in 26 minutes, but after three days the volume reduced itself to 350 gallons per minute.

With such a column of water in No. 2 Pit exercising great pressure on the tender Wealden strata, it was considered advisable to let No. 1 fill up to the same level in order that this outside pressure might be neutralised.

This incident occurred in April, and nearly nine months elapsed before sinking could be resumed in No. 2 Pit, up and down which the water-barrel travelled night and day unceasingly, and as rapidly as the engines could wind. Thus only was it possible to keep the inflow under control and enable work to proceed in No. 1. At 990 ft. an inset was made in this pit, in which were erected two Evans direct-acting straight-line pattern ram pumps, cylinders 24 in. bore, rams 10 in. in diameter with a 2-ft. stroke. Each pump has a capacity of raising 350 gallons per minute against a head of 600 ft., with a steam pressure of 100 lbs. per sq. in. The total capacity of these pumps is 42,000 gallons per hour, and they deliver their water at the 600-ft. inset.

As the sinking progressed pulsometers were employed to bring the water from the pit-bottom to the pumps, and after their installation efforts were made to divert all the Hastings water from No. 2 to No. 1. These efforts were eventually successful, though it was found difficult to win it away from its long attachment for No. 2. Ultimately, all but a small proportion was raised by the 990-ft. pumps, and the sinkers were once more able to enter this pit.

1910.

By mid-January No. 1 Pit reached the top of the gravelly bed at the base of the Hastings at 1,028 ft.; this proved thicker than had been anticipated, the Oolites not being met with before 1,035 ft. The upper 3-ft. were found to be much disintegrated and corroded, owing to the action of the water in the overlying bed. At 1,038 ft., however, the sinkers' picks struck the hard and solid rock with a sound that was as music in the ears of all who heard it.

The gravel bed separating the fresh-water Wealden from the marine Oolites was found to consist of a loose conglomerate of sand and shingle, with quantities of semi-carbonised driftwood and numbers of large water-worn pebbles of coal, that must have been denuded from some not very distant outcrop. These coal pebbles indicated that the Oolites did not persist throughout the coalfield—a fact since established by later borings. The position of the shafts at the opening of this year (1910) was thus:—

No. 1, depth 1,014 ft. Sunk during the past 6 months, 172 ft.

No. 2, depth 995 ft. Sunk during the past 8½ months, 13 ft.

It must not be inferred that this slow progress was due to any lack of capacity or energy on the part of the engineering staff. Mr. M. Griffith having resigned in 1909, the position of manager was now held by Mr. T. W. Austin, with Mr. H. J. Wroe as assistant manager; Mr. Geo. H. Hollingworth, of Manchester, was the Company's consulting engineer.

The passage through the Wealden series was extremely difficult and, of necessity, tedious. It was during this period that so much trouble was experienced from the action of the fine silt of the Hastings beds which led to frequent stoppages of the pumps, the valves of which it made to resemble kitchen colanders.

Mr. Martin (H.M. Inspector of Mines), in his annual report for 1909, says:—

> "These beds present considerable difficulty, not so much from the quantity of water, as with the strata which consists practically of sand, which almost dissolved in water and ran at the

sides wherever given the least opportunity. It got into the pumps, playing havoc with the valves, which it threatened to choke."

Another obstacle to progress was the fact of the strata not being sufficiently firm to support the bricking curbs. This deficiency had to be made good by driving a series of heavy baulks of timber into the sides of the pits, leaving projecting ledges upon which the iron bricking curbs rested. The fitting of these "ersatz" curb-beds was a tedious and tricky job.

The lesson to be learned from these operations is obvious, viz., that in sinking through the treacherous Lower Greensand and Wealden series two shafts with powerful pumping equipment, and preferably going down in stages, are a *sine qua non*. Had the Tilmanstone Pits been started simultaneously, with proper equipment, it would have been comparatively easy to deal with the water which, in fact, was never in such quantity, up to this stage, as to present any serious engineering difficulty. The Hastings silt could have been successfully dealt with by Sulzer pumps. A practical demonstration of this statement is furnished by No. 3 Pit, which was commenced in August, 1910, when the difficult passage of the sand-bed loomed large on the horizon, and which was sunk into the Coal Measures in two years and two months, as against six years in the case of Nos. 1 and 2.

CHAPTER XI.

East Kent Colliery, continued. More Water difficulties. Electrical Pumps installed. Capital raised to £500,000.

"What dreadful noise of water in mine ears,"

—RICHARD III.

But to resume. Once in the Oolites, the sinkers made good headway, and by March 7 No. 1 was down to 1,083 ft., all but 17 ft. of which had been bricked; this represented 50 ft. of sinking and 30 ft. of bricking for four weeks' work—a very different record from those of many weary months past. No. 2 was then down to 1,011 ft., and was also practically bricked up.

Sinking in both pits proceeded normally, and on May 21 No. 1 had reached 1,140 ft. The Coal Measures were then very near as to distance, but, as events unluckily proved, so very distant as to time. At this point sinking stopped while No. 2, then at 1,087 ft., was being continued to the same level. Meanwhile, in view of the conditions at the junction of the Secondary rocks and the Coal Measures at Shakespeare Cliff, where the Upper, Middle and Lower Lias were represented by a thickness of 87 ft., and the uncertainty as to whether these beds extended to Tilmanstone, a test borehole was put down some 10 ft. below the bottom of No. 1. This resulted in the tapping of a small feeder of water, not more than 8,000 gallons an hour, which was easily plugged off.

No. 2 Pit reached the same level as No. 1, viz., 1,140 ft., on July 10, so that, with two shafts within 30 ft. of the Coal Measures, everyone concerned felt that he might safely engage in the pleasurable occupation of counting his chickens!

Towards the end of the month another hole was bored into the junction bed from the bottom of No. 2 Pit, which it was intended should go down into the Coal Measures and, incidentally, demonstrate whether or no any further feeders existed.

At 1,158 ft. the demonstration was forthcoming with a vengeance! A very large volume of water

THE ORIGINAL WINDING ENGINE AT No. 1 PIT TILMANSTONE, BY WHICH THE SHAFT WAS SUNK TO 1,130 FEET.

Permanent Winding Engines, No. 1 Pit, Tilmanstone.

was met with, the pressure being such as not only to render futile all attempts to plug the borehole, but to cause it to burst through the pit-bottom. The water brought with it several hundreds of tons of sand, and it was only with great difficulty that it was kept from flooding the pump inset at 990 ft.

Thus the counted chickens, after the manner of their kind, failed to hatch out. Such a great inrush of water took the management completely by surprise, but it must be borne in mind that they had been advised over and over again that no great volume need be anticipated. Even the Government Inspector of Mines, Mr. Joseph S. Martin, in his 1909 Report, written just after No. 1 Pit had been taken safely into the Oolites, expressed himself thus:—

> "Some people anticipate an inflow of water on the head of the Coal Measures, but I, personally, feel that if any such difficulty should arise there —which I do not anticipate—it will not be anything like so great as in the Hastings Beds, and it may be accepted that from an engineering point of view the Colliery is won."

There is no little irony in the fact that the publication of the Government Blue Book, from which the above extract is taken, coincided almost to the day with the flooding of No. 2 Pit with water from the Junction bed!

Although only some 30 ft. of strata intervened, more than two years were to elapse and many thousands of pounds were to be expended before the shafts had been safely taken into the Coal Measures. The management has been much criticised for putting down the borehole from the bottom of No. 2 Pit, which was not only unprovided with pumps, but lacked even any connection at pit-bottom with No. 1, where there was a powerful pumping installation, and from which shaft, moreover, a large quantity of water could have been raised with a water-barrel. The volume of water given off from this junction bed, when it came to be seriously tackled, proved to be about 2,000 gallons per minute; but when the pressure had been taken off it was reduced to 1,600 gallons per minute, to which must be added about 200 gallons which came down from the Hastings beds, or 1,800 gallons in all—no inconsiderable quantity when the depth is taken into account.

But what added so materially to the engineering problem was the fine sand with which, as I have mentioned, the water was charged. This was ruination to the valves of the steam pumps, and occasioned many stoppages for renewals. A similar trouble had been experienced with the water from the Hastings beds, but in that case it was a fine, silty slime that was responsible for the mischief, although to a much lesser extent.

Difficulties, however, as has been said, were made to be surmounted, and those at Tilmanstone, after the first shock of disappointment, were faced in this spirit. For one thing it was decided, after much consultation with expert advisers, to put down a third shaft, 19 ft. in diameter, not only as a precautionary measure against any further unforeseen difficulties, but because it would ultimately serve to increase the coal-winding capacity of the colliery. No. 1 Pit, it will be remembered, was only 14 ft. in diameter and largely taken up with steam pipes and delivery ranges. The first sod of the third Pit was turned on August 9, 1910.

An electrical installation, together with an equipment of Sulzer pumps, was now under consideration. These pumps having proved their worth under like conditions elsewhere, notably at Thorne Colliery, where 7,500 gallons of sandy water per minute were raised, gave every promise of being equal to the present occasion—a promise that was amply fulfilled. A change from steam to electricity, was further indicated, and greatly facilitated by the formation of the East Kent Electric Power Company, Limited, whose first station it was proposed should be erected at Tilmanstone.

Pending a definite decision regarding the electrical pumping installation, to find the money for which promised to be no light task, additions were made to the steam pumps in the hope that they would put the management "top side" of the water, and enable the sinking to proceed.

The remainder of the year was occupied in their establishment and in generally improving the surface equipment. A new lattice headgear and powerful winding engine were erected at No. 1 Pit. The latter was manufactured by Messrs. Markham & Company, Chesterfield, and consists of a pair of

Diagrammatic Section showing General Position of the Tilmanstone Pits after the Water from the Junction Bed had burst up the Bottom of No. 2 Pit.

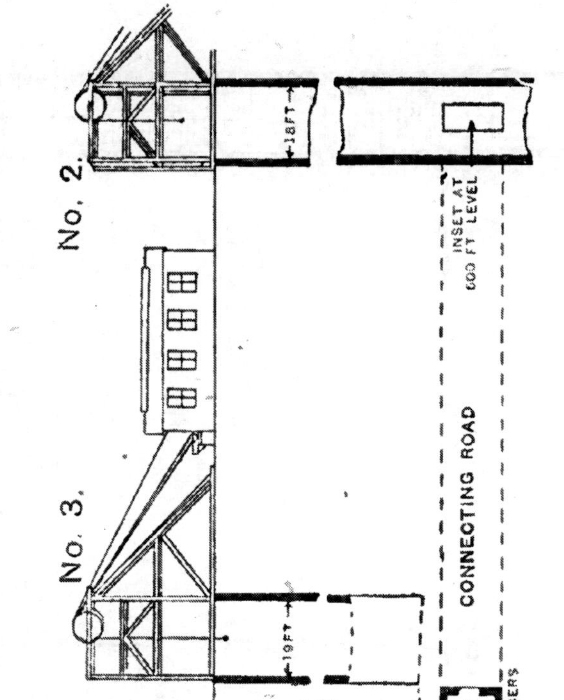

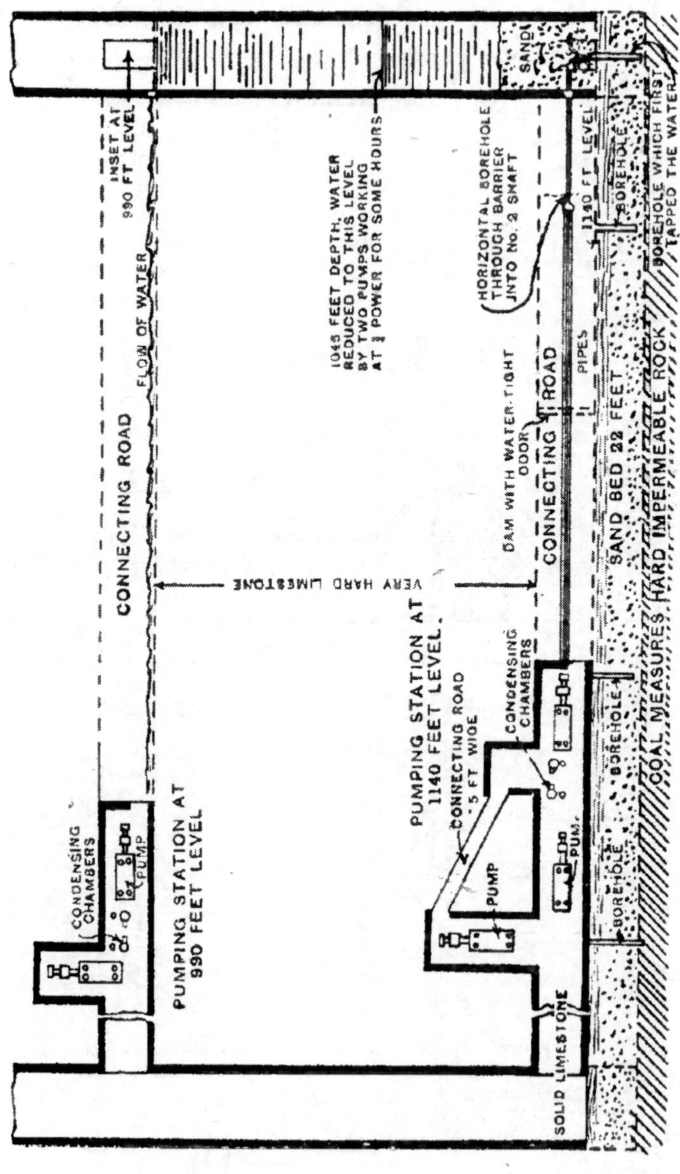
CONNECTING ROAD
INSET AT 990 FT LEVEL
FLOW OF WATER
REDUCED TO THIS LEVEL
BY TWO PUMPS WORKING
SAND
HORIZONTAL BOREHOLE THROUGH BARRIER INTO No. 2 SHAFT
1140 FT LEVEL
BOREHOLE
BOREHOLE WHICH FIRST TAPPED THE WATER
PIPES
DAM WITH WATER-TIGHT DOOR
CONNECTING ROAD
SAND BED 22 FEET
HARD IMPERMEABLE ROCK
COAL MEASURES
VERY HARD LIMESTONE
PUMPING STATION AT 1140 FEET LEVEL
CONNECTING ROAD 5 FT WIDE
CONDENSING CHAMBERS
PUMP
CONDENSING CHAMBERS
PUMP
PUMPING STATION AT 990 FEET LEVEL
SOLID LIMESTONE

horizontal cylinders 32-in. bore by 72-in. stroke, Cornish inlet and Corliss exhaust valves. It is fitted with a steam reversing gear, a Whitmore steam brake, and overwinding prevention gear. The drum is 20 ft. in diameter and 10 ft. wide.

1911.

The accompanying plan shows the general position of the pits at the beginning of the year 1911. During the whole of the year not a single foot was sunk in either No. 1 or No. 2 Pit, but No. 3 made good progress through the chalk and gault. I will not inflict upon my readers a tedious recital of the varied troubles that almost daily confronted an anxious and harassed staff. A brief summary will, I am sure, sufficiently indicate how heart-breaking their experiences must have been.

My abbreviated narrative, however, should convey some useful lessons to others who may be faced with similar problems in course of the opening up of this new field, the geological features of which differ so materially from those of other coalfields in this country.

At the beginning of the year there was no connection between Nos. 1 and 2 below the 990-ft. level. The water was still coming up the disastrous borehole into the sand bed from No. 2 pit-bottom, and there was nearly 100 ft. of accumulated sand standing in this shaft.

Efforts were made to un-water No. 2 by means of the steam pumps, no electrical plant having yet been ordered. It will be remembered that the water from the sand bed was brought to the pumps in the inset at 1,140 ft. in No. 1 Pit, by means of boreholes in the connecting road. By February 9 the water level in No. 2 had been lowered some 50 ft., when a sudden rush of sand up the boreholes necessitated the closing of their valves to save the pumps from being overwhelmed. This resulted in No. 2 again filling up to the 990-ft. inset.

March 27 was another black day. A pipe in the steam range in No. 1 burst, and was only replaced by the time the water had risen to within 15 in. of the workmen. Pumping was immediately resumed, but a few hours later another similar pipe burst, and this time both pits filled to within a few feet of the 600-ft. inset.

This catastrophe proved the final argument that closed the discussion as to the electrical equipment, and in April orders were placed for an extensive plant.

THE SWITCHBOARD; TILMANSTONE POWER HOUSE.

At this juncture Mr. Burr pleaded his ignorance of electrical matters as a reason for handing over his responsibilities as managing director, so far as the colliery works were concerned, to Mr. John Hamilton, the proprietor of the Auldton, Over Dalserf and Woodside Collieries, Lanarkshire. It was hoped that Mr. Hamilton's experience with electrical installations would prove of great service to Tilmanstone, in which colliery he and a large number of his Scottish friends were interested.

A change also was made in the management of the colliery, Mr. H. J. Wroe, the under-manager, being put in charge.

Nothing further in the way of pumping was attempted beyond keeping the water below the 600-ft. insets in both shafts; and April, May, June, July, August and September were chiefly occupied in the construction and equipment of the electrical power house, and in perforce adding to the water supply of East Kent millions upon millions of gallons from Tilmanstone's subterranean and inexhaustible resources. No amount of pumping has ever made any appreciable difference in the volume of water at their disposal.

The turbines were in running order by the end of September and the Sulzer sinking pumps had their trial run on October 8. These worked splendidly from the start, and by mid-November the water-level was down to 920 ft., while the last day of the year saw No. 1 Pit completely unwatered. The following is the schedule of the pumping plant at this time in operation:—

No. 1 Pit.

600-ft.—4 Evans horizontal ram steam pumps: Aggregate capacity, 170,000 gals. per hour to the surface.

990-ft.—2 Evans horizontal ram steam pumps: Aggregate capacity, 2,000 gals. per hour to 600-ft.

1,140-ft.—3 Evans horizontal ram steam pumps: Aggregate capacity, 90,000 gals. per hour to 600-ft.

No. 2 Pit.

600-ft.—One six-stage horizontal stationary Sulzer pump: Capacity, 72,000 galls. per hour to the surface.

Two four-stage high-lift Sulzer sinking pumps; each of a capacity of 1,200 gals per minute, against a manometric head of 870 ft.

Power.

Ten Lancashire boilers 30-ft. by 8-ft. 6-in. Insured for a working pressure of 150 lbs. to the sq. in.

Two high-pressure Westinghouse steam turbines, rated at 1,000 kw. at 80 per cent. power factor. Speed, 3,000 r.p.m.

Four Babcock and Wilcox patent water-tube boilers (each having 4,020 sq. ft. of heating surface) constructed for a working pressure of 200 lbs. per sq. in. with induced draft, and fitted with the makers' integral superheaters. Working in conjunction with these boilers is a Green's fuel economiser, with 400 tubes arranged in two groups.

Before the electrical pumps were started the late Lord Merthyr, who was a shareholder in the East Kent Colliery Company, was requested to nominate an engineer to pronounce a benediction upon the plant. Accordingly, Mr. John Hutchinson (general manager of the Lewis Merthyr Collieries) inspected and reported favourably on the whole scheme, although he stated that, in his opinion, the question of installing electrically-driven pumps ought to have been considered as soon as the water was met with in the shingle bed at the base of the Hastings. That this was not done he considered showed a lack of energy and forethought on someone's part, as it was neither economical nor advisable to carry steam pipes to such depths in sinking pits.

I ought, perhaps, to have mentioned that at the beginning of the year the capital of the Company was raised from £250,000 to £500,000, and various issues of this new capital were made from time to time to provide funds for carrying out the works I have described.

CHAPTER XII.

East Kent Colliery, concluded. Sinking through the Junction Bed. The coal at last. Financial difficulties. A Receiver appointed. Re-organisation of the Company New Directors elected. Outputs, 1913-1918.

"The future is of more consequence than the past,"

—DOANE.

1912.

The opening days of this year were occupied in overhauling the pumps at 1,140 ft. and 990 ft. that had been so long submerged. There was also a considerable amount of repair work to be done in the shafts, while the removal of the accumulation of sand in No. 2 delayed the unwatering of that pit. The steam and delivery pipes in No. 1 from 600 ft. to 1,140 ft. had also to be duplicated, as it had become apparent that considerable reliance would have to be placed on the steam pumps at the pit-bottom until three more horizontal Sulzer pumps had been provided.

It will be noted that even now the actual passage through the Junction bed had not been attempted. There seems to have been a general disinclination, or fear, to "grasp the nettle" until No. 3, which, on February 24, was down to 1,015 ft., had reached the same level as the other pits—and the extra Sulzer pumps were in position.

At the beginning of March one of the boreholes at 1,140 ft. was opened, and the water coming to the pumps comparatively free from sand, the water level in No. 2 was soon reduced to 1,050 ft. Two further boreholes were opened by March 20, when the sand bed gave off about 1,800 gallons a minute, besides which there were 250 gallons a minute coming down from the Hastings beds, which had also to be raised to the surface.

By the end of March the position was that No. 3 was down to 1,078 ft., or within 62 ft. of the other pits; that 22 ft. of sand still remained to be got out of No. 2; that it was only just possible to keep No. 1 dry; and that there was no prospect of sinking until the further Sulzer horizontal pumps were available, delivery of which was still nearly four months distant.

On April 9 the last of the sand was cleared out of No. 2 Pit, but there was naturally a great deal of straightening up to be done, and in particular the plugging of the borehole in the pit-bottom was a work of time, and sinking was still something to be looked forward to.

The three extra Sulzer pumps, to which I have referred, were still in the makers' hands, and it was not until early in September that they were ready for their trial runs. It was only after their efficiency to throw 1,000 gallons of water each from 1,140 ft. to the surface had been demonstrated, that it was decided that sinking might safely be resumed in this pit. This work, accordingly, started on September 16 from 1,140 ft., which depth, be it remembered, had been reached so far back as July 10, 1910.

Similarly, No. 1 Pit broke new ground some three weeks later, and sinking was recommended from 1,140 ft., the depth which it had reached no less than two years and four months earlier.

No. 3 followed into the limestone on the top of the sand bed on October 7. But this Pit, my readers will remember, had been commenced only on August 9, 1910, so that it had been carried down to 1,140 ft. while its fellows had been standing at that level for over two years.

The sinking of these three pits through the sand bed, even with the splendid service of pumps now at the command of the management, proved no easy task. By October 25 all three were actually in the loose sand; the water was continually dodging from one pit-bottom to the other, and the pump valves were being subjected to great wear and tear. As the pits progressed a number of pulsometers were employed in bringing the water to the stationary pumps at 1,140 ft., and these proved very effective. Finally, after an anxious three weeks, No. 3, on November 1, achieved the distinction of being the first to enter the Coal Measures.

Nine days later No. 1 followed suit, but it was not until December 12 that No. 2 attained the desired goal. The accompanying photograph of No. 2 pit-bottom on the eve of fixing the last segment of tubbing graphically indicates the volume of water which had held up all progress

INFLOW OF WATER AT NO. 2 PIT-BOTTOM, TILMANSTONE, BEFORE FIXING FINAL SEGMENT OF TUBBING.

in Nos. 1 and 2 for the preceding two years. For various reasons it was not considered advisable to seal off this water entirely, and, moreover, the tubbing was not of such thickness as to warrant this being attempted. A certain quantity was therefore allowed to come up the boreholes in the connecting road between the two shafts, and this still continues to be pumped.

1913.

With all three shafts into the Coal Measures, sinking proceeded normally, and after passing through some thin veins, the 5-ft. seam, which is being worked to-day, was struck on March 12, 1913. Thus, after many trials and tribulations, the Tilmanstone Colliery became at last an accomplished fact.

It is easy to be wise after the event, and, looking backward over the records of this sinking, to point out how and where mistakes were made. We must remember, however, that, apart from the Dover pits, no previous sinking in England had been done through the treacherous water-bearing series in the Secondary Rocks.

Not one of the engineering staff engaged at Tilmanstone had been connected with the Dover works, so that the conditions which they had to face were totally different from any they had previously experienced. The original Tilmanstone management, moreover, gave an all too ready credence to the optimistic assurances of their technical advisers to the effect that they need not anticipate the same water difficulties that beset the pits under Shakespeare Cliff.

In support of this statement I produce the following extract from a report to the Concessions Company, under date February 7, 1905, by Mr. Maurice Griffith, afterwards the first manager of Tilmanstone:—

> "Professor Boyd Dawkins (our greatest geologist) has given you the knowledge that the coal seams under your areas can be reached without the same water difficulty which was encountered by my late father at Dover."

Thus it came about that not until 1911 was any provision ever made in advance of instant necessity. The records show that the guiding principle was to go blithely ahead in a happy-go-lucky spirit, always assuming that difficulties were not only non-existent, but non-existing, until flooded pits proved the contrary. The wish, of course,

The East Kent Colliery Company, Limited. General View of Tilmanstone Colliery.

was at all times father to the thought, because the corollary of difficulties was money, and money itself was a difficulty.

I have purposely refrained from dealing with the financial history of this company; to have done so adequately would have unduly lengthened my narrative, and, except perhaps for the actual shareholders, the practical record is of greater interest than the financial. Still, as the doings of the East Kent Colliery Company have bulked somewhat largely in the public eye, it might be well to emphasise the fact that its trials and tribulations were greatly augmented by its chronic lack of cash.

The unfortunate record of the numerous companies associated with the Shakespeare Cliff pits had the natural result of creating an element of distrust in all Kent Coal enterprise. Not even the proving of the good seams at Waldershare was sufficient to convince the public of the great possibilities attaching to this extension of the coalfield. Or if in a measure these were realised it was not to an extent sufficient to outweigh the distrust of a personnel compromised by association with the previous failures in Kent.

Although the time occupied in this sinking was unduly long, I am sure that many of my readers have knowledge, personal or acquired, of other such instances, and they will appreciate what is involved in raising, from a depth of 1,140 ft., 1,800 gallons per minute of water heavily charged with fine sand. Reimer's well-known work "Shaft Sinking in Difficult Cases" furnishes several classical examples of sinkings extending over many years, even when backed with unlimited money and every engineering device known to science.

Those of my readers who may desire more exact technical details of the electrical pumping installation and its working will find further particulars in a Paper by Mr. H. J. Wroe, the manager, read before the London Branch of the Association of Mining Electrical Engineers on February 8, 1914. (See "Proceedings," Vol. V., 1913-14.)

Work was forthwith started on roads through the Shaft Pillar, and on the first longwall face being opened up the roof and general working conditions were found to be favourable; while the coal was of excellent quality, as will be seen from the following analysis :—

Analysis by Mr. Geo. R. Hislop, F.C.S.
Proximate (Dry Basis).

	Per cent
Volatile matters	22.12
Fixed carbon	68 69
Sulphur	2.30
Ash	5.87
Water	1.02
	100.00
Coke per ton of coal	75.16

Ultimate (Dry Basis).

	Per cent.
Carbon	79.12
Hydrogen	4.66
Oxygen	5.90
Nitrogen	1.13
Sulphur	2.30
Ash	5.87
Hygroscopic moisture ...	1.02
	100.00

Evaporative power, 14.17 lbs. of. water from 212 deg. Fah. to steam.

Calorific power in Centigrade heat units=7609 Calories.

It was, however, a great disappointment that the coal should have proved unsuitable for household purposes; being very fragile, the greater bulk of it is marketable only in the form of slack. Had the seam been hard, its low volatile contents would not have been a bar to its domestic use in the local markets, where it would have commanded a price that undoubtedly would have yielded a large margin of profit.

1914-1918.

In the beginning of 1914 the output averaged about 400 tons per diem, and all went well until March 30, when there came a break in the roof, which was succeeded by an inrush of water to the workings amounting to some 800 gallons a minute.

This brought coal-getting to a standstill, and threw a great strain on the pumping equipment, which now had to deal with some 3,000 gallons per minute. By May 5, however, the colliers were able to resume work on the coal to the rise.

The Company's operations having been carried on so far at a loss, a financial crisis now arose. An extraordinary general meeting was held in Dover on May 20, at which a reconstruction scheme was put forward for consideration. There was a good deal of opposition and nothing definite resulted, save that a few weeks later—no action having been taken in the meanwhile—the colliery passed into the hands of a receiver.

On March 24, 1915, the debenture holders were called together by the receiver to approve a draft contract for the sale of the colliery to Mr. R. Tilden-Smith. The terms suggested were such as to evoke determined opposition, the leaders of which being Mr. George Thomas, of Dover, and Mr. Arthur Wells, of Canterbury.

A further meeting was held on April 21, when a shareholders' committee was formed to assist the board in getting out some scheme that would not entirely denude the ordinary shareholders of their interests.

Mr. J. J. Clark, the chairman of Snowdown Colliery, was chairman of this shareholders' committee, which, on May 12, put forward its proposals. These provided that the existing debentures were to remain in force; that the Company's creditors were to receive 4 per cent. income bonds in discharge of their claims; and that £150,000 perpetual second mortgage 6 per cent. debenture stock was to be created; this stock was also to carry the right to three-fourths of the profits available for dividend in each year.

A sufficient amount of this debenture stock was taken up in due course to pay out the receiver, who accordingly retired at the end of November, 1915, since when the Company has remained master in its own house.

Its tenure, nevertheless, is none too assured, for the majority of the first mortgage debentures being in one hand, assent to the committee's scheme was secured only on the Company's undertaking to sink the shafts to one of the deeper seams.

Owing to the incidence of the war this obligation has remained in abeyance. It will have to be faced very shortly, and a substantial sum will be required for the work, which, it is hoped, will be forthcoming from the unissued balance of the second mortgage debentures.

In the directors' report accompanying the accounts to December 31, 1915, the services of Mr. J. J. Clark, Mr. George Thomas and Mr. Arthur Wells in saving the Company from extinction were handsomely recognised. The directors were not able to submit a profit and loss account, but stated that the colliery was in good working order, and that the output averaged about 2,000 tons per week.

The ordinary general meeting was held on May 24, 1916, the most important business at which being the appointment of new directors, as provided for in the reorganisation scheme.

The Board consisted, in 1913, of Mr. Arthur Burr, Mr. Henry G. Gompertz, Mr. John Hamilton, Professor W. Galloway, Mr. H. W. Marley and Mr. Arthur Wells, but since 1914, owing to various reasons, only the three last-named have remained in office.

The new Board as constituted in 1916 was as follows :—Professor W. Galloway (chairman), Mr. H. W. Marley, Mr. P. G. Agelasto, Mr. George Thomas and Mr. Arthur Wells, all of whom still occupy their seats.

The profit and loss account to December 31, 1916, submitted at the ordinary general meeting on September 15, 1917, showed a gross working profit of £5,156, of which, after deducting administration and general expenses, only £1,002 remained to the credit of the account.

A considerably better showing was made in the following financial year, the gross working profit to December 31, 1917, amounting to £18,657, which the directors stated would have been materially increased but for the calling-up of men for the Army and for the great lack of housing accommodation. In order to improve the financial position of the Company and supply the funds required to take the shafts down to one of the deeper seams (a contingent liability towards the first mortgage debenture holders, to which I have already drawn attention), an option to purchase the £75,000 unissued 6 per cent. second debenture stock was given to Messrs. Schneider et Cie., proprietors of the famous Creusot Works in France, who, however, decided not to exercise it. This was probably owing to the negotiations which they were initiating direct with the parent companies for the acquisition of extensive mineral areas.

The following table shows the yearly output of the Colliery from the first raising of coal in 1913 :—

		Tons.			Tons.
1913	...	40,054	1917	...	135,350
1914	...	82,310	1918	...	129,600
1915	...	41,546			
1916	...	103,040	Total	...	531,900

In August, 1919, Mr. Wroe resigned his managership of Tilmanstone to take up a similar position with the Guilford Colliery Co. His successor at Tilmanstone is Mr. T. M. S. Ritchie.

CHAPTER XIII.

1907.—*South Eastern Coalfield Extension.—A Speculative Proposition. Its Capital Increased. Debentures created in* 1911. *The Schneider Option. Its Surplus Assets. List of Borings. Thinning-out of Water-bearing Strata. Mr. Burr's Retirement.*

"Everything is sweetened by risk."—ALEX SMITH.

The next in sequence of the companies formed in 1907 was the

SOUTH EASTERN COALFIELD EXTENSION, LIMITED.

(Registered June 6, 1907.)

Capital, £25,000 in 23,500 ordinary and 1,500 founders' shares, all of £1 each, the ordinary shares being entitled to a preferential non-cumulative dividend of 12 per cent. per annum; the balance of profits available for distribution being divisible as to 67 per cent. to the ordinary shares and 33 per cent. to the founders' shares. Each subscriber of twenty-five ordinary shares was entitled, by way of bonus, to an allotment of one fully-paid founders' share; and an extra founders' share was allocated to "all subscribers of every £100 who pay up in full on allotment."

There was no board of directors, Mr. Arthur Burr being self-appointed director-general for life, his remuneration to be 20 per cent. of the net profits. The company was somewhat in the nature of an overflow of the Concessions Company. The circular, issued by Mr. Burr, by way of prospectus, stated that the Concessions Company had reached the limit of its expansion, and was unwilling to undertake any further responsibilities, while there were yet some thousands of acres of speculative value which it was desirable to keep from falling into the hands of competitors. Mr. Burr further stated in the same circular that:—"As a proposition, however, I prefer to place it before my friends as speculative, and as such I now ask those who avail themselves of the right to subscribe for shares to so regard it."

By the light of later events it will be seen that it is unfortunate for Concessions shareholders that their capital was not directly increased, and these areas, which were really not so speculative as was represented, secured for their benefit. That Concessions were the losers is borne out by a statement in what Mr. Burr termed a "standard communication" to some of his more intimate correspondents, under date June 18, 1907, which reads thus:—

> "The areas which will be acquired by the new company will have a much greater commercial value than any of the Concessions, and therefore, comparing capitals, acreage, quality, etc., South Eastern shares will really be considerably more valuable than even Concessions."

Mr. Burr undertook that his 20 per cent. remuneration should cover general administration expenses, and also disbursements for promotion. This latter consideration he evidently overlooked, and by retaining for his own benefit a number of the founders' shares, as promotion profit, he rendered himself accountable for a large sum of money —for which judgment was given in an action brought by the company after his retirement from the management.

During the first twelve months of its existence, only 12,000 ordinary shares were allotted, the remaining 11,500 not being offered until June, 1908, when they were issued at a premium of 5s. per share to existing members of the company, and at a premium of 10s. per share to shareholders in Concessions and other allied companies. In a covering memorandum addressed to shareholders of Kent Coal Concessions, Limited, Mr. Burr wrote as follows:—

> "I venture to tender my advice to every shareholder in Concessions not to miss the opportunity of participating also in the Extension. It may so happen that, although unexpected by me, this will soon prove to be of greater value and potentialities than even our Concessions areas. The prospects at least are such

as deserve serious consideration, and I shall always regret that the element of risk originally present necessitated the formation of an overflow company."

From these small beginnings this Extension Company, whose capital was increased in September, 1909, and again in July, 1911, by the creation of a further 15,500 and 40,000 ordinary shares respectively, has gradually acquired a paramount position in the Coalfield. Its freehold and leasehold minerals largely exceed those of Concessions. There is no doubt that it has reaped where it has not sown, for it never could have attained its present status but for the pioneer work of the original Parent Company. This fact is recognised in the circular above mentioned, which stated that—"By way of acknowledgment and return for the use of exclusive geological evidence and knowledge, a substantial interest in the profits of the Company will be secured to the Concessions Company."

The only attempt to fulfil the obligation, thus admitted, was the allotment of 500 founders' shares to Concessions—which they parted with at £2 per share—so that the substantial interest in the profits of the Extension Company that was to be secured has not materially benefited Concessions shareholders.

During the years when the Extension Company was aggrandising itself, largely at the expense of Concessions, certain moral inter-company rights were created under the "community of interest" policy, of which the shareholders have heard so much in the past. Owing, however, to Mr. Burr's retirement in 1914, when the Articles of Association were amended to enable directors to be appointed, the control passed into the hands of Mr. Dewrance and his colleagues, who are now in charge of practically all the companies formerly under the direction of Mr. Burr, and these moral rights have gone by the board—of necessity, no doubt. On this point it is instructive to recall the following paragraph from Mr. Burr's report submitted to the Extension shareholders at their general meeting on July 25, 1911:—

"I have stated that with respect to the Concessions Company what has been accomplished within the last two years is phenomenal. Of the two companies, in comparison, the Extension Company has been the more successful in increasing the acreage of minerals acquired, and has, in fact, gone beyond the limit of its acknowledged sphere of influence. Capital for capital its acreage is out of all proportion to that of the Concessions Company, thanks largely to the geological guidance of this latter company's borings, for which it has not fully contributed—a point that I shall in common justice feel called upon to raise upon some future occasion."

The Concessions shareholders have little reason to be satisfied with their position in this connection, for upon them fell the heat and burden of the day, and their share of the harvest—as legally determined—promises to be but meagre in comparison with what is morally their due. The Extension Company, nevertheless, did not rely entirely on the work of its allied undertakings. It prosecuted a vigorous policy of exploration, and put down several boreholes, all of which proved the existence of good payable seams throughout its areas. The chief of these were at Walmestone, Stodmarsh, Trapham, and Woodnesboro'. Another boring, at Mattice Hill, went down in very faulty ground, but even so it disclosed two workable seams of navigation steam coal.

These borings are all situated in the northern part of the coalfield, and, notwithstanding that the records of the Secondary strata are very poor, there is yet ample evidence of the persistent thinning out of the bad sinking ground between the base of the gault and the top of the Coal Measures. The lack of precise information is due to the holes having been taken as far as the Coal Measures with the chisel. It is to be regretted that the diamond crown was not brought into use when the base of the gault was reached, in order that the composition of the Hastings and Wealden series might have been accurately determined. This information would be of inestimable value when the time comes for sinking pits. Sufficient data, however, have been obtained to establish the fact that these treacherous beds have very materially attenuated, as will be seen from the following representative boring section :—

Section of Borehole at Walmestone (74 *ft. O.D.*).

	Ft.	in.	
Tertiary	137	0	
Chalk	796	0	
Gault	113	0	
Lower Greensand ..	17	0	
Wealden	12	0	
Coal Measures			at 1,075 ft.
Sandstone	362	0	
Coal Seam	3	3	at 1,437 ft.
Bind	142	0	
Coal Seam	1	6	at 1,519 ft.
Sandstone and Bind	223	0	
Coal Seam	1	6	at 1,802 ft.
Bind	23	0	
Coal Seam	3	1	at 1,825 ft.
Bind	13	0	
Coal Seam	1	8	at 1,837 ft.
Bind	15	0	
Coal Seam	1	9	at 1,852 ft.
Bind	58	0	
Coal Seam	3	5	at 1,910 ft.
Bind	38	0	
Coal Seam	6	3	at 1,948 ft.
Bind	9	0	
Coal Seam	1	6	at 1,957 ft.
Bind	21	0	
Coal Seam	6	1	at 1,978 ft.
Bind	31	0	
Coal Seam	5	10	at 2,009 ft.
Bind	6	0	
Coal Seam	1	6	at 2,015 ft.
Bind	99	0	
Coal Seam	3	7	at 2,114 ft.
Bind	162	0	
Carboniferous Limestone... ..			at 2,276 ft

The chief points to note are that the boring, which started at 74 ft. O.D. in the Tertiary (Eocene) Beds well towards the northern boundary of the Coal Basin, shows that the Greensands and Wealden have thinned perceptibly, while the Oolites have entirely gone.

The Coal Measures thus directly underlie the Wealden. All the coals in this section belong to the Middle Measures, and the following analysis of the 6 ft. 1 in. seam may be accepted as fairly representative, thus :—

Volatile matters ...	22.81	per cent.
Fixed carbon ..	72.13	,, ..
Sulphur	0.70	,, ,,
Ash	4.36	,, ,,
	100.00	

Evaporative power 14 78 lbs of water.

Calorific power in Centigrade heat units=7,936 Calories.

In October, 1911, the Extension Company created £80,000 of debentures in bonds of £10 each, redeemable at £12, or, at the option of the holders, partly in its own shares and partly in those of the Concessions and Extended Extension companies. The market value of all these shares being now so much below the prices at which they were to be accepted, by way of redemption, there is no prospect of this option being exercised. Therefore, under present arrangements, the debentures will have to be paid off in cash six months after the declaration of Peace. Subscribers were allowed to underwrite their applications at a commission of 10 per cent., so that, in effect, the issue price was £90.

The main object with which the debentures were created was to enable the Company to associate itself with the other Parent Companies in acquiring areas, mostly freehold as to minerals, on joint account. Substantial acreages were thus secured in various parts of the field.

In this connection, it should be noted that some of the obligations under which, as I have stated, the Extension Company rests towards Concessions may be deemed to be discharged, for the latter has secured to itself a larger interest in these joint acquisitions than its cash contribution towards their purchase in reality warrants.

In January, 1915, a further obligation was incurred by the Extension Company when it joined with the other members of the group then (and

Group taken at Fredville Boring in 1906.

Left to right—A. Burr, M. Burr, G. H. Hollingworth, F. C. A. Golden, W. Boyd Dawkins, C. H. Smithers, Foreman Borer.

now) under the chairmanship of Mr. Dewrance, in raising £90,000 for general purposes, and, *inter alia*, for deepening one of the shafts at Snowdown Colliery to test the lower seams, particulars as to which will be given when the latter Company's operations are under review. The Extension Company's liability in respect of this £90,000 was shown in the last published accounts, to December 31, 1917, to be a little over £20,000 at that date.

In July, 1917, a combined meeting of the South Eastern Extension, Kent Coal Concessions, and Extended Extension Companies was held, at which the directors gave full particulars as to the respective assets and liabilities of each of these companies. The value of the former being based on the price at which an option to purchase a considerable acreage had been given to the well-known French firm, Messrs. Schneider et Cie.

By way of introduction, and somewhat in the form of apology for the pre-eminent position of the South Eastern Extension Company, it was pointed out that it had a very much smaller capital than Concessions; that it had been formed at a later date, and that it had not been subjected to the same ruinous administration expenses.

The meeting was informed that this company's estate comprised 2,864 acres of freehold minerals and 18,692 acres of leasehold minerals. Its total assets were valued at £525,485, whilst the whole of the liabilities, including debentures, premiums, interest and contingencies, estimated on a most liberal scale, were given as £221,243, thus showing a surplus of assets over liabilities of £304,242.

In a winding-up two thirds of the surplus would be divisible amongst 63,762 ordinary shares, and the balance amongst 1,500 founders' shares, representing about £3 per share to the ordinaries and £67 per share to the founders. When in due course the time for division arrives it will be interesting to see how nearly the actual results approximate to these estimates.

1918.

The last Ordinary General Meeting of the Company was held on December 18, 1918, when the Chairman stated that French buyers were coming forward with offers for half their areas, and that it was quite remarkable what a lot of applications they were getting from people who wished to acquire areas in Kent. This Company's prospects, therefore, may be regarded as extremely bright, and if the present board's expectations are realised it will be a striking tribute to the judgment of the previous management under whose *régime* all its assets were acquired.

The Extension Company's addition to our knowledge of the geology of the coalfield is greater than that of any other individual contribution, for the reason that its five boreholes—which each proved workable seams—penetrated the Carboniferous Limestone. Thus the northern and north-western boundaries of the basin have been clearly indicated. Those companies, therefore, whose late arrival on the scene resulted in their having to content themselves with areas in the Isle of Thanet up to, and under, the Thames Estuary, now find themselves in the unenviable position of the Foolish Virgins of Scripture. The following is the list of the Company's borings:—

	O.D.	Total Depth.	Carboniferous Limestone.
Walmestone ...	74ft.	2,285ft.	at 2,276ft.
Trapham ...	59ft.	3,226ft.	at 2,775ft.
Stodmarsh .	87ft.	2,263ft.	at 2,145ft.
Mattice Hill ...	11ft.	2,075ft.	at 2,051ft.
Woodnesboro' ..	51ft.	2,663ft.	at 2,621ft.
Total		12,512ft.	

These borings established beyond doubt the fact already indicated in some of those on Concessions' areas, viz., that the Lower Coal Measures are non-existent in East Kent. Thus the thickness of coal throughout this section of the Extension Company's areas is much less than that proved in the central portion of the Coal Basin, where the Transition Series obtains, and where the depth of the Carboniferous Limestone permits of a greater vertical thickness of the Middle Coal Measures.

The evidence of the above borings further shows conclusively that the northern areas of the Extension Company run almost up to the boundary of the coalfield, and that those companies owning minerals north of the River Stour cannot reasonably expect any extensive section of their property to yield them much coal.

By way of compensation, however, all the borings in question show that the Secondary Strata have thinned out very materially, in some instances even to the point of extinction. The only water that could possibly give any real trouble will be met with in the chalk, but, having regard to the success of the cementation process at Chislet (of which more anon), no serious engineering problem is involved.

CHAPTER XIV.

1907.—Guilford Syndicate.— Pits started at Waldershare on the Estate of Lord Guilford. Haulage difficulties cause stoppage. Insufficient Capital. Several attempts to promote Colliery Company. Property sold to the Forges de Chatillon. Shareholders lose their entire Capital. Mr. Burr's Retirement.

> "Lord Stafford mines for coal and salt,
> The Duke of Norfolk deals in malt,
> The Douglas in Red Herrings."
>
> —HALLECK.

We now come to the formation of

THE GUILFORD SYNDICATE, LIMITED.

(Registered August 2, 1907).

Capital, £40,000 in Ordinary shares of £1 each.

The Syndicate was formed to take over from the Fonçage Syndicate all its rights and interests in the Guilford (Waldershare) Colliery section, comprising 1,500 acres, to a lease of which Fonçage was entitled under agreement with Kent Coal Concessions, Limited, together with works, buildings and plant, as a going concern.

There was no board of directors, the management being vested in the Fonçage Syndicate as managers. Mr. Arthur Burr being life manager of that Syndicate, it follows that the affairs of the Guilford Syndicate were entirely in his hands. As in the case of some of the other companies of which Mr. Burr was the sole manager, he was supposed to be assisted by a committee of shareholders, but it must not be assumed that in practice this implied any controlling influence.

No shares were offered to the public, the privilege of an allotment being reserved to shareholders in the allied companies—unfortunately for them, as will be seen.

The colliery abuts on to Singledge Lane, which separates it from Waldershare Park—the seat of the Earl of Guilford—and is within a mile and a half of the Waldershare boring.

My readers will remember that it was owing to the delays at this boring that the Sondage Syndicate started the 7-ft. exploratory shaft at Tilmanstone; it was for the same reason that the Fonçage Syndicate appeared upon the scene and commenced a similar shaft at Guilford. This shaft had reached a depth of 300 ft. in October, 1906, when, as in the case of Tilmanstone, the proving of the good seams in the Waldershare boring resulted in the adoption of a more ambitious sinking programme.

The Fonçage Syndicate thereupon increased its capital to £20,000 in order to provide an adequate sinking plant and surface equipment for the purpose of starting two 18-ft. shafts. Not that it was thought possible to complete the sinking with this amount of capital; the intention was to carry on in the hope of, before very long, selling the undertaking at a substantial profit.

Singledge Lane, as its name might imply, had not been constructed to stand much heavy usage, and in the winter months its deficiencies as a road were particularly apparent. The extraordinary traffic on the local roads generally resulted in exorbitant claims for compensation by the District Council, so that it soon became necessary to suspend operations at Guilford until come connection could be made with the South-Eastern and Chatham Railway. It was decided that this should take the form of a tramway, but as a matter of fact no connection of any description was made until the East Kent Light Railway linked up the colliery with the main line some five years later, the consequence being that work had frequently to be suspended for months at a time.

In May, 1907, when one of the 18-ft. shafts (No. 3) had been sunk to 265 ft., and the other (No. 2) to 30 ft. only, Concessions, by arrangement with the Fonçage Syndicate—attempted the flotation of a company to take over the works. A draft prospectus was prepared for "The Guilford (Waldershare) Colliery Company, Limited," Capital £300,000, the chairmanship of which was provisionally accepted by the Earl of Essex. The names of Mr. James Matthews, of Messrs. Hawthorn, Leslie, & Company, and Mr. Isaac Storey, of Messrs. Storey Brothers, Lancaster, also figured as directors. It was found impossible, however,

General View of the Guilford Colliery.

to raise the necessary working capital, and the scheme had to be abandoned. It was in these circumstances, therefore, and as an alternative, that the Guilford Syndicate was formed to relieve Fonçage of its responsibilities, to refund its cash expenditure and to enable work to be once more resumed.

The managers of the Syndicate did not expect that their small resources would enable the Colliery to be established as such, but in the circular under date July 27, 1907, by way of prospectus, inviting applications for its shares, it was estimated that one 18-ft. shaft could be sunk to workable coal for £12,000, and then :—

"Upon completion of such sinking it is suggested that the undertaking shall be sold to a company to be then promoted upon terms and conditions as to price and capitalisation as will then, and having regard to the altered circumstances, appear fair and reasonable."

"As a suggestion, a sale price of the undertaking of £500,000 would not be unreasonable, with a working and development capital of £200,000. Upon such capitalisation, and after allowing a preferential dividend of 10 per cent. upon such development and working capital of £200,000 (£20,000 per annum), even the published estimates based upon the smaller output, with a selling price of 14s. per ton, excluding all profits from fireclay, would give a 20 per cent. return upon the £700,000."

"The above suggested sale price of the undertaking would give to the shareholders in this Syndicate a return of about £5 for a £1 share."

The following figures were also given in the same circular under the heading of "Appropriation of Capital":—

	£
To the Foncage Syndicate for purchase of mineral areas and works, plant, machinery, etc... ..	18,000
Preliminary expenses	300
Supplementary machinery, winding engines, ordinary and reserve pumping plant for contingencies	2,500
Sinking to, say, 1,600 feet if necessary	12,000
For contingencies	7,200
	£40,000

If courage were the sole criterion by which such adventurous spirits were to be judged, the founders of Guilford could surely claim some high distinction. The managers of the Syndicate must have drawn their inspiration from Shakespeare, whose famous exhortation, "Be bloody, bold and resolute," might well have been inscribed upon its seal! I venture to think that any of my readers who are colliery men would have experienced cold shivers down their spines, and tremblings in the knees, had the Fates decreed that they should work to such figures.

Although it is anticipating my story, I may as well state now that, without reaching the coal, the Syndicate's expenditure amounted to £150,000, exclusive of the small sum of £36,000 representing unpaid debenture interest!

To resume. The 7-ft. exploratory shaft was enlarged to 12 ft., and has since been used for the water supply of the colliery. No. 2 Pit remained stationary for many months at 30 ft., but sinking was carried on intermittently in No. 3 until October, 1908, when, at a depth of 752 ft., work had again to be suspended for the winter months owing to haulage difficulties. The unmetalled Singledge Lane had become well-nigh impassable.

However, as the Tilmanstone Pits were at this time making fair progress, it was thought that the delay would be positively advantageous in that Guilford could probably be disposed of at a good price when its sister colliery was raising coal—which was confidently anticipated would be the case within a few months. This anticipation, as my readers will have already learnt, was far from realisation, and the long delay in getting the Tilmanstone shafts through even the Hastings Beds emphasised the desirability of continuing the Guilford sinking, the idea being that Guilford should form a second string in case the difficulties at Tilmanstone proved insurmountable. In December, 1909, preparations were made for continuing work in No. 2 Pit, for it had become patent to everybody that no real progress was possible without this second shaft. By the end of the following May it had reached a depth of 270 ft., at which juncture sinking had to be stopped pending the arrival and erection of more powerful winding engines, those already installed having reached the limit of their capacity.

At this time only £22,000 of the Syndicate's capital had been issued, whereas the expenditure to date had amounted to £40,000, the difference having been provided by a loan from the East Kent Contract and Financial Company, whose affairs

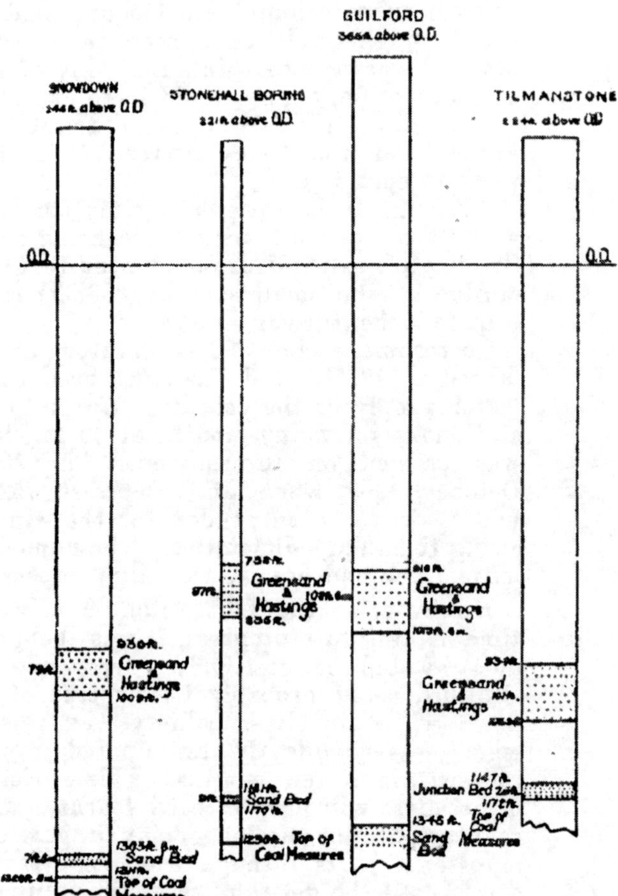

Diagram showing comparative Positions of the Greensand and Hastings Strata and the "Junction" Sand Bed at three important Points on the Coalfield.

will be the next to engage our attention. Guilford shareholders were accordingly advised of the necessity for raising more money, it being pointed out that it would be well to avoid selling until Tilmanstone was raising coal. When that happy condition of things obtained, a sale should return to them "from £10 to £15 for every £1 invested "!

It was not, however, possible to await that glad event, so a second effort to form a company for taking over the Guilford Pits was made in July, 1910, when the Syndicate's shareholders were informed that the "Guilford (Waldershare) Coal & Fireclay Company, Limited," was about to be registered with a capital of £460,000. The capital was to be divided into 700,000 participating preference shares of 10s. each, 200,000 ordinary shares of 10s. each, and 200,000 founders' shares of 1s. each, of which the preference shares would be underwritten and offered for public subscription.

This company had been for some time in the gestatory stage, but in November, 1910, it seemed likely to see the light of day, for the shareholders were advised that:—"Arrangements are being completed for the transfer of the Guilford Colliery from the Syndicate (the small capital of which has long been exhausted) to the large company. The legal details have been settled and the prospectus is in the hands of the stockbrokers who will undertake the underwriting of the capital."

References to this proposed company continued to appear from time to time in circulars issued to the Syndicate's shareholders, but Somerset House was never called upon to provide it with a birth certificate.

Nevertheless, by means of further loans from the Contract Company, sinking was resumed, and continued, though somewhat spasmodically, until the end of 1910, when Nos. 2 and 3 Pits were down to 480 ft. and 850 ft. respectively. During 1911 a similarly slow rate of progress obtained, and it was not until November of that year that both shafts had been sunk and bricked to 900 ft. So far no difficulties whatever had been encountered in the sinking; the chalk water was first met with at 280 ft., and continued down to 330 ft., the total quantity amounting to 100 gallons per minute. This was raised by the suction barrel until it was successfully sealed off by brickwork coffering.

It was now essential that pumps should be installed before attempting the passage of the Lower Greensands and Wealden. Accordingly two Evans double-acting ram pumps were erected in an inset at 613 ft., their united capacity being 800 gallons per minute. At the same time 1,440 tons of tubbing for lining the shafts through the bad ground were put on order. The accounts to October 31, 1911, were not submitted to shareholders until the general meeting held on January 8, 1912, when the total expenditure on the colliery was shown to have been just on £84,000, of which the Contract Company had advanced no less than £43,000.

I might mention, incidentally, that the management had been advised professionally, in 1907, that the two 18-ft. shafts could be sunk to 2,000 ft. for £40,000, whereas more than twice that amount had been expended in carrying them down to half that depth.

During 1912 no sinking whatever was done, the management being engaged in the profitless occupation of marking time until direct communication with the South-Eastern and Chatham main line could be established. This long-desired and most essential connection was not effected until October of that year, when the East Kent Light Railway track was brought up to the Pits.

Hereupon another attempt was made to secure the requisite funds for resuming the sinking, and in November, 1912, the shareholders were advised that :—" The East Kent Light Railway having now been connected with the Guilford Colliery, in order to provide funds for the continuation of the sinking to workable seams of coal the Guilford Syndicate, Limited, has decided to create and issue £80,000 of debentures." The issue price was £85, less a 5 per cent. underwriting commission to shareholders, and it was stated that the Syndicate would at once " proceed to the formation and registration of a company to acquire the Guilford Colliery as a going concern."

Nevertheless, it was not until the middle of 1913 that any practical steps were taken towards the formation of this company, the third to be projected. On July 1 of that year a circular was issued convening an extraordinary general meeting of the Syndicate for the purpose of sanctioning the proposed sale to a new company to be entitled The Guilford Collieries & Fireclay Company, Limited, the capital of which was to be £467,500. The purchase consideration was fixed at £233,500;

but, like the two attempted flotations which had preceded it, this scheme also proved abortive, with the result that ten months later, when the pits had been sunk to within 80 ft. of the Coal Measures, a sale was effected that will yield to the Syndicate only about one-third of that amount. But I am anticipating.

The proceeds of the debenture issue enabled sinking operations to be resumed, No. 2 getting to work in February, 1913, and reaching 1,272 ft. in the following September, by which time No. 3, re-started in April, had been taken down to a like depth, or, to be exact, to 1,269 ft.

No particular difficulties were met with in the passage through the Lower Greensands and Wealden, the water in which was entirely shut off by means of tubbing from 1½ in. to 2¼ in. in thickness. Of this tubbing, 192 ft. were fixed in No. 2 Pit and 163 ft. in No. 3. It is interesting to note that the Oolites were met with at 1,038 ft., only 3 ft. lower than at Tilmanstone, and that the passage of the Greensands and Wealden was accomplished in one-tenth of the time. The thickness of these beds proved to be 117 ft., as against 101 ft. at Tilmanstone, but the object lesson afforded by the latter had been taken to heart, and no attempt was made to sink through this bad ground at Guilford until the necessary equipment for properly tackling the job had been provided. This shows that the long delay at Tilmanstone was due mainly to artificial rather than natural causes.

In the early part of 1914 an inset was made at 1,264 ft in No. 2 Pit with a view to putting down a 3-in. borehole to test the Junction Bed. Every precaution was taken to secure control of the water, so that there should be no repetition of the dire results that followed the similar exploration in No. 2 Pit at Tilmanstone.

The boring went very slowly for the first 18 ft., the ground being hard limestone (Bathonian), but from thence downwards rapid progress was made through soft, sandy clays. These would indicate the presence of a substantial amount of Lias, though the débris from the borehole was insufficient for a definite pronouncement as to this.

At 1,316 ft. water was met with, which came up the tubes at the rate of 300 gallons per minute;

this was dealt with by winding, and the borehole was continued, in soft ground, to 1,346 ft., when what is believed to be the Junction Bed was reached. A considerable volume of water heavily charged with sand then made its way up the tubes, the quantity being such as to necessitate the with-

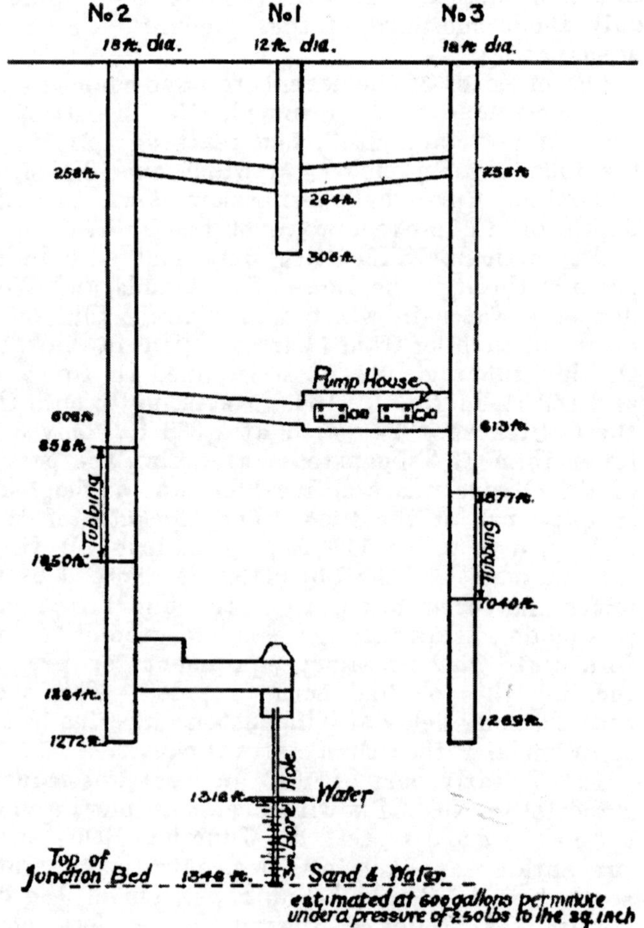

Diagrammatic Section of the Guilford Pits when the Syndicate ceased Work.

drawal of the boring rods and the closing of the controlling valve. So that, as the boring did not actually enter the Coal Measures, the thickness of this last water-bearing bed was not determined.

Nothing further was done at these pits, and the

position at the cessation of work is clearly shown in the accompanying plan.

The Guilford Syndicate now found itself in extremely grave financial difficulties; its third promotion scheme had failed; its capital had long since gone; the proceeds of the debenture issue had been expended, and over £40,000 was owing to the Contract Company. The situation evidently called for an explanatory circular from Mr. Burr, which was duly forthcoming, under date March 14, 1914, and from which I quote :—

"All shareholders will recognise that inability to finance the scheme adopted at the meeting held on July 10 last year rendered it impossible to carry it out as intended. The Balkan troubles and the consequent state of the money market reacted upon our enterprise.

"Under the circumstances, the managers of the Guilford Colliery were compelled to restrict their operations to sinking under conditions of extreme economy, hoping to be able to continue the shafts to a good workable seam of household coal, and thus remove all difficulties of a financial character. In this they were unfortunately disappointed, for on reaching the Junction with the Coal Measures it was our misfortune to encounter similar engineering obstacles as those which were met with at Tilmanstone, although on a much smaller scale.

"There are two alternatives :—(1) To sell the undertaking, provided that satisfactory terms can be obtained, and negotiations upon the subject have been under consideration now for several months; (2) to provide a sufficient sum to continue the pits through the Junction Bed to a good seam of coal—an engineering operation that does not appear to present any serious difficulties in view of the experience gained at Tilmanstone, but it will involve finding a sum of at least £40,000 to be on the safe side.

"My advice to the shareholders is to await the issue of the negotiations, or at all events for a month or six weeks . . . ."

Within the above suggested period, during which shareholders were to wait, Micawber-like, for something to turn up, a transaction took place which resulted not only in their being effectually relieved of their existing financial embarrassments, but of their entire future interest in the Colliery, as will presently be seen. This further kaleidoscopic change in the situation naturally demanded yet another explanatory circular, which was issued under date May 5, 1914. In this circular Mr. Burr stated that:—

"I have, acting in your interests and in conjunction with my colleagues on the board of the Concessions Company, felt it my duty to enter into an agreement for a joint sale of the Colliery and a valuable mineral area (leasehold) belonging to that Company . . . . with the effect, I hope and believe, of securing all who are interested in the Guilford Colliery from loss. This sale, however, is subject to confirmation, and I am therefore inviting both share and debenture holders to meet me, when I shall be in a position to give full details. . . . ."

After a *résumé* of the position of the pits and references to the uncertain amount of expenditure that would be involved in taking them through the Junction Bed, Mr. Burr stated that "the immediate prospect of financing the company appears hopeless," and he continued—

"Because I recognised the impossibility of raising further and sufficient capital I invited the firm with whom I was negotiating to make an inclusive offer for both the areas and the Guilford Pits.

"There is not the smallest doubt that whoever exploits this Colliery with adequate cash resources, and, of course, good engineering, will own one of the big prizes in colliery enterprise.

"I cannot conclude this letter without attributing a full share of responsibility for the practically compulsory sacrifice of this splendid asset to the persistent and organised attacks and misrepresentations of the 'Pall Mall Gazette' and other journals, which have made it quite impossible to raise capital in England for legitimate development and enterprise in respect of a proven colliery area, in respect of which large sums of shareholders' money have already been expended."

The promise to submit this agreement to the shareholders for confirmation was not fulfilled. It was discovered that their assent was not necessary under the Articles of Association, and as the terms of the sale could not possibly prove palatable to them it was thought that no useful purpose could be served by calling them together. The debenture holders, however, had to be treated with more respect. At a meeting in Dover on June 4, 1914, they passed a resolution confirming the sale of the whole of the Syndicate's undertaking—including 2,800 acres of adjoining leasehold minerals belonging to the Concessions Company (who were parties to the agreement as joint vendors)—for the lump sum of £150,000. The purchasers were La Compagnie des Forges de Chatillon, Commentry et Neuves Maisons. No attempt was made to apportion the purchase consideration between the two vendor companies, the debenture holders agreeing that this important question should remain open for amicable settlement—or, failing that, by arbitration.

This was to prove the last important administrative act performed by Mr. Burr in connection with his later series of Kent Coal companies—companies which he had created and which he had brought to the verge of success, but which, perforce, he was to leave in the hands of others; others less endowed with his imaginative faculties and perennial optimism, but more amply equipped with true commercial instincts and common sense.

Owing to the outbreak of war the contract with the Forges de Chatillon remained in abeyance, and it was not until March, 1919, that the first instalment of the purchase money was paid over to Mr. Burr's successors in office. The directors duly advised the shareholders of this payment in a circular dated March 15, 1919, at the same time expressing their regret—

"That there is not the slightest prospect of the shareholders of the Syndicate receiving anything, as the claims of the debenture holders amount to £124,000, made up of £80,000 for principal and £44,000 for interest, and in addition the unsecured creditors of the Syndicate amount to about £50,000. In fact, therefore, even if the whole £150,000 of the above purchase consideration were receivable by the Syndicate it would not be sufficient to discharge the claims of the debenture holders and the unsecured creditors."

Under the agreement of May, 1914, already referred to, the apportionment of the proceeds of this sale was to be settled between Concessions and the Syndicate—or, failing agreement, by arbitration. The debenture holders were accordingly called together on March 24, 1919, when three of their number were elected to confer with the Concessions Board with a view to an amicable settlement.

Thus the Guilford shareholders were not even invited to attend the obsequies of the Syndicate, which had received its death-blow in May, 1914. At such a ceremony I doubt if their feelings would have permitted them to enact the part of "mutes."

In anticipation of an earlier completion of the sale the purchasers had formed an English company under the title of

THE GUILFORD WALDERSHARE COLLIERY COMPANY, LIMITED.

(Registered June 11, 1917.)

Capital, £240,000 in ordinary shares of £1 each.

Directors.—Messrs. Camille Constant Cavallier, Leon Alphonse Levy, Jacques Emilie Aguillon, Charles Emile Heurteau, Theodore Laurent, Marcel Dumins, Felix Le Breton, and Paul Nicou. Registered offices: 3, Gray's Inn Place, London, W.C.2.

The Guilford Pits, when they came into the possession of their new proprietors, were full of water to within about 260 ft. of the surface, but they were speedily emptied. Monsieur Francois, whose name is widely known in connection with the cementation of water-bearing strata, has undertaken the sinking of the pits into the Coal Measures, and is confident that his process will enable him to accomplish this successfully. Local engineers are following his operations with much interest, but, so far as I can judge, are preserving an open mind with reference to the work. They certainly hope that Monsieur Francois' expectations will be realised and that he will succeed in transforming the heavily water-logged Junction Beds into a compact sandstone.

Comparative Table of Secondary Rocks from the Surface to the Top of the Oolites in the four principal Sinkings in Kent.

	Dover.	Guilford. Ft.	Tilmanstone Ft.	Snowdown. Ft.
O.D.	50	365	224	214
	Depth from Pit Bank			
Chalk	166	766	750	739
Gault	301	910	9[illegible]4	930
Folkestone beds	3[illegible]6	9[illegible]5	939	931
Sandgate beds	388	951	972	967
Atherfield clay	431	985.9	974.6	977
Wealden	481	1004	1007	985
Hastings	516	1027	1035	1009
	Thickness of Strata.			
Chalk	166	766	750	739
Gault	135	144	184	191
Folkestone beds } Bad ground	5	5	5	1
Sandgate beds } Bad ground	82	35	33	36
Atherfield clay } Bad ground	43	24.9	2.6	10
Wealden } Bad ground	50	28.3	32.6	8
Hastings } Bad ground	25	23	28	24.6
	215	117	101	79.6

Some differences may be observed in the figures given for these subdivisions from time to time. It is impossible to secure uniformity for the reason that the colliery records are made indiscriminately from first one and then another of their pits. In the Wealden and Hastings Beds, particularly, the thicknesses are seldom identical in both shafts at any of the sinkings.

CHAPTER XV.

1907.—*East Kent Contract and Financial Co.—The Honest Broker. Community of Interest. Inter-Company Transactions. Large Sums advanced to Allied Companies. Undertakes to construct Light Railway. Contract gets out of its depth. Mr. Burr gives up Control. Concessions issues Convertible Preference shares. Further Borings in Progress.*

> "Out of my lean and low ability,
> I'll lend you something."—SHAKESPEARE.

The year 1907, so prolific of Kent Coal Companies, was now drawing to its close, but was not destined to end without a further addition to the family, which was duly registered on December 13 under the title of

THE EAST KENT CONTRACT AND FINANCIAL COMPANY, LIMITED.

Capital—£50,000 in 48,000 ordinary shares and 2,000 deferred shares, all of £1 each. The ordinary shares are entitled to a preferential non-cumulative dividend of 20 per cent. per annum, after payment of which the profits available for distribution in each year belong as to 75 per cent. to the ordinary and 25 per cent. to the deferred shares.

As in so many of these companies, there was no board of directors, Mr. Burr being director-general, assisted—according to the circular issued by way of prospectus—" by an Advisory Committee of Shareholders." This advisory committee, however, had no corporeal existence, and the Company's affairs were under the sole control of the director-general, whose remuneration was to be 10 per cent. of the profits.

The circular stated that the main object of the Company was to facilitate and hasten the development of the Coalfield " by creating an intervening agency between the Concessions Company, in the provision of money necessary for the legitimate exploitation of its minerals, and the investing public seeking safe and remunerative employment for its savings, to the manifest advantage of both.'' In this way it was proposed to exclude the groups of financiers who were represented—erroneously, as I think—to be hungering after promotion profits in connection with the enterprise. It was not suggested, however, that such profits would not be made—far otherwise—for in a covering letter to prospective subscribers, accompanying the circular, Mr. Burr stated that—

> "Notwithstanding the great advantage to the Concessions Company, as in the case of the Sondage Syndicate, the profits of the Financial Company will be enormous, and the shares must soon be of great value, probably 10 or 20-fold appreciation within the first twelve months.''

This obvious pandering to the cupidity of human nature scarcely squares with a preceding paragraph in the document from which I am quoting :—

> "It (the Company) is a necessity, and it is no less a necessity that its control should be in my hands as disinterested and seeking mainly advantages for the Concessions Company. Otherwise, its utility would not be so obvious, as independent management would only consider its own shareholders and aim at making too large profits at the expense of the Parent Company."

The "necessity" for such a company was perhaps more obvious than the "necessity" for its control being vested solely in a director-general who already held the affairs of all the other allied companies rather more than less in his own hands. With a responsible board of directors the same advantages might have been secured as have followed the operations of similar financial companies in other industrial fields.

As events proved, however, the communal manner in which the Contract Company's cash resources, those of its director-general and of the other Companies of the group, were dealt with, have resulted in its affairs becoming so hopelessly involved as to be almost inextricable. Between the many companies which came to be known as the "Burr Group" there naturally existed a community of interest, inasmuch as their aims were identical and shareholders' investments were in very few instances confined to one company.

But community of interest was held to imply also community of cash, and inter-company loans inevitably followed when any one of the Group had succeeded in filling its coffers. These loans, however, were not made direct from the lending to the spending company—it was a point of honour that the Contract Company should be permitted to enact its rôle of "honest broker," and even an honest broker does not "broke" for nothing.

Thus it would happen that the managing director of Concessions (Mr. Burr) would interview the director-general of Contract (Mr. Burr) with a view to a loan. Contract, not having any money at the moment, would approach the director-general of, say, South Eastern Coalfield Extension (Mr. Burr), borrow the required sum from that company and make the loan to Concessions. Therefore the utility of the East Kent Contract & Financial Company, Limited, was, as its promoter proclaimed, "obvious." How otherwise could the cash in the coffers of the South Eastern Coalfield Extension have found its way into those of Concessions?

As evidence of the intricate inter-company financial operations, in all of which the Contract Company served as a conduit pipe for the cash, I reproduce the following list of credits and debits from the balance-sheet to December 31, 1917, issued by the present board :—

Amounts owing to Contract by allied Companies.

	£	s.	d.
Kent Coal Concessions, Ltd.	56,116	12	5
South Eastern Coalfield Extension, Ltd. ..	15,403	15	9
Extended Extension, Ltd.	14,232	4	11
Concessions, Extension and Ex-Extension jointly	6,148	7	11
East Kent Colliery Co., Ltd.	15,819	7	10
Snowdown Colliery, Ltd.	19,390	19	2
Guilford Syndicate, Ltd	42,736	16	2
South East Kent Electric Power Co., Ltd ...	5,152	12	6
	£125,770	16	8

Of the above amounts, that shown as owing by the East Kent Colliery Company has since been discharged by an allotment of 4 per cent. income bonds, the value of which is more or less hypothetical. As regards the sum of £42,736 due from the Guilford Syndicate, not a single penny of that amount is recoverable, so that in this transaction alone the Contract Company was shorn of almost its entire share capital. That such a sum of money should have been loaned to one of the allied undertakings without a vestige of security was surely stretching the "community of interest" beyond all reason.

Similarly in connection with the loans to Snowdown Colliery, Limited, the Contract Company is in the position of an unsecured creditor, and though the consequences are not likely to be so disastrous as in the Guilford case, there is even less excuse for the lending company's unprotected position.

In addition to the debts scheduled above, the balance-sheet shows an amount of £50,000 as owing by the former director-general. This claim, it is only right to say, is not admitted; and, as the transactions upon which it is based may form the subject of legal proceedings, no further comment is permissible. I am of the opinion, however, that in any circumstances its value is not even problematical.

Amounts Owing by Contract to Allied Companies

	£	s	d.
Intermediate Equipments, Ltd.	29,041	8	7
Foncage Syndicate, Ltd.	14,125	12	3
Sondage Syndicate Ltd.	4,577	19	1
Deal and Walmer Coalfield Extension, Ltd. ...	998	4	6
Concessions, Extension and Extended Ext., balance due on joint cash account	11,209	4	7
East Kent Light Railway Co., Ltd.	8,886	14	0
	£68,839	3	0

The Contract Company's ability to discharge the above debts naturally depends upon the extent to which it succeeds in collecting the sums previously shown as due to it.

I do not propose to give more than a brief sketch of the Contract Company's career. In any case it would be impossible to follow the intricacies of its financial operations, while its general relations with the allied companies will appear as each of these is severally dealt with.

The Company's capital, of which only £18,000 had been issued up to the date of its statutory meeting, was at all times inadequate for its purposes. To have successfully carried out all the business in which it engaged would have demanded not less than £1,000,000 of capital. Even in January, 1911, when the second general meeting was held, the issued capital was only £33,000—notwithstanding which the chairman stated that the Company had succeeded in raising on its own credit, and lending to the spending companies, no less than £125,000. At this meeting dividends of 40 per cent. to the ordinary and 100 per cent. to the founders' shares were confirmed. In moving the adoption of the accounts, the Chairman said:—

> "We have not looked for profits. I may safely tell you that the Contract Company has only had one idea in its head—if a Contract Company can have a head—and that has been to render services mainly to Tilmanstone, but also to the other collieries in course of formation, in order to facilitate the sinking of the pits to the coal—and so to establish this great enterprise upon a rock, the foundations of which even the waves of the English Channel could not shake."

For a company that did not look for profits, Contract was singularly fortunate in having profits thrust upon it; that such was its experience is shown by the following extracts from the director-general's report to the shareholders, dated July 30, 1913, covering the accounts to December 31, 1912:—

> "This Company, established in 1907, has now returned to its ordinary shareholders dividends as follows:—In 1908, 10 per cent.; in 1909, 15 per cent.; in 1910, 15 per cent.; in 1911, 50 per cent.; in 1912, 20 per cent. (interim) = 110 per cent. on the ordinary shares. To its deferred shareholders:—In 1911, 100 per cent.; in 1912, 50 per cent. = 150 per cent. on the deferred shares, and the Company's assets, although much undervalued, by far exceed its paid-up capital.
>
> "For the year under review, the following interim dividends have been made, which require the sanction of the shareholders:—December 27, 1912, 10 per cent. on the ordinary shares; April 11, 1913, 10 per cent. on the ordinary shares."

Swollen profits in the case of companies sometimes leads, as with individuals, to swollen heads, for Contract had now embarked on a business that was to involve it in great financial embarrassments. My statement that £1,000,000 of capital would not be too much for its requirements is amply borne out by a further extract from the document quoted above :—

> " This Company had entered into contracts of a most profitable character with the East Kent Light Railways for the construction of its line of railway as authorised, viz. :—

	Estimated cost, including lands and minerals thereunder.
Original Order, 1911	£240,000
Extension Order No. 1 (1911)...	120,000
" " No. 2 (1912)...	60,000

> and supplementary contracts are about to be entered into for further construction in respect of supplementary extensions, plus further orders granted, the estimated cost of which, including purchase of lands and underlying minerals amounting to £300,000, makes a total of £720,000, in addition to which applications are now before the Commissioners for powers to construct further extensions for the service of collieries about to be established within the Coalfield, and many other important sinkings are in contemplation, in respect of which still further extensions may be necessary."

The Contract Company acted as promoter of Snowdown Colliery, Limited, Intermediate Equipments, Limited, Deal and Walmer Coalfield Extension, Limited, South-East Kent Electric Power Company, Limited, and further acquired by purchase the Pluckley Clay Works, near Ashford. At these works most of the bricks used in connection with the various sinkings were made, but the plant and machinery were of a very antiquated type and the kilns, with one exception, were also quite out of date. Notwithstanding the high prices charged for their products, the works were carried on at a loss.

The chief undertaking, however, in which the Contract Company adventured was the East Kent Light Railway. Jointly with Concessions, and other companies of the group, Contract put forward applications to the Light Railway Commissioners for a series of lines to serve the collieries in course of construction and others that were projected.

Following upon the issue of the necessary orders, Contract promoted the East Kent Light Railway Company, Limited, whose affairs are of sufficient importance to be dealt with separately—which will be done in due course; for the moment we are concerned only with the financial matters between these two companies.

It was in this connection that Contract got so far out of its depth by undertaking the construction of the several lines for which orders had been obtained, in consideration of the allotment of practically the whole of the shares and debentures which the Light Railway Company was authorised to issue.

As I have already stated, the Contract Company's resources were insufficient for carrying out works of such magnitude; the performance of the obligations involved consequently depended upon the shares and debentures in question being converted into cash. Had they been marketable at anything like their face value, the construction of the line might have proved a profitable business for Contract, but, unfortunately, the prices realised fell far short of its expectations.

As in the case of the Guilford Syndicate, the Contract Company passed out of the hands of Mr. Burr into those of Mr. Dewrance and his colleagues. During the war period the new board has found much occupation in endeavouring to straighten out this company's affairs, and as none of the directors is drawing any fees it is to be hoped that the task is proving a labour of love.

In the early days of the war it was mutually agreed that repayment of all outstanding inter-company loans should be postponed until six months after the Declaration of Peace. Similarly, construction work on the Light Railway has been suspended The time is fast approaching, however, when the affairs of the Contract Company, as, indeed, of those of all the allied companies, will press for settlement. As to what the issue will be I do not care to prophesy. I am certain, though, of one thing—and that is that shareholders, who at one time could have sold their shares for £5 or

£6 apiece, may consider themselves extremely fortunate if the par value is ever again established.

With the history of the East Kent Contract and Financial Company I have completed my record of the various subsidiary companies formed in 1907, so I will now resume my story in chronological order, letting the affairs of the parent company (Kent Coal Concessions, Limited) run through it as its *Leit motif*, so to speak.

1908.

There are still several later allied companies to be dealt with, and when they have received as much attention as their importance warrants, my readers should have a clear understanding as to their functions and performances in the Kent Coal scheme of affairs.

The most important of these later companies, and the only one created in 1908, is The Snowdown Colliery, Limited, which was registered on March 26, and with which I will deal in detail after narrating whatever may be of general interest concerning Concessions' operations during that year.

In the early part of January some French capitalists were seriously contemplating the purchase of a colliery area from Concessions, and they deputed the well-known engineer, Monsieur A. Fonville, to examine and report on the coalfield.

Having the knowledge of the troubles at Shakespeare Cliff in mind, Monsieur Fonville advised that the Greensands could not be sunk through without the aid of the Kind-Chaudron system, and the implied cost of sinking probably accounts for the fact that nothing came of the negotiations.

Towards the end of the year Monsieur Fonville again visited the field, and, finding that the Tilmanstone Pits had got through the danger zone of the Greensands, he changed his view materially, and stated that:—

> "This horizon, which inspired such fear, owing to the precedent at Dover, offers no danger in this part of Kent, owing to the thinness and distance from the outcrop and sea."

Beyond his expressed opinion that the Kent Coalfield was a continuation of the Pas de Calais basin, there is nothing of particular interest in Monsieur Fonville's report.

By the middle of the year Concessions' exchequer was getting low, and with the continuous increase in option rents, and in boring expenditure, it was essential that further working capital be raised. At the beginning of the year Concessions ordinary shares were being dealt in at £3, but in June they were a dull market at 37s. 6d. There was therefore no possibility of getting the required money by a fresh issue of ordinaries without depressing the price still further.

Consequently it was decided to create a new class of shares having such attractive possibilities as might ensure their being subscribed for. An extraordinary general meeting of the preference shareholders, therefore, was held on July 24, when resolutions were passed authorising the creation of 50,000 convertible preference shares, ranking *pari passu* with the existing preference shares, of which 16,841 were still unissued. These were added to the 50,000 new shares, and became convertible likewise. The conversion privilege was the right to exchange into ordinary shares of the Company on July 1, 1910, upon the holder giving six months' previous notice in writing of his desire so to do.

An issue of 40,000 of the new shares was made, to Concessions shareholders only, at a premium of 15s. per share, subject to a rebate of 10s. per share to allottees who had not sold any of their ordinary shares at less than 37s. 6d. up to the date when the conversion right matured. A further 5,000 were offered, on similar terms, to shareholders of the allied companies—not being members of Concessions.

The Company's original capital of £50,000, in 48,500 ordinary and 1,500 deferred shares, had now expanded into £200,000, divided thus:—

33,159 cumulative 10 per cent. preference shares.
66.841 convertible non-cumulative 10 per cent preference shares.
98,500 ordinary shares.
1,500 deferred shares.

Borings were in progress during this year on Concessions' areas at Goodnestone and Barfreston, but as they were not completed until 1910 and 1912 respectively, it would be premature to give their sections now.

CHAPTER XVI.

1908.—*Snowdown Colliery started by the Fonçage Syndicate. Heavy feeder of water in the Chalk. Company formed to take over the work-Mr. Burr as managing director. Easy sinking to base of Galut. No water difficulties. Costly methods of raising capital. Coal at last. First in the Field. Board of Directors appointed. 4 ft. 5 in. seam at 3,000 ft.*

"Success is a fruit slow to ripen."—ANON.

1908.

There is, therefore, nothing further of a practical nature to chronicle concerning Concessions itself in 1908. Tilmanstone, as has already been seen, was monopolising the stage during this period—though a rival, that was destined to be foremost in the race to the coal, appeared on the scene, when, on March 26, there was registered the only subsidiary company formed this year, viz. :—

THE SNOWDOWN COLLIERY, LIMITED.

The inception of the Snowdown Colliery is due to the initiative of the Fonçage Syndicate. Early in September, 1906, the Syndicate's operations at Guilford were brought to a standstill owing to the cartage difficulties, to which reference has already been made. Thereupon they bethought themselves to transfer the scene of their activities. Even before coal was actually proved in the Fredville boring they entered into negotiations with the Concessions Company which resulted in the Syndicate obtaining an option over 1,500 acres of minerals, and three days after the first 18-in. seam of coal had been pierced work was commenced on the site of the present colliery.

As in the case of Guilford it was the intention of the Syndicate to do a certain amount of work, and then to dispose of their interests in this colliery section at a profit. Unfortunately, owing to meeting with a big water-bearing fissure in the Upper Chalk, the Syndicate found itself with a wet pit and a dry purse before 300 ft. of sinking had been accomplished. The conditions, consequently, were such that there was little prospect of being able to pass on their responsibilities to any outsiders; therefore it was determined to form a company for this purpose, the shares of which should be offered only to existing members of the allied group.

It was in these circumstances that the Snowdown Company came into being, with the object of taking over the pits and establishing the colliery which has since achieved the distinction of being the first in Kent to raise coal from a seam that was to be worked thereafter on a commercial scale. The accompanying photograph of the first hoppit of coal brought to bank from these pits is therefore not without historic interest.

A certain amount of interest also attaches to the sinking at Snowdown if only for the reason that the geological conditions there proved so different from those at Tilmanstone. Except for the setback due to the large volume of water met with in the Upper Chalk at about 260 ft. from the surface, which entailed the abandonment of No. 1 Pit, no serious engineering difficulties were encountered. Therefore, had it been possible to devote to Snowdown a modicum of the energy and a fraction of the money that were for so long, and so unavailingly, expended at Tilmanstone, the critics who shrieked (like Lloyd George's "wild men" at Paris) through the keyhole of Concessions' board room for tangible results, would have had their mouths effectually closed, and their discordant voices silenced, several years before that happy consummation was rendered possible.

The Snowdown Colliery, Limited, was registered with a capital of £251,250 in 150,000 preferred ordinary shares of £1 each, 100,000 ordinary shares of £1 each, and 25,000 founders' shares of 1s. each. The preferred ordinary shares are entitled out of the profits in any one year, to a non-cumulative preferential dividend at the rate of 10 per cent per annum; and of the balance remaining for distribution one moiety is payable to Kent Coal Con-

THE FIRST HOPPIT OF COAL RAISED AT SNOWDOWN COLLIERY, NOVEMBER 19, 1912.

cessions, Limited, and one moiety is divisible as to one-third to the holders of the preferred ordinary shares, one-third to the holders of the ordinary shares, and one-third to the holders of the founders' shares. The whole of the ordinary shares were allotted to the Fonçage Syndicate by way of purchase consideration.

The East Kent Contract and Financial Company acted as promoters and were allotted 15,000 of the founders' shares with the option to take up at par any of the remaining 10,000 of such shares as were not subscribed for in connection with the first issue of preferred ordinaries. This issue was limited to 50,000 shares, and subscribers had the right to an allotment at par of 10 founders' shares in respect of every 100 preferred ordinaries applied for; and also to an option to take up an equal number of preferred ordinary shares at par, either on May 1, 1909, or October 1, 1909. In respect of every 100 shares subscribed for under this option the Contract Company undertook to give five founders' shares by way of bonus.

This is unquestionably an involved and complicated financial scheme, and it is not surprising that there are few shareholders to-day who have more than a hazy notion as to the respective rights attached to the several classes of shares.

Contract undertook to manage the affairs of the Snowdown Company, until such time as it should be raising coal, with the assistance of two members of the board of Concessions, viz., Mr. H. A. Johnston, the chairman, and Mr. H. S. Close. As the management of the Contract Company was vested solely in the person of Mr. Burr, and both these assistant directors were resident in Ireland, it may readily be understood that their office was a sinecure.

The colliery is situated about nine miles from Dover, midway between Adisham and Shepherdswell Stations on the South-Eastern and Chatham main line, with which it is connected by a siding The actual site is within 200 yards of the Fredville boring, and it may be desirable before we come to deal with the sinking to give details as to the strata that had to be pierced.

Comparative Figures re Fredville Section, 259 *O.D.*

Strata.	Figures given in boring sections.			As proved in No. 3 Pit 243 O.D
	Boyd Dawkins.	Malcolm Burr.	Conces-sions Co.	
	Ft. in.	Ft. in.	Ft. in.	Ft. in.
Chalk	800 0	800 0	800 0	739 0
Gault	148 0	147 0	148 0	191 0
Folkestone beds,				1 0
Sandgate beds,	51 0	52 4	50 0	36 0
Atherfield clay				10 0
Wealden ..	36 0	35 0	37 0	8 0
Hastings ..				24 6
Oolites	323 0			293 0
Sandbed		350 6	316 0	8 0
Lias	10 6			16 6
Coal Measures at ..	1,368 6	*1,375 0	1,351 0	1,327 0

* I have given Dr. Burr's figures as published in "Science Progress," January, 1909, but they are incorrect as they add up to 1,384 ft. 10 in. instead of 1,375 ft. as printed.

The greatest disparity between the above records occurs in connection with the Gault. It is practically impossible to determine, in a boring put down with a chisel, where the Chalk ends and the Gault begins, and for this reason the published boring sections should not be accepted as accurate in respect to the relative thicknesses of these strata. The totals from the surface to the top of the Lower Greensands, however, may be generally relied upon.

When the Pits were taken over from the Fonçage Syndicate, early in 1908, they were down to less than 300 ft., and, as I have already mentioned, No. 1 was water-logged and derelict. The purely local character of the trouble which necessitated its abandonment is evidenced, however, by the fact that No. 2, only 50 yards distant, met with very little water in the Chalk and was carried down without any difficulty.

The enterprise as a whole always had more water than money at its disposal, Tilmanstone in particular proving a drain in more senses than one. Consequently the Snowdown Colliery Company, like its contemporaries in the field, was compelled to take up its burden insufficiently supplied with funds. Hence it will be seen that work was carried out sporadically, and sinking to the Coal Measures, which might have been accomplished within two years, occupied more than twice that time.

No. 3 Pit, which was started to replace No. 1, was down to 360 ft. by August, 1909, No. 2 meanwhile standing idle at 270 ft. as when the Fonçage Syndicate handed it over. By November, 1910, the respective depths were .—No. 2, 896 ft., and No. 3, 396 ft. It was not until towards the end of 1911 that both shafts had reached 917 ft., which was as near to the base of the Gault as was thought prudent to sink until provision had been made for dealing with the expected water in the Lower Greensands and Wealden.

1912.

An inset, therefore, was made at 720 ft. in No. 2 Pit, in which were erected three Evans "Cornish" compound engines with double-acting ram pumps, the capacity of each being 500 gallons per minute. The early portion of the sinking had been done with a very temporary, not to say trumpery, plant, but No. 2 was now equipped with winding engines by Markhams, of Chesterfield, having 30-in. cylinders, 60-in. stroke, with Corliss exhaust valves. Drum, 14 ft. diameter by 9 ft. 6 in. wide. Like the winding engines at Tilmanstone, these are fitted with the Whitmore brake and over-winding prevention gear.

At No. 3 Pit a pair of Worsley-Mesnes piston-valve winding engines were installed. These have cylinders 25 in. in diameter with 48-in. stroke, and are fitted with Melling automatic expansion gear (giving a range of cut-off from 0 to 90 per cent.) and a steam reverser. The drum is 13½ ft. diameter by 8 ft. wide.

Power is supplied by five Lancashire boilers, three of 8 ft. by 30 ft. and two of 9 ft. by 30 ft., the draught for which was furnished by a Weber ferro-concrete chimney, 110 ft. high with an internal diameter of 5 ft. I might mention, incidentally, that this was the first and last of these chimneys erected on the coalfield; it proved a failure, and has long since been replaced.

When the tubbing, which was manufactured by the Butterley Company, was on the ground and the curbs from which it was destined to be hung were completed, the crucial moment had arrived. It is a commonplace in mining that you cannot see beyond the length of your pick: what difficulties lay hidden beneath the few feet of compact Gault in the pit-bottom, who could say? Certainly, none would dare to prophesy. But the plunge from ignorance to knowledge had to be

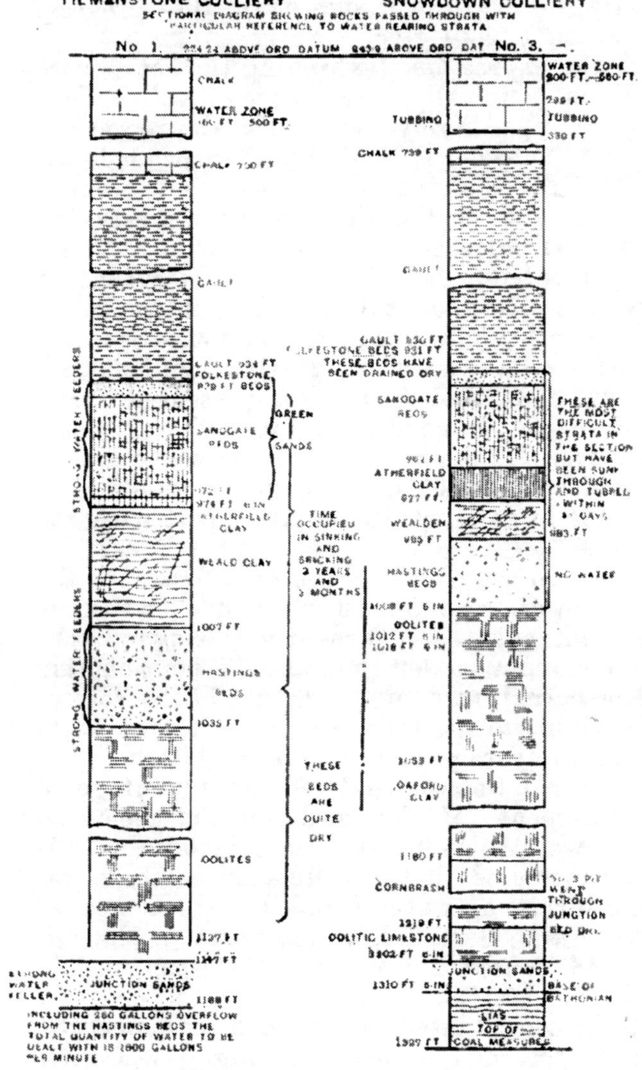

made and so with hopes for the best, and not unnatural fears for the worst, an exploratory bore-hole was started.

The results justified the most sanguine hopes, and heartfelt sighs of relief were emitted when little more than a trickle of water was met with in penetrating the upper portion of the treacherous Greensands. When the shafts were well into these beds the water naturally increased, but at its maximum it never caused any material delay in the sinking—as will be shown in the progress records which I shall give.

If ever the expression "whipping the cat" were justified, as pictorially descriptive of bitter unavailing regrets, surely this was the occasion. Sinking at Snowdown had been suspended for months in order that the entire energy and finance at the command of the Concessions undertaking might be concentrated on Tilmanstone. There Nature presented more than one barrier that at times seemed insurmountable, and that consumed not only month upon month of precious time, but thousands upon thousands of dearly-bought money.

At Snowdown no such barriers presented themselves; even the dreaded Junction Bed was shorn of its terrors. Thus the future of the whole undertaking had been needlessly mortgaged in the misplaced attempt to reach the winning-post with the wrong horse.

The plan on page 178 graphically presents the contrast between the Snowdown and Tilmanstone sinkings, not only as regards the passage of the Greensands and Wealden, but also of the Junction Bed. The actual rate of progress at the former from the Gault to the Oolites was 23 ft. per week, as against an average of 14 in. at the latter.

Not only did Snowdown have the advantage of better equipment for the task, but the geological conditions were substantially more favourable. It will be remembered that at Tilmanstone there was a violent inrush of water from the gravel bed at the base of the Hastings, which burst in the pit-bottom and caused several months' stoppage in the sinking. At Snowdown this gravel bed was found to be consolidated into a hard conglomerate.

Sinking proceeded normally through the Oolites —in one week No. 3 was sunk 20 ft. and bricked 40 ft., which constitutes a record for the coalfield—and the management enjoyed freedom from anxieties until they were approaching the sand bed, when the fact that its level was 150 ft. lower than at Tilmanstone gave them furiously to think.

The "Beresford" Seam a Few Feet in from the Shaft; Snowdown Colliery, January, 1913.

The sinking staff at the colliery was not considered competent to deal with the anticipated difficulties, so this section of the work was entrusted to the well-known firm of Messrs. Eaton, Son & Hinds. However, here again Nature proved in a complacent mood, and No. 3 Pit had quite a dry passage, while the water met with in No. 2 was not sufficient to retard its progress.

By October 26 the pits at both Snowdown and Tilmanstone were in the sand bed. At the former there were 372 ft. between the base of the Gault and the top of the sand bed, and the time occupied in taking the pits down this length was five months. Whereas at Tilmanstone, while the distance between the same two points was only 206 ft., the sinking took no less than three years and ten months! The causes of this disparity in the rate of progress have been fully dealt with in my record of the Tilmanstone sinking.

At the latter the sand bed interposed between the base of the Oolites and the top of the Coal Measures, and consequently this bed—which persists throughout the greater part of the Coalfield—by usage has become known as the "Junction" Sand-bed, or Junction Bed. In the districts in which the Lias is met with it naturally does not form any such junction.

There are 17 ft. 6 in. of Lias at Snowdown between the base of the sand bed and the Coal Measures; hence it was that Tilmanstone was the first to enter the Promised Land, the frontiers of which for so long had been successfully defended by Nature. Snowdown was a good second, however, entering the Coal Measures seven days later: but, as I have already stated, Snowdown Colliery was the first to gladden the eyes of Kent Coal devotees with a sight of black diamonds—not in negligible quantities from an 8-in. borehole, but in full measure and overflowing from an 18-ft. shaft.

1913.

The first two coal seams met with being only 18 in. in thickness, sinking proceeded to the "Beresford" 4 ft. 4 in. seam, which was reached on January 2 of the above year at a depth of 1,490 ft. The accompanying photograph (page 180) shows the seam at a few feet from the side of the shaft.

It is generally believed, though to my mind it is an open question, that the seams being worked at Snowdown and Tilmanstone both correlate with the 6-ft. 1-in. of the Barfrestone boring section. The Beresford seam is certainly much higher in volatiles, and would give a better yield in by-products, than the Tilmanstone seam, but it is suggested that these differences are only such as are common to the same seam when worked in different localities.

As soon as the first heading had been driven a few feet a representative sample of the coal was submitted to Mr. Geo. R. Hislop, who reported as follows, under date January 26:—

Mineralogical Characters.—The coal possesses considerable lustre and brownish-black streak; fracture partly defined by organic remains, and partly coarse, angular and crystalline; cross-fracture small cubical, semi-resinoid and crystalline; partly finely columnar between the several lines of stratification, and with shining planes in the natural partings; moderately cohesive and very compact; under heat it intumesces and agglomerates; coke, silvery; colour of ash, brown; thickness of seam, 47 in.; mean specific gravity of the coal, 1,276 (water 1,000); weight of one cubic foot, 79.75 lbs.

Chemical Analysis.

	Per cent.
Volatile matters (containing 0.44 of sulphur) ..	29.02
Coke consisting of carbon 62.59, sulphur 0.28, ash 6.07	68.94
Water expelled at 212° Fah.	2.04
	100.00

Practical Results.

Gaseous Products.

Gas per ton of coal at 60° Fah. and 30 in. bar ..	12,465 cub. ft.
Gas from one cub. ft. of the coal	438.43 „
Specific gravity of the gas	430 (air 1,000)
Hydro-carbons absorbed by bromine	4.00 per cent.
Durability of 1 cu . ft. by 5-in. jet flame ..	35 min. 12 sec.
Value of 1 cub. ft f gas in sperm	403.2 grains
Value of gas from 1 ton of coal in sperm ..	717.98 lbs.
Illuminating power of gas in standard candles (per No. 2 met. burner)	16.8 candles
Sulphuretted hydrogen (H_2S) in foul gas ..	1.00 per cent.
Carbonic acid (CO_2) in foul gas	3.25 „
Carbonic oxide (CO) in foul gas	6.25 „
Sulphur eliminated with volatile products ..	9.85 lbs

Liquid Products.

Tar per ton of coal	9.65 gals
Ammoniacal liquor per ton of coal , ..	8.75 gals.
Strength of ammoniacal liquor .. .	8.0 deg. Twadd
Hygrometric water per ton of coal .	5.37 gals.
Aqueous absorbent capacity of coal (determined by complete saturation)	2.56 per cent.

Solid Products.

Coke per ton of coal	1,544.25 lbs.
Carbon in the coke	91.20 per cent.
Ash in the coke	8 80 ,,
Sulphur in coke per ton of coal	6.27 lbs.
Heating power in 1 lb. of coke (water from boiling point into steam)	12.51 lbs.

Remarks.—"This is an excellent gas and coking coal, and as such it yields a large volume of good gas and affords 13.77 cwts. per ton of fine, massive and firm coke, with a minimum of breeze. As a house coal it gives excellent heat, possesses great durability, and contains a very moderate amount of sulphur. Compared with Main Lesmahagow cannel coal, represented by 100 (calculated on the bases of a production of 13,000 cub. ft. of gas and 1,535.5 lbs. of sperm value per ton, and having regard also to the value of the secondary products and the cost of the purification of the gas), this coal is equal to 51.48."

With a view to establishing the commercial value of the "Beresford" coal, it was arranged to test it at the Tilmanstone electric power station against the coal they were using there which came from the Lewis-Merthyr Collieries. The result was entirely satisfactory, as will be seen by the following report (dated March 11, 1913) from the electrical engineer, Mr. G. F Metzger :—

Result of Coal Test at Tilmanstone Power Station. Quality of Coal used, Snowdown Colliery, "Beresford" Seam, large Coal.

Babcock & Wilcox boilers, hand-fired, induced draft.
Heating surface of each boiler, 4,020 sq ft.
Grate area of each boiler, 76 sq ft.
Steam pressure, 200 lbs. per sq. in.
Temperature of superheated steam, 500 to 560 deg Fah.

Analysis of the coal as given by G. Lloyd Jones (Principal of West Ham Testing Laboratory), and as published in the "Electrical Review" of February 28, 1913 :-

	Above shale band. Per cent.	Below shale band. Per cent.
Volatile matter	27.98	28.26
Coke	70.34	69.76
Ash	7.20	6.11
Fixed carbon	63.14	63.65
Moisture (hygroscopic)	1.68	1.98
Sulphur (separately determined) ..	1.32	1.29
Calorific value (as dried)	13,990 B.T.U.	14,180 B.T.U.
Net effective calorific value (as fired)	13,136 B.T.U.	13,454 B.T.U.
Evaporative power (as fired) ..	13,79 lbs. of water from and at 212 ° F.	13.92 lbs. of water from and at 212° F.

Duration of test: From 11.0 a.m., March 5th, to 6.35 p.m., March 6th, 1913—31 hours 35 minutes.
Quantity of coal used: 26 tons, 19 cwts. 3 qrs. = 60,452 lbs.
Coal burnt per hour .. .. 1,919 lbs.
Total units generated 26,764

Comparisons.

	Welsh coal.	Snowdown coal.	Difference in favour of Snowdown coal.
Superheat obtained ..	550° F.	560° F.	10° F.
Temperature of feed water	230° F.	250° F.	20° F.
Lbs. of coal per unit generated	2.30	2.25	0.05

For reasons which will presently appear obvious, I shall feel compelled to confine my later records of Snowdown to documents which have already been published. But before any such restriction is placed upon my pen I must refer to certain administrative acts by which the financial position of the Company was seriously compromised prior to the election of a regular board of directors.

In August, 1912, at which time the Company was largely indebted to both the Contract and Concessions Companies, the director-general of Contract, in his office as managing director of Snowdown, determined upon an issue of £50,000 of 10 per cent. debentures to be redeemable in five years. The terms upon which these debentures were offered to shareholders were so extremely—not to say recklessly—liberal that it is not surprising they were speedily subscribed for. The issue price was £80 per £100 debenture, and allottees had the right to subscribe for 30 preferred ordinary shares, at par, any time within twelve months of the shafts entering workable coal, in respect of each £100 of debentures allotted. Further, they received from the Contract Company—by way of bonus—ten (1s.) founders' shares of the Snowdown Company.

The option over the preferred ordinary shares, contrary to expectations, proved of no particular value, but as the founders' shares changed hands as high as £2 10s. per share after coal was raised, this bonus represented a further substantial reduction in the cost of the debentures—to those at least who realised the shares.

Notwithstanding the given-away-with-a-pound-of-tea class of terms, a guarantee of the issue was effected under which the Company paid the guarantors a fat fee, and also gave them an option over the whole of the available unissued preferred ordinary shares (some 68,000) for a period of twelve months from the date when workable coal was reached in the shafts.

The guarantors were not called upon to take up any debentures, neither did they exercise any of their option; but they effectually prevented the Company from issuing its shares, as it might so easily have done. "Thus bad begins, and worse remains behind."

The "Beresford" seam was struck on January 2, 1913, and according to the Articles of Association steps should have been taken immediately towards the election of a regular board. Nothing was done, however, in this direction for some months, during which the director-general of Contract, in his capacity as managing director of Snowdown, went ahead and still further complicated the financial affairs of the Company by creating another 50,000 preferred ordinary shares and an additional £100,000 of debentures. At this time, be it noted, there were 68,000 preferred ordinary shares still unissued and unissuable, except under the above-mentioned option.

The obvious course, and one which would have presented no difficulty, as was pointed out at the time to the ruling power, was to obtain the consent of the existing debenture holders to this increase; instead of this a most costly form of procedure was adopted, for it was decided to make the new issue of debentures £150,000 and to redeem the existing bonds, which had been issued only so recently as August, 1912. Under this arrangement the Company was made to pay £20 for the use of £80 for less than twelve months, plus 10 per cent. interest on £100=32½ per cent. on £80.

Interior of Workshops, Snowdown Colliery, 1913.

Holders of the original issue received yet other *bonnes bouches*, for the new debentures, into which practically all of them exchanged, were issued at £90, with a bonus of two each Snowdown ordinary and founders' shares, then officially valued at £1 and £2 10s. per share respectively. So that—to summarise—an original investment of £80 yielded as follows:—

£110 of new 10 per cent. debentures, issued at £90 and redeemable in three years at £100.

12½ per cent. interest on £80 for 10½ months.

An option over 30 preferred ordinary shares of the Company for 12 months after workable coal was reached in the shafts.

Twelve founders' shares, valued at £30.

Two ordinary shares, valued at £2.

Six months' interest on £100 in respect of a like number of weeks.

The last item needs a word of explanation. Under the terms of the new issue, dated June 10, 1913, subscribers paying in full on allotment were entitled to a full six months' interest to August 1. Therefore, as the old debentures were treated as cash, holders who exchanged into the new issue received six months' interest in respect of these six weeks; and as they were also paid their fixed 10 per cent. up to the date of exchange, they thus received double interest over a period of 4½ months, or the equivalent of 25 per cent. per annum on their £80. Comment on such frenzied finance is superfluous.

This issue of £150,000 of debentures was actually made at the beginning of June, 1913, within a fortnight of the general meeting at which shareholders elected their first directors, who were Mr. J. J. Clark, J.P. (Chairman), Professor W. Galloway, F.G.S.; Mr. Henry S. Close, J.P.; Mr. J. A. Bell-Beattie, Mr. A. E. Ritchie, Mr. Archd. Bryson, and Mr. Arthur Burr. The two last-named resigned their seats at the end of 1914, and death robbed the remaining directors of a highly-esteemed colleague in the person of Mr J. A. Bell-Beattie in 1917. These vacancies were not filled, but, as under the articles of association the Concessions Company was entitled to nominate two directors—a right which, so far, it had not exercised—in 1916 Mr Walter F. Moens, their general manager at Dover, was appointed to the board to represent Concessions' interests.

Two months after their election the new directors issued a circular to the shareholders, in which they stated that the output would be restricted to 500 tons per week, pending the erection of a washing plant to enable the coal to be sent out in a more marketable condition than was possible by merely screening it.

As further evidence of the intrinsic value of the "Beresford" coal, and of its suitability for bunkering purposes, the following letters to the Company's selling agents were embodied in the circular:—

DOVER, August 22, 1913.

MESSRS. MOWLL & COMPANY, LIMITED, DOVER.

DEAR SIRS,—Referring to the bunker coals you delivered to the s.s. "Herdis," twenty tons small nuts from Snowdown Colliery, I beg to state that we, the undersigned, tried the coal first in donkey boiler and then in main boiler for getting steam, and have to report that the coal has shown itself to be an excellent steam coal for this steamer. Although the coal is small nuts as we asked for, as soon as it goes into the fire it cakes together and provides a very strong heat. Some slight smoke is shown when the coal is put in the furnace, but this immediately passes away and continues smokeless. From residue point of view, this coal gives very little slag and ashes and considerably less than East Coast coal we usually get on board this steamer. We consider after this trial that the coal is more economical than the usual Welsh bunker coal we get from Bristol Channel Ports.

We usually take twelve hours to get steam on main boiler, but with Snowdown coal we get steam in much less time, and with much less consumption of coal.—Yours faithfully,

(Signed) Y. WEBE (Master).
J. N. TONGSTAD (Chief Engineer).

BLYTH,
August 24, 1913.

MESSRS. HICKIE, BORMAN & WOODS, DOVER.

DEAR SIRS,—Please inform shippers of my bunker coals in Dover that the coals proved to be very good coals indeed, no trouble whatever in keeping steam, and very little ashes. The consumption was very much less, too, than with any other sorts we have had on board. We made the run from Dover to Blyth in 29 hours, which proves the coals to be good.—Yours faithfully.

(Signed) Y. WEBE
(Master, s.s. "Herdis").

1914.

In the Directors' report of June 23, 1914, covering balance-sheet to March 31 of that year, it was stated that when the board came into office in June, 1913, about 800 tons per week were being raised from the "Beresford" seam. The coal, however, though excellent for steam and gas purposes, being rather friable and productive of a large percentage of slack, it was considered desirable to try and develop one of the lower seams. Coal suitable for domestic consumption obviously could not fail to prove extremely profitable, and it was confidently hoped that such would be met with.

Coal-winding, therefore, was suspended in No. 3 Pit and sinking with three shifts was commenced, while in No 2 coal-winding was restricted to one shift, the other two being devoted to sinking. Unfortunately, at the end of February, 1915, when No. 2 was down to 1,744 ft., sinking in this pit had to be suspended for financial reasons, the company's resources being only sufficient to cover the cost of sinking No. 3, which was kept going with three shifts, as before.

This Pit passed through two of the seams of the Barfrestone boring at 1,898 ft. and 1,961 ft. respectively, but they were not sufficiently promising to work, and sinking was continued to 2,236 ft., where, on May 18, the 4-ft. 7-in. seam of the Barfrestone boring was reached. It proved to be somewhat thinner in the Pit than in the boring, but being a seam of hard bright coal it was named the "Snowdown Hard." The following is an analysis of a pit sample:—

	As received. Per cent.	As dried. Per cent.
Volatile matter	23 29	23.54
Coke	75 66	76 46
Ash	4.45	4.50
Fixed carbon	71 21	71 96
Hygroscopic moisture	1.05	--
Sulphur (separately determined)	0 95	0,96

Thermal Values.

	Available as received. B.T.U.	As dried. B.T.U.
Calorific value	14.209	14,790
Carbon equivalent	—	13,895
Evaporative Power (lbs. of water from and at 212° F. per lb. of coal).. ..	14.71	15.31

As this seam promised to yield better results than the "Beresford," the directors were anxious to resume sinking in No. 2 Pit, for until both shafts were into the coal it could not be worked on a commercial scale. An issue of preferred ordinary shares was therefore made, but owing to the sudden outbreak of war the response was insufficient to justify an allotment, and the application moneys had to be returned.

The outbreak of war also made it necessary for the directors to approach the debenture holders with a view to obtaining their consent to forego the payment of any interest until six months after the Declaration of Peace, and a similar arrangement had to be made with respect to the repayment of their principal.

On October 14, 1914, the debenture holders assented to the creation of £50,000 of 7 per cent. prior lien bonds ranking in priority to their security, and these bonds were duly created and issued.

1915—1919.

Early in 1915 the Concessions' directors decided that it would strengthen their hands in negotiating for the sale, or lease, of their minerals if one of the existing shafts on their areas was sunk to the bottom of the Coal Measures. After careful consideration, No. 2 Pit at Snowdown was decided upon, and mutually satisfactory arrangements were made between the two companies for the carrying out and financing of this work.

When the Pit reached 3,007 ft., on April 6, 1917, it entered a 4-ft. 5-in. seam of solid coal, having no partings, which correlated exactly with a similar sized seam at the Barfrestone boring, distant a little over 1¼ miles. The following is a representative analysis of this deep seam :—

	Per cent.
Volatile combustible matters	20.97
Fixed carbon	75.65
Ash	2.55
Moisture (212° Fah.)	0.83
Calories 8,606 ; B.T.U. 15,490.	100.00

During the first two years of the war the Company was able to increase its output, although to a much less extent than would have been the case in normal times, and by the beginning of 1917 it was producing about 3,000 tons weekly. Thereafter, owing to the man-power demands of the military authorities, and to the patriotic manner in which the men voluntarily offered themselves for service, the figures showed a substantial retrogression, and during 1918 the output barely averaged 2,000 tons per week. At the time of writing (July 1919) production is on the up-grade, but some time must elapse before the ground lost during the war is fully recovered.

It is thus evident that the slow development of this Colliery is due to the abnormal conditions it encountered immediately upon entering upon its active existence, and the shareholders and management alike are the victims of circumstances over which they veritably have had no control.

Official statistics have shown that the Kent Coalfield has the highest percentage of men joining the Colours of any colliery district in the Kingdom, and the Snowdown Colliery was the leading factor in the establishment of that pre-eminence. If, therefore, the results have not proved satisfactory from a financial point of view, "Snowdown" may take a reasonable pride in its record of patriotic service, and might indeed be called to the bar of public opinion and pronounced "to have deserved well of its country."

CHAPTER XVII.

1909.—*Concessions increases its Mineral Areas. Rebuffed by Ecclesiastical Commissioners. Questions in Parliament. Many valuable Coal Seams. The Coal proves of high quality. Extended Extensions, Limited. A 9 ft. 4 in. seam at Ripple. Mr. Burr retires in favour of Board of Directors. Valuation of Company's Minerals.*

"When the judgment's weak the prejudice is strong,"
—O'HARA,

1909.

In resuming my chronological record of Kent Coal Concessions, Limited, I find that there is little more in the way of practical developments to chronicle for the year 1909 than for its predecessor. The exploitation of the Company's minerals was still being held up owing to the difficult sinking conditions at Tilmanstone and the consequent delay in reaching the coal.

Concessions, however, found some compensation for this delay, which, by keeping possible competitors out of the field, enabled it to secure additional mineral rights and to fill up some of the blanks on its plan, thus linking up several detached properties into compact unbroken areas. The pursuit of this programme—which was also adopted by the South-Eastern Coalfield Extension, Limited—brought both companies into conflict with the Ecclesiastical Commissioners, who are large landowners in Kent, and who have achieved the distinction of putting more obstructions in the way of the developing companies than any of the private landlords. And that is saying something.

The plan on page 194 shows an area of about 215 acres at Coldred belonging to the Ecclesiastical Commissioners practically surrounded by freeholds and leaseholds of the Concessions Company. Not only did Concessions wish to link up their minerals by means of this inter-locked area, but also to acquire the right to lay rails to connect the Guilford pits with the South-Eastern and Chatham Railway at Stonehall.

On November 18, 1909, Concessions' solicitors made formal application for a lease of the Commissioners' minerals under these 215 acres and under a further 1,000 acres to the north-west. I quote the following extracts from the solicitors' letter to the Commissioners:—

"Our clients instruct us to inform you that they are ready to take up at once a lease for the usual term of 60 years of the minerals of both the above blocks, and, with regard to Coldred, to work the minerals at an early date, as soon as the pits can be completed at the adjoining Guilford Colliery; and with regard to the other block, which we understand is over 1,000 acres, to sink within twelve months pits either on the land in question or land adjacent thereto, and to work the minerals as soon as such pits can with every possible engineering expedition be carried down to the coal seams. In the meantime our clients are prepared to pay a dead rent of £1 per acre for three years, such dead rent to be increased after three years, until the minerals are worked and the dead rent is merged into royalties, thus affording you a guarantee that the minerals will be vigorously worked.

"Our clients also desire to have facilities for laying a railway over the surface of the Coldred portion to connect the adjoining pits already sunk at the Guilford Colliery with our clients' freehold at Stonehall, which abuts on the southern part of your land at Coldred; they would guarantee to at once start work on this railway, and thus be able to give employment practically at once to some 200 hands.

"Our clients are the only persons who have spent money, which amounts to at least £30,000, on borings and explorations, and who have any geological knowledge of the coalfield inland from Dover, and are thus in possession of the necessary information to enable any of the areas to be properly worked.

"Under these circumstances they consider that the terms now offered are advantageous to you as landlords, and, moreover, such as you could not possibly obtain elsewhere; in fact, the

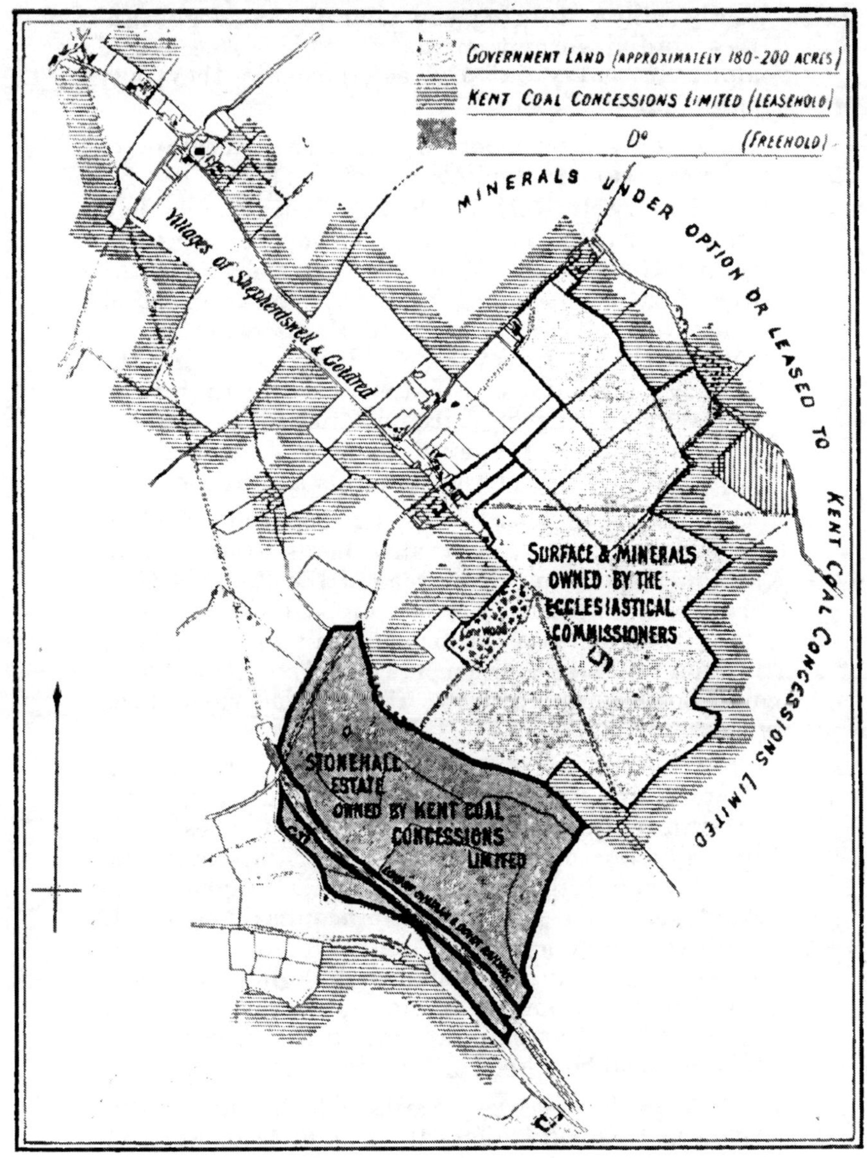

Coldred property is entirely surrounded by property over which our clients have acquired the mineral rights, and our clients inform us that it

would be impossible for any other person or company to work the minerals underlying your Coldred property.

"Our clients ask us to state that they are perfectly willing to give you all reasonable guarantees and information as to their status and ability to carry out any engagements they may enter into."

Under date November 23, 1909, the Secretary to the Commissioners replied as follows:—

"The Ecclesiastical Commissioners have had under consideration the application contained in your letter of the 10th inst. on behalf of the Kent Coal Concessions, Limited, for the grant of a lease of the minerals underlying their lands within the parishes of Coldred, etc., in the County of Kent, and I am directed to inform you that in existing circumstances the Commissioners are not prepared to entertain the proposals for a lease of the minerals in question."

Earlier in the year the South Eastern Coalfield Extension, Limited, had also made similar proposals in respect to other areas of the Ecclesiastical Commissioners within the proven coalfield, and had met with the same uncompromising negative. Thus, under date August 11, the Extension Company's solicitors wrote to the Commissioners as follows:—

"We are acting on behalf of the South Eastern Coalfield Extension, Limited (which is a subsidiary Company to Kent Coal Concessions), in acquiring options for mining rights over the area extending—roughly—from Wingham to Sandwich. We have already acquired on behalf of this Company—and paid for—options over 4,000 acres, and we should be glad to know whether the Commissioners would feel disposed to grant this Company an option over their lands in the neighbourhood of Eastry."

"Very shortly, the terms which the South-Eastern Company offer are a sum calculated at the rate of 10s. per acre for a three years' option. This sum, together with the legal and other expenses on the usual scale, is payable in advance on the grant of the option."

The reply which the Company's solicitors received some three months later was brief—not to say laconic—I quote it in full :—

"November 5, 1909.

"Your letter of August 11 last has been submitted to the Ecclesiastical Commissioners, and I am directed to inform you that they are not prepared to entertain the application contained therein."

Feeling that an obstructive attitude, both unreasonable and unbusinesslike, on the part of an important public body could be but the result of prejudice or ignorance, the Company's solicitors called upon the Secretary to the Commissioners, hoping that a personal interview would promote a better understanding. Unfortunately the interview proved as fruitless as the correspondence which had preceded it, but, nevertheless, the solicitors returned to the charge, and on November 16 wrote another letter to the Secretary clearly setting out the Company's aims, and practically inviting the Commissioners to name their own terms. I quote one or two paragraphs as follows:—

"Our clients feel confident that if the Commissioners could be satisfied of the actual position of the undertaking at the present time, and of the sound financial position of the allied companies, they could not, as a public body, refuse to allow the proper development of their minerals by the only companies in a position to develop them effectively.

"They have, therefore, instructed us to ask you to put before the Commissioners the following proposal:—

"The Commissioners, at our clients' expense, to appoint a practical mining engineer to visit the Company's Pit at Tilmanstone, where every facility will be given him to make a thorough investigation, to examine, so far as our clients are at liberty to disclose the same, the results of the various borings, to see the areas already acquired by the two Companies, and to make such inquiries as the Commissioners may desire into their financial position.

"If, as our clients cannot doubt, the result of such inquiry is satisfactory, they would ask that the Commissioners should themselves state upon what terms they will grant the option or lease desired over the land in the Eastry district and over Bramling Court Estate (as soon as the present contract in that case has expired), and we are instructed to add that *any practically reasonable terms will be agreed to.* In saying this, our clients are confident that the Commissioners will not ask for terms so prohibitive as to hamper the successful development of the Coalfield, which is a matter of the very greatest importance, not only to East Kent, but to the whole country."

The reply to the above was a curt negative expressed with the greatest economy of words:—"I am directed to inform you that the Commissioners are not prepared to reconsider their decision in this matter."

It is extremely improbable that any public body ever received so advantageous an offer, the acceptance of which under no possible circumstances could have prejudiced them, but on the contrary, must have yielded a substantial sum in immediate cash, with the promise of large annual royalties as and when the coal was worked.

It is an open secret that the Commissioners were prejudiced against the Kent coal companies for purely personal reasons, which may explain, though it does not justify, their dog-in-the-manger attitude. Their churches within the Coalfield, however, did not scruple to make clamant appeals to the charity of Mr. Burr. To them there was no taint upon money that was to be had for the asking, but their controlling authority, sublimely indifferent to their necessities, declined to enter into business relations with his companies. The parochial requirements of the district could have been amply provided for out of the revenues from the Ecclesiastical Commissioners' minerals. A medium surely more consistent with the dignity of the Church of England than the employment of begging letters.

An object lesson on the abuses inseparable from bureaucratic control is afforded by the fact that in 1911 the same Commissioners leased a different portion of their minerals, on infinitely less favourable terms, to a syndicate of German origin (of which I shall have something to say later) registered as the Anglo-Westphalian Kent Coal Syndicate. But the pioneers of the field, whose discoveries had attracted the attention of the Westphalian magnates, feel some satisfaction in the knowledge that the greater part of this area contains little or no coal. And the Ecclesiastical Commissioners now find that they have refused the substance and grasped the shadow!

I do not cherish the hope that my comments will ruffle the serenity of their permanent officials, or render them any more alive to the duty they owe the nation to facilitate the exploitation of their minerals. I am mindful of the old adage that you cannot disturb the slumbers of an elephant by scratching matches on its hide.

Returning to the year under review, 1909, the borings in various parts of the Coalfield during this period were still further demonstrating the mineral wealth of the basin. In September Concessions issued a statement, upon the authority of its consulting engineer, Mr. Geo. H. Hollingworth, showing that within the preceding two months 57 ft. 7 in. of coal had been proved, bringing the aggregate up to no less than 257 ft. in 79 seams. No attempt at any correlation having been made at this period, it will, of course, be understood that these figures include the same seams, perhaps, in some instances, more than twice over.

At Barfrestone a 6-ft. 1-in. seam had been proved in July—this being the thickest yet met with on Concessions' areas. The following analysis of a bore-hole sample by Mr. Geo. R. Hislop shows that this seam can hold its own for quality with the leading coals of a similar character in other districts:—

Analysis of the 6-ft. 1-in. seam at Barfrestone.

Proximate analysis.	Dry basis. Per cent.
Volatile matters	25.49
Fixed carbon	68.53
Sulphur	1.06
Ash	4.92
	100.00
Coke per ton of coal	78.83

Ultimate analysis.	Dry basis. Per cent.
Carbon	83.62
Hydrogen	5.30
Oxygen	4.54
Nitrogen	0.56
Sulphur	1.06
Ash	4 92
	100.00

Evaporative power, 15.12 lbs. of water from and at 212 deg. Fah.

Calorific power in Centigrade heat units, 8,119 calories.

Remarks.—"This is a remarkably fine coal. It possesses heating power equal to the finest Welsh coals, and is well adapted alike for steam raising, household use, and the manufacture of lighting and power gas. It contains moderate amounts of both sulphur and ash, and is, indeed, without one detracting property. It is essentially, therefore, a valuable coal for gas, steam, and household purposes."

Another very valuable seam, 3 ft. 9 in. in thickness, was proved about the same time in the Goodnestone boring, some three miles to the north of Barfrestone. The following analysis, also by Mr. Hislop, shows this coal to be of quite exceptional quality:—

Proximate Analysis.

	Dry basis. Per cent.
Volatile matters	20.64
Fixed carbon	74.75
Sulphur	0.74
Ash	3.12
Water	0.75
	100 00
Coke per ton of coal	78.20

Ultimate Analysis

	Dry basis. Per cent.
Carbon	89.05
Hydrogen	4.88
Oxygen	1.74
Nitrogen	0.42
Sulphur	0.77
Ash	3.14
	100.00

Evaporative power, 15 86 lbs. of water from and at 212 deg. Fah.

Calorific power in Centigrade heat units, 8.516 calories.

Remarks.—"This is an exceptionally pure and valuable coal for household use and steam raising purposes, and as such it is not surpassed, if indeed equalled, by any known coal of its class. A coal containing 94.5 per cent. of heat-producing elements, as this one does, is entitled to be classed as an ideal coal."

The discovery of these two seams, and of others scarcely less important, together with the fact that, having got through the Greensands and Wealden series, the Tilmanstone Pits promised an early entry into the Coal Measures, combined to attract capital to the Concessions Company, thereby enabling it to consolidate its position.

Towards the end of the year a question arose with regard to certain areas that it was important to keep from falling into competitive hands. Concessions' directors were not disposed to increase their obligations, and the South-Eastern Extension Company had also reached the limit of its then resources. It was determined, therefore, to create yet another company in order to acquire these areas, and thus there came into being the Company known as—

EXTENDED EXTENSION, LIMITED.

(Registered November 26, 1909.)

Capital.—£50,000 in 47,000 ordinary and 3,000 founders' shares, all of £1 each, of which 43,000 ordinary and 3,000 founders' shares are issued and fully paid. The ordinary shares are entitled to a preferential non-cumulative dividend of 12 per cent. per annum, the remaining profits divisible in each year belonging as to 67 per cent. to the holders of the ordinary shares, and 33 per cent. to the holders of the founders' shares.

Here again there was no board of directors, Mr. Burr being self-appointed life-manager at a remuneration of 20 per cent. of the net profits.

The Company was formed to adopt certain agreements with the East Kent Contract & Financial Company, Limited, and with Messrs. Arthur and Malcolm Burr, relating to the acquisition of mineral areas in Kent and to the management of the Company's business.

In 1911 £50,000 of 6 per cent. debentures, redeemable at a premium of 20 per cent. in November, 1914, were created, but of these only £10,000 were issued. Their repayment is long overdue, but holders have agreed to waive payment of both interest and principal until six months after the declaration of Peace.

The Company has a further liability in connection with the joint issue of first mortgage trust bonds, created for the general purposes of this and the other parent companies of the group, and, *inter alia*, for furnishing funds for the deep sinking at Snowdown Colliery. This liability will, it is estimated, amount to £22,680 at the end of the redemption period.

Mr. Burr was in sole control of this Company's affairs until August, 1914, when he relinquished his position. Meetings were then held for the purpose of amending the Articles of Association in order that a regular board of directors might be appointed. The committee of shareholders who had stepped into the breach when the affairs of all the parent companies were drifting into a state of hopeless confusion, were duly elected, and this Company, like the others of the "Burr Group," passed into the hands of Mr. Dewrance and his colleagues, the new board being constituted thus:—Mr. John Dewrance (Chairman), The Earl of Darnley, Lieut.-Col. J. P. Dalison, Mr. Stuart D. Greig, and Mr. William P. Studholme.

Under Mr. Burr's management valuable mineral areas, both freehold and leasehold, had been acquired, and the Company was responsible for one of the most productive borings on the Coalfield—viz., that at Ripple, on a site just 2½ miles due west of Walmer.

The Ripple bore is interesting from the fact that, commencing at 68 ft. O.D., the Coal Measures were entered at, about, only 925 ft. from the surface. The contractors were the Internationale Bohrgesellschaft who took the hole down to 3,317 ft. in nine and a-half months. Nothing but the chisel was used down to 1,317 ft., and their "bull-at-a-gate" methods preclude any classification of the 92 ft. of strata between the base of the Gault and the Coal Measures. In fact, they only realised that they had passed through the Secondary Rocks when they blundered into about 1 ft. of coal at 925 ft.

The next 1,100 ft. proved to be barren ground consisting almost entirely of sandstones, but between 2,225 ft. and 3,169 ft., at which depth the Carboniferous Limestone was entered, the aggregate coal proved totals 52 ft.. At 2,800 ft. the boring section shows a 10-ft. seam, 9 ft. 4 in. of which is without any parting. This is quite one of the best, if, indeed, not the very best of the seams proved on the Coalfield. The analysis of a borehole sample by Mr. G. R. Hislop is as follows:—

	Per cent.
Volatile matter	10.71
Fixed carbon	84.26
Sulphur	0.63
Ash	4.40
	100.00

Evaporative power, 15.56 lbs. of water.
Calories, as per Thomson's calorimeter, 8,355.
Weight per cubic foot, 83.56 lbs.

Report.—"This is a remarkably good smokeless navigation steam coal, admirably suited also for general furnace work and slow-combustion stoves. It contains fully 92½ per cent. of heat-producing elements and moderate amounts of ash and sulphur. It will burn freely and leave an ash which will not flux into a hard clinker. In every respect, therefore, the coal is one of high commercial value."

The mineral areas proved by the Ripple boring are included in the option granted to Messrs. Schneider et Cie, and at a joint meeting of the parent companies held in London in July, 1917, the directors gave the following information as to the assets and liabilities of Extended Extension, Ltd., the value of the former being based on the prices fixed in the above option:—

Assets	£
955 acres freehold minerals at £40	38,200
1,848 acres leasehold at £21	38,808
Value of surfaces purchased on joint account ..	34,561
Value of share in freehold minerals purchased on joint account	58,760
Value of share in leasehold ditto purchased on joint account	36,771
East Kent Colliery Co. 2nd mortgage debentures	9,500
Holdings in other allied companies	7,463
	224,063
Less total liabilities	91,692
	£132,371

The surplus, when realised, will be employed first in returning the capital on £43,000 of ordinary and £2,989 of founders' shares; the balance would then be divisible in the proportion of two-thirds and one-third to the holders of the ordinary and founders' shares, who should thus receive about £2 and £15 per share respectively.

CHAPTER XVIII.

1910.—*Attention centred on Tilmanstone. The Coalfield extending. The Concessions Group. Summary of results. Deal and Walmer Coalfield, Limited. The Oxney Boring. Whitaker's prophecy fulfilled. Smokeless Navigation Steam Coals. The Messrs. Burr retire. Company's Minerals under Option to French Group. East Kent Light Railways Company. Branch lines to Collieries. A growing traffic. Future Prospects.*

"Thine was the prophet's vision"—LONGFELLOW.

1910.

This year's record of Kent Coal Concessions, Limited, need not occupy us for long, as the chief events concerning the coalfield are more particularly associated with the work of its subsidiary companies, and are dealt with elsewhere in my narrative.

Tilmanstone was still the centre of attraction, and in the early part of the year its prospects were most promising. The various borings continued to bear witness to the extraordinary mineral wealth of the field, and great efforts were made to ensure that the pick of the coal-basin should be secured to the allied companies.

There was an all-round rise in share prices, and the opportunity to secure further funds without increasing the capitals of the existing companies was seized upon by the familiar expedient of creating new ones. Thus it was that the Deal and Walmer Coalfield, Limited, came to be registered. The same excuse was made for this new entrant on the scene as had done duty in similar circumstances previously, for Mr. Burr stated that:—

"The proposition had been under consideration for two years, but for reasons that were justified by the then existing conditions, both financial and geological, it was not entertained by the Concessions Company, which was pledged to its shareholders to incur no risks, while the site was quite outside the sphere of influence of the Extension Company.''

But after the Deal and Walmer Company was launched it was discovered that "Circumstances, and later geological knowledge, have considerably modified the element of risk."

Before dealing with this new venture, however, a review of the work of the whole group will not be out of place.

In order to demonstrate the financial strength of the undertaking the balance sheets of all the allied companies and syndicates were made up to April 30, 1910, and these, together with some particulars of the work done, were published as an advertisement in the financial dailies. I give this information in a summarised form, as under:—

Company.	*Issued Capital.*	*Cash at Bank.*
	£	£
Kent Coal Concessions, Ltd. ..	199,939 ..	9,098
S.E. Coalfield Extension, Ltd. ..	40,500 ..	5.226
Sondage Syndicate, Ltd. ..	5,000 ..	5,268
Extended Extension, Ltd. ..	26,175 ..	5,207
Fonçage Syndicate, Ltd... ..	20,000 ..	5,325
East Kent Colliery Co., Ltd. ..	218,655 ..	11,877
Guilford Syndicate, Ltd. ..	28,182 ..	6,017
E.K. Contract & Fin. Co. Ltd. ..	32,483 ..	15,624
Snowdown Colliery, Ltd. ..	150,723 ..	7,281
	£721,657 ..	£70,923

According to the official statement the total *cash* subscribed and paid up in respect of issued capital amounted to £393,679.

Total depth of shafts sunk, 4,706 ft.

Total depth of all borings, 13,744 ft.

Total coal proved in seams of 2 ft. and over, 55 ft.

Total number of such seams—15, averaging 3 ft. 8 in.

Total cost of borings to parent companies, £64,389.

Total approximate extent of proven mineral areas, 90 sq. miles.

Total amount of cash dividends paid, £26,341.

I will now give a brief summary of the activities of the latest company to be formed for the purpose of acquiring areas, with a view to proving their minerals and sub-leasing them to colliery companies. Its title, as I have mentioned, is—

THE DEAL AND WALMER COALFIELD, LIMITED

(Registered May 24, 1910.)

Capital.—£100,000 in 90,000 ordinary and 10,000 deferred shares, all of £1 each, of which 34,129 ordinary and 9,164 deferred have been issued. As customary there was no board of directors, the management being vested in Dr. Malcolm Burr as director-general for life at a remuneration of 20 per cent. of the profits, with Mr. Arthur Burr as "honorary consulting governor" at a remuneration of 1 per cent. of the profits, and Mr. J. Loudoun Strain, as consulting engineer.

This Company was promoted by the Contract Company, but its operations were confined within a restricted sphere, and only a small acreage of minerals was secured. The results, while of great interest geologically, are not likely to prove very satisfactory financially.

It will be remembered that, following upon the discovery of coal in the Brady boring, Whitaker stated that the prolongation of the Coal Measures should be sought in the vicinity of St. Margarets. This is an important historical pronouncement that, singularly, has escaped mention in any of the voluminous Kent Coal literature that has come within my purview. I consider that I am justified in designating Whitaker's statement as historical, for had it been listened to, and his advice acted upon, the history of the Coalfield would have run on very different lines. However, his was "a voice crying in the wilderness," and under the less inspired direction of Etheridge, Boyd Dawkins, Brady and others, the explorers turned their faces to the west—with the barren results that I have already chronicled.

I emphasise the mis-direction to the west at the risk of being charged with labouring the point unduly, but I am seeking to unravel the tangled skein of facts concerning the Kent Coalfield, to establish the truth as to the various stages of its development, and to see that honour is given where honour is due.

Thus, in 1891, Whitaker advised a boring at St. Margarets, but it was not until 1910 that the Deal and Walmer management, for quite unconnected reasons, started a bore-hole at Oxney, only 1½ miles from the locality which Whitaker had recommended 19 years previously.

The Oxney boring was begun on April 21, 1910, by Messrs. Mather & Platt, who carried it down to 834 ft. in three months, when Messrs Vivian took over the work, boring a further 969 ft. in sixteen months, only in their turn to relinquish the hole to the Tréfor Company, who bored 1,940 ft. in eight months. The final depth being 3,743 ft., leaving off in the Carboniferous Limestone.

The section of this boring, so far as the imperfect records through the Secondary Rocks enable it to be determined, is as follows:—

	Ft.	in.
Drift, ...	21	0
Chalk and Gault, ...	813	0
Folkstone Beds, ...	1	6
Sandgate Beds, ...	19	6
Atherfield Clay, ...	10	0
Greensands, ...	31	0
Wealden, ...	39	0
Oxfordian, ...	3	0
Bathonian, ...	90	0
Oolites and Lias, ...	93	0
Coal Measures entered at	997	0
Transition Coal Measures	778	0
Middle Coal Measures	1,927	0
Total thickness of do., ...	2,705	0
Total thickness of seams over 1 ft. ..	65	10

	Ft.	in.	Ft.
The first thick seam is	5	7	at 2,431
The second do., ...	6	6	at 2,615
The third do., ...	4	4	at 2,846
The fourth do., ...	11	4	at 3,195
The fifth do., ...	9	0	at 3.271
The sixth do., ...	7	10	at 3,382
The seventh do., ...	4	9	at 3,396

Practically all these coals are of the navigation steam class, and the analyses of the two upper seams, which I set forth below, may be accepted as typical of the whole:—

Analysis of the 5-ft. 7-in Seam, by Geo. R. Hislop.

	Per cent.
Volatile matter	13.82
Fixed carbon	81.89
Sulphur	1.55
Ash	2.74
	100.00

Calories as per Thomson's calorimeter = 8,071.

Evaporative power = 15.03 lbs. of water from and at 212 deg. Fah.

Remarks.—This is a valuable navigation steam coal, containing as it does 91.5 per cent. of heat-

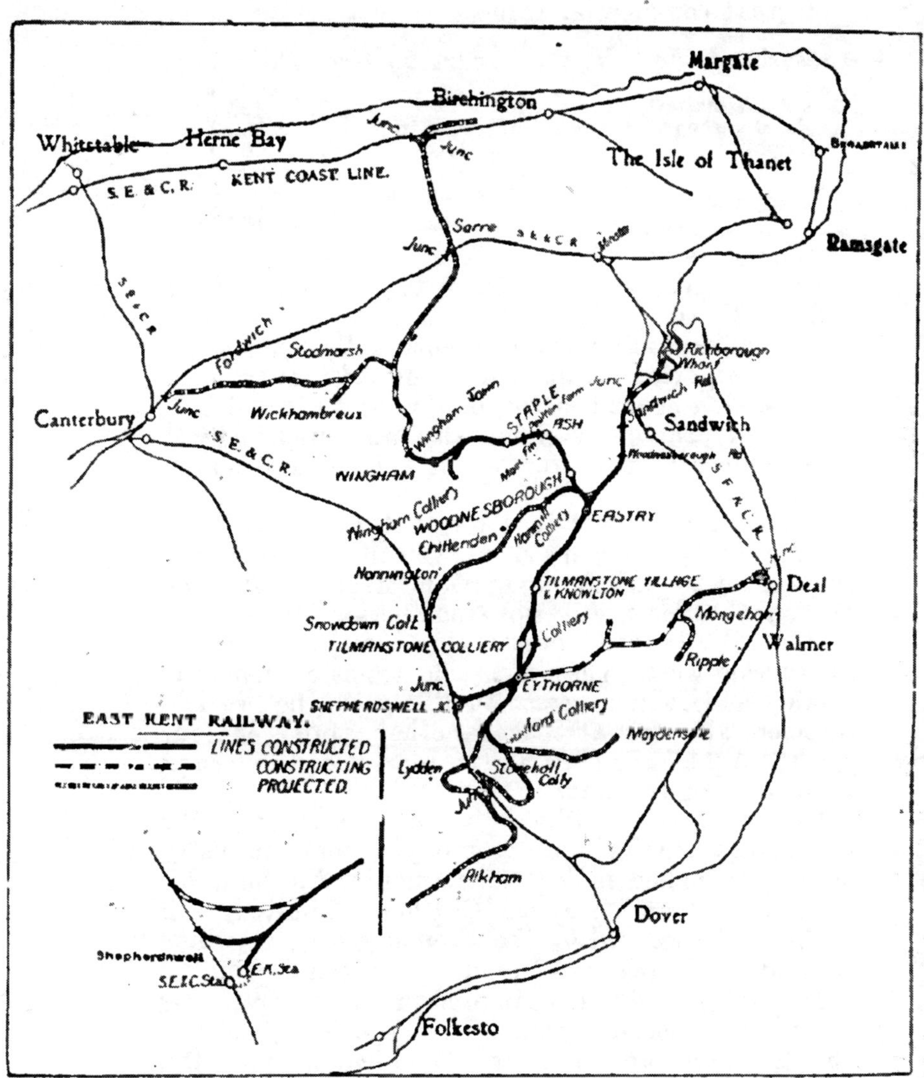

Sketch Map Showing East Kent Railway as Constructed, in Progress, and Projected, and its Connection with the South-Eastern & Chatham Railway.

ing elements, and possessing an evaporative power of 15 lbs. of water from and at 212 deg. Fah. into steam. In all respects the coal is one of great commercial value.

Analysis of the 6-ft. 6-in. seam by Geo. R. Hislop.

	Per cent
Volatile matter	13.71
Fixed carbon	83.20
Sulphur	0.99
Ash	2.10
	100.00

Calories as per Thomson's calorimeter = 8,189.

Evaporative power = 15.25 lbs. of water from and at 212 deg. Fah.

Remarks.—This is an exceptionally fine smokeless navigation steam coal of the Admiralty class. Possessing great heating power, and a small content of ash, it is chemically and physically a valuable coal alike for steam raising and household use.

The lower seams of 11 ft. 4 in., 9 ft. and 7 ft. 10 in. having only 10 per cent. volatile matter are classed as smokeless navigation steam coals, and are suitable for use in slow-combustion stoves.

Had Whitaker's prescience been appreciated at its true worth, these valuable seams of smokeless steam coal, which are not likely to be worked commercially for at least another three or four years, might have been at the service of the Grand Fleet during the war.

Unless Mr. Smillie's views regarding the nationalisation of the country's coal industry become embodied in legal enactments, the minerals of the Deal and Walmer Coalfield, Limited, will probably be worked by the French group, to whom they are now (July, 1919) under option.

In 1914 Mr. Burr relinquished his control over all the Concessions group, with the exceptions of the Sondage and Fonçage Syndicates, and Dr. Malcolm Burr also resigned his position as director-general of the Deal and Walmer Company. Following the procedure of the other parent companies, meetings were held to amend the Articles of Association, and thus enable a regularly constituted board of directors to be appointed. Upon completion of the necessary formalities Mr. John Dewrance and his colleagues were elected directors,

East Kent Light Railway.
Cutting Leading to Tunnel through Golgotha Hill, Shepherdswell.

and the Company's affairs still remain in their hands.

The most important event of 1910, in connection with the development of the Coalfield, was the advent of

THE EAST KENT LIGHT RAILWAYS COMPANY.

This was promoted by Kent Coal Concessions in conjunction with all the principal companies of the allied group.

The first application before the Light Railway Commissioners was heard in Canterbury on October 17 and 18, 1910, but the Order under which the Company was incorporated was not made until June 19, 1911.

Several further applications were allowed from time to time as the boundaries of the proven coal-field were extended by one successful boring after another. The total length of the authorised lines now amounts to 65 miles, of which about 20 miles have been constructed.

The accompanying map clearly shows the comprehensive manner in which the field will be articulated when all the projected lines link up with those already constructed. In settling the various routes the promoters naturally were guided by their knowledge as to where the big traffic was most likely to be forthcoming, and it was unfortunate for the Company that the line to Sandwich had not been completed when war broke out. Had this connection existed the many thousands of tons of Tilmanstone coal for Government use at Richborough could have gone direct, instead of by a roundabout route over the South-Eastern and Chatham line.

While the East Kent Light Railway was promoted principally in the interests of the collieries, the Commissioners took care that the requirements of the agriculturists were not overlooked, and the farmers on the routes already opened up have not been slow to recognise the facilities now at their command. The passenger traffic is insignificant at present, but in the future, when the large number of collieries projected are each employing from 1,000 to 3,000 men, an important revenue must be realised from this service.

A contract was entered into between the Railway Company and the East Kent Contract and Financial Company, Limited, under which the latter undertook to construct all the lines for which orders were, or might be, granted, in consideration of the allotment of practically the whole of the share and debenture capital issuable under such various orders. These securities were issued as the work progressed, and were marketed as best they could by the Contract Company, whose financial resources, as I have already explained, were totally inadequate for the proper performance of its undertaking.

It was not until April, 1912, that any prospectus was issued; shareholders in the allied companies were invited then to subscribe for 50,000 shares. This issue, though made nominally by the Railway Company, was in reality made on behalf of the Contract Company as a means of putting it in funds. The following particulars are abstracted from the prospectus:—

The East Kent Light Railways Company, Limited.
Authorised capital, £240,000.

(With powers to issue part of the capital as preference capital, and to borrow).

Directors.—Mr. Henry Western Plumptre, Mr. William H. Richmond Powell, Mr. Arthur H. Loring, Sir Henry E. Dering, Bart., Mr. Arthur Burr, and Dr. Malcolm Burr, D.Sc.

Engineer.—Lt.-Col. H. F. Stephens, A.M.I.C.E.

The prospectus stated that:—"The Contractors' temporary line connecting Tilmanstone Colliery with the South-Eastern and Chatham Railway's main line at Shepherdswell has been in operation for nearly five months, during which time it has carried upwards of 10,000 tons of material to this colliery, the revenue from which has shown an ample return on the capital outlay, besides effecting considerable economy for the colliery in haulage charges and extraordinary traffic claims."

The necessity for the temporary track to Tilmanstone will be appreciated by a glance at the accompanying photograph (page 210) of the heavy work in piercing Golgotha Hill, which confronted the contractors at the start of the line proper. The hill was negotiated partly by cutting and partly by a tunnel, about 600 yards in length, the spoil from which was utilised in making the embankment that leads to the main line system. This is the only piece of heavy work that has been necessary, the lie of the country rendering the remainder of the lines very easy of construction. The following are the tonnages of traffic originating on this Railway during the past four years:—

	Tons.		Tons.
1915	15,886	1917	132,275
1916	70,898	1918	129,604

The slight decrease in 1918 was due entirely to the effect of war conditions on Tilmanstone, but the current year is certain to show a large increase. Not only has Tilmanstone's weekly output materially improved, but the resumption of sinking operations at Guilford is already providing a substantial additional tonnage, which will expand into big figures when, in the near future, the producing stage is reached at this colliery.

The Company's engineer, Lieut.-Colonel H. F. Stephens, whose work in connection with similar lines is known to everybody in the railway world, is also acting as general manager of the Company. It is fortunate that the practical work should be in such competent hands, particularly as there is not a single member of the board who has had the slightest experience of railways other than as a passenger. Sir Henry E. Dering and the Messrs. Burr are no longer directors of the company, nor have their places been filled.

There is every probability of this Railway Company becoming one of the most paying propositions in connection with the Coalfield. Whatever may be the financial results attending the operations of the present colliery companies, it is certain that the Coalfield will be vigorously developed during the next few years, and that a very large tonnage will originate on these lines. Having regard to the short haulage involved the working results cannot fail to prove extremely satisfactory to the shareholders, and as they will have been some years without any return on their investments no one should grudge them a due recompense when the dividend stage is reached.

CHAPTER XIX.

Medway Syndicate. Two Abortive Borings. Ebbsfleet Syndicate. Lydden Boring a Success. Failure to Unwater Tilmanstone Pits. Goodnestone Boring. Mr. John Hamilton joins the Board of the East Kent Colliery. Closing the "Book."

> "Attempt the end, and never stand to doubt;
> Nothing's so hard but search will find it out."
> —HERRICK.

Owing to the severance of the friendly relations between Mr. Burr and Professor Boyd Dawkins, which had existed from the days of the Kent Coal Exploration Company of unhappy memory, the latter ceased to be officially connected with the Concessions group of companies. This breach between two of the pioneers of the Coalfield led to the formation of a rival exploring company, which was registered in 1910 under the title of

THE MEDWAY COAL EXPLORATION SYNDICATE, LTD.

Capital, £12,500 in shares of £1 each. As to the genesis of this Syndicate, there is no doubt, to my mind, that the collapse of the Concessions Company was looked for by a certain section of the landowners in Kent, who therefore busied themselves in seeking another source from which to draw the revenues which they feared they were about to lose. Boyd Dawkins having no longer any official connection with the Kent Coal companies, whose accredited geological adviser he had been for some years, it is not perhaps surprising that his co-operation should have been invited.

The Concessions Company, however, though at times severely pressed, surmounted its difficulties and maintained its boundaries inviolate. Thus it was that Boyd Dawkins' new friends were compelled to go further afield, and another abortive attempt was made in a westward direction to locate the prolongation of the Coal Basin.

Lord Harris was the moving spirit in this enterprise, and, as will be seen by the following extract from my Press cuttings book, the leading local paper of his district spread itself in a somewhat amusing fashion over his venture—even removing Tilmanstone Colliery to Canterbury in order to bring the proven coal some ten miles nearer to the site of the Medway Syndicate's operations!

> "Reports state that mainly through the endeavours of Lord Harris, a company called the Medway Coal Exploration Syndicate has been formed with a capital of £12,500 to carry out boring operations for coal in the neighbourhood of Sittingbourne. Professor Boyd Dawkins, the eminent geologist, who located the coal which is now being worked at Tilmanstone Colliery, Canterbury, is of opinion that a seam of coal would be found under Sittingbourne. Borings will be commenced almost at once at a spot about two miles north-west of Sittingbourne, and not far away from the River Medway. The scheme is backed by London financial houses whose speciality is mining."

When the bore-hole in question was down to about 5.0 ft. the "Daily Express" of October 10, 1910, gave great prominence to the work of the Syndicate, emphasising its importance with the bold head-line, "Millionaires Hunt for Coal." Certainly that fortunate class was well represented on the Syndicate's share register, as witness such names as the following:—Mr Evelyn de Rothschild, Mr. F. Eckstein, Mr. Otto Beit, Mr. Sigismund Neumann, Mr. Malcolm Christopherson, the Hon. Kenelm Pleydell Bouverie, Mr. John Arnold, Mr. S H. Sands, Mr. Robert Hilder and the Consolidated Gold Fields of South Africa, Limited. But Nature is no respecter of persons, and the millionaires' search for coal at Sittingbourne went unrewarded—though our geological knowledge was enriched by the definition of yet another district where coal was *not*.

This disappointment led to another exploratory boring, the site selected being on the Chilham Castle estate some three miles south-west of Canterbury. But although it was within a stone's throw, so to speak, of the proven coalfield, all previous experience had tended to show that this would prove to be the wrong side of the Dover-Canterbury Road

The results, as might have been anticipated, were negative.

The following are the sections of these two unproductive borings:—

Bobbing, near Sittingbourne. 120 *O.D.*

	Ft.
Thanet sands	42
Chalk	692
Gault	144
Lower greensands	55
Oolites (unclassified)	67
Oolites (Bathonian)	90
Silurian	70
Total depth from surface	1,260

Chilham, near Canterbury. 40 *O.D.*

	Ft.
Thanet sands	21
Chalk and gault	603
Lower greensands	42
Oolites (unclassified)	268
Oolites (Bathonian)	145
Lias	24
Silurian	51
Total depth from surface	1,154

The first company to acquire minerals in East Kent outside the charmed circle of the Concessions group was the

EBBSFLEET COAL SYNDICATE, LIMITED,

(Registered September 20, 1910).

Capital, £15,750 in 15,000 participating preference shares of £1 each, and 15,000 deferred shares of 1s. each. The former are entitled to a cumulative dividend of 7 per cent., and to the whole of the profits until the entire amount of the preference capital paid up has been refunded, after which they are entitled to one-quarter of the profits over and above their fixed 7 per cent. dividend. The remaining three-quarters of the profits available for distribution belong to the holders of the deferred shares. The capital was later increased to £20,850 in 20,000 participating preference shares of £1 each and 17,000 deferred shares of 1s. each. The directors were Messrs. M. H. Robinson, J.P. M.I.C.E. (chairman), J. H. Snow, G. E. Solley, S. F. Staples, M.I.C.E., G F. Vye and E. E. Wastall, J.P.

The Syndicate was promoted by St. Augustine's Links, Limited, who were also the principal vendors, for the purpose of purchasing and developing 777 acres of minerals near Ebbsfleet, abutting on Sandwich Harbour. It was stated in the Prospectus that the promoters

> "feeling confident of the presence of coal under the property mentioned, and being desirous of having their opinion verified by a leading expert, placed the facts before Mr. W. Whitaker, F.R.S., who, after a careful examination of the property in question, and of the neighbourhood, has reported to them on the subject in the form of a memorandum, from which the following is an extract:—'It is a reasonable inference that there is a great probability of Coal Measures being found in the neighbourhood of Ebbsfleet, and it is highly probable that the underground plane of the older rocks will be only 1,000 ft. below Ordnance Datum, or, say, from that to 1,100 ft. The evidence we have justifies the making of a boring to prove the beds.'"

The anticipated profits as set out in the prospectus were of no mean magnitude, for, on what was stated to be a reasonable basis, they were estimated at £120,000 per annum for a period of 18 years. It was stated further that

> "on the figure mentioned each £500 invested would receive (besides a 7 per cent. dividend for 18 years and the return of the capital in full) other dividends amounting to over £17,000, and this without reckoning the dividends upon 25 of the deferred shares received by the subscribers as practically a bonus."

Bearing in mind all that has happened in connection with the Coalfield during the nine years that have elapsed since I first read this prospectus, I feel that undue optimism in respect to Kent Coal was not confined to the original pioneers of the field.

The Ebbsfleet Syndicate put down a boring on an alluvial flat of the River Stour commencing at only 10 ft. above Ordnance Datum. The following is a summary of the full detailed section of this boring which appeared in an Appendix to the "Report of the Geological Survey" for the year 1911:—

Ebbsfleet Boring.

		Ft.	In.
Estuarine alluvium and Thanet sands	..	110	0
Chalk..	..	785	0
Gault	..	110	0
Folkestone beds	..	30	0
Sandgate beds	..	6	0
Weald clay	..	15	0
Coal Measures	at	1,056	0
Coal (1 ft.)	,,	1,100	6
Coal (9 in.)	,,	1,130	9
Carboniferous Limestone	,,	1,159	0
Bottom of borehole..	..	1,389	0

Before considering the bearing of this boring in relation to those of Concessions and its allied companies, it is interesting to compare the section with that of a borehole put down in 1896-7 near the French coast between Capes Gris-Nez and Blanc-Nez, known as the

Sondage de Strouanne.

	Ft.
Chalk (Cenomanian, Albian and Aptian) ..	259
Wealden	293
Coal Measures, with three thin seams of coal..	406
Carboniferous Limestone penetrated	29

The Ebbsfleet boring, while naturally greatly disappointing to the exploring Syndicate, is extremely valuable from a geological point of view. It demonstrated beyond question the northern boundary of the Coal Basin, as that at Brabourne had proved the southern limit, though not with such exactitude.

The nearest borings to Ebbsfleet at which coal has been proved are those at Ash, only 1¾ miles to the south-west, and Mattice Hill, just 2¾ miles due south; whereas there is a stretch of five miles between Brabourne, where the Coal Measures are non-existent, and Elham, the nearest boring where coal was discovered. Thus the Ebbsfleet boring gives the exact northern limit of the Coalfield, but the southern boundary, while sufficiently known for all practical purposes, is not absolutely defined from the scientists' point of view; it probably runs equi-distant between the Brabourne and Elham boreholes.

The failure of the Ebbsfleet bore to realise the Syndicate's great expectations did not entirely damp the ardour of the directors, who transferred the scene of their operations to a point farther south, near Deal. This brought them to the confines of Lord Northbourne's property, whose minerals the Concessions had long tried in vain to secure. At this period, however, his lordship had arranged for their exploitation by the Betteshanger Syndicate (of which more anon), and the two Syndicates

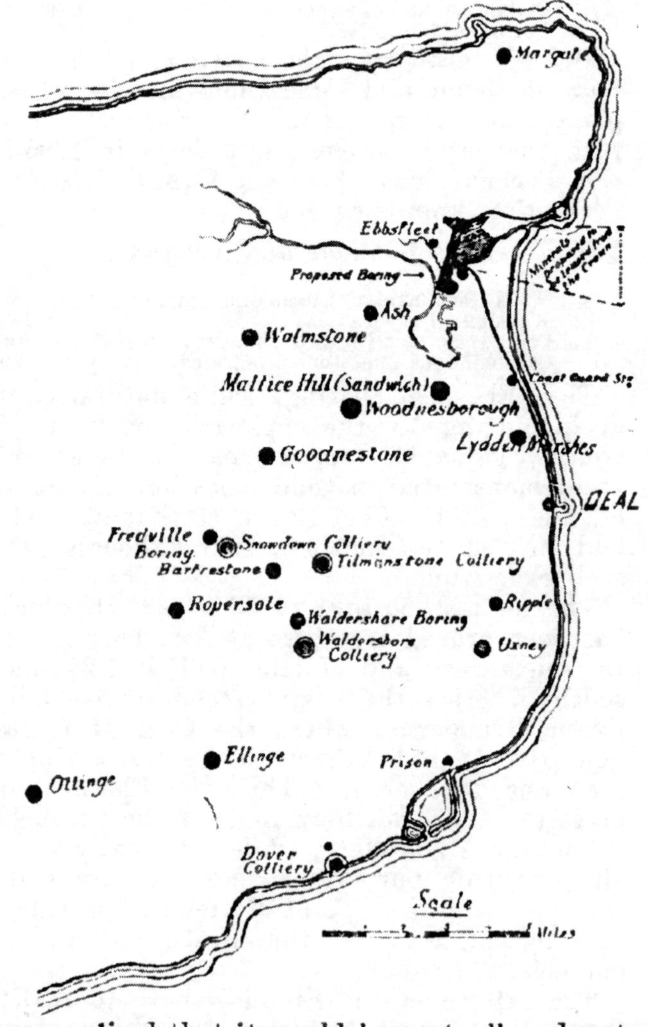

soon realised that it would be mutually advantageous to come to a working agreement. One of the fruits of this arrangement was that Betteshanger shared the cost of the Lydden boring, the site of which, and that of Ebbsfleet, are shown on the accompanying map.

Having come sufficiently far south to be within the boundaries of the already proved Coal Basin, the results at Lydden were quite satisfactory, as witness the following section:—

Lydden Valley Boring, O.D. 20.

	Ft.	In.		Ft.
Chalk	750	0		
Gault	128	0		
Oolitic Sandstone	61	0		
Coal Measures			at	939
Coal Seam	1	6	,,	1,086
Coal	0	9		
	0	6	,,	1,104
Coal Vein	0	4	,,	1,169
Coal Seam	3	7	,,	1,252
Coal Vein	0	6	,,	1,382
Coal Seam	1	3		
	1	10	,,	1,480
Coal Seam	1	1	,,	1,531
Coal Seam	5	4	,,	1,543
Coal Seam	4	6	,,	1,551
Coal Seam	4	9	,,	1,590
Coal Seam	1	3	,,	1,623
Coal Vein	0	4	,,	1,699
Coal Vein	0	10	,,	1,820
Carboniferous Limestone			,,	1,959
Total depth bored from the surface				2,240

It will be seen that the boring proved about 21 ft of coal within the easy working depth of less than 1,600 ft. At the annual meeting of the Syndicate held on December 30, 1913, the chairman stated:—

> "I believe I am within the truth in claiming that we have a greater thickness of payable seams within, say, 500 yards from the surface—that is, within an easy, workable and economical depth—than any other borehole in Kent has revealed."

The chairman was fully justified in making this claim, the strict accuracy of which I can confirm. The coal in the principal seams is of quite excellent quality, and the following analysis of the 5 ft. 4 in. seam, in particular, leaves little to be desired:—

	Per cent.
Volatile matter	17.00
Fixed carbon	78.24
Ash	3.80
Sulphur	0.96
	100.00
Calorific value	15,102 B.T.U.

The coming of war caused the collapse of certain negotiations for the establishment of a colliery to work the Syndicate's minerals, and during the past few years the directors have had an anxious and trying time. Owing, however, to their untiring efforts, and to the unfailing support given them by a small but helpful body of shareholders, the directors have been enabled to carry on and preserve their property intact.

The Ebbsfleet Syndicate contains within itself all the elements of a successful commercial undertaking. While the profits suggested in its prospectus are not, nor indeed ever were, possible of attainment, yet, if legislation does not rob them of their just dues, the shareholders should have every reason to be satisfied with the return they will receive on their investments.

1911.

The last attempt to unwater the Tilmanstone Pits by means of the steam pumps was made in the early part of the above year, and having proved unsuccessful the promise of a speedy entrance into the Coal Measures had faded away. Concessions shareholders were naturally much depressed, for birds of ill omen were fluttering around and croaking direful prophecies of coming disaster. In order to reassure the faint-hearted it was officially stated that:—

> "The prospects, both permanent and near, of the Tilmanstone Colliery are as bright as could be desired, and are in no way prejudiced nor rendered less certain by the irritating delay, which is purely of a physical and temporary character, presenting no substantial engineering difficulty, but calling for patience, caution, and no little outlay in cash."

Some comfort for the present and hope for the future were afforded by the results at the various borings, of which nine were in active operation at this period, yielding a plethora of good seams and extending the known boundaries of the Coalfield. Also it was being clearly demonstrated that in the later extensions there existed no such formidable physical conditions as obtained at Tilmanstone.

The Goodnestone boring, in particular, had proved a rich series of seams pertaining to the Middle Coal Measures, as will be seen from the section below.

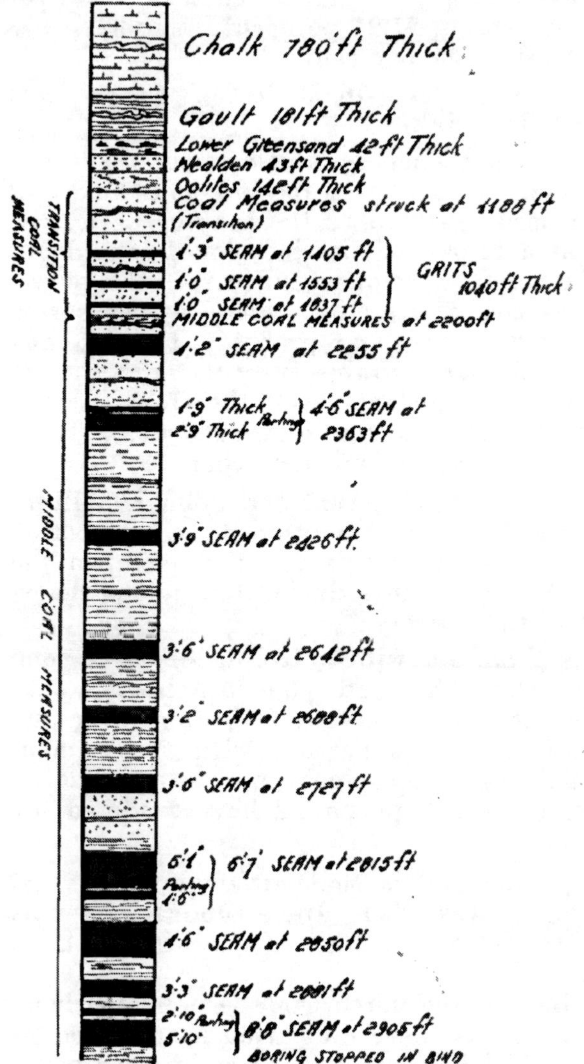

Mr. Geo. R. Hislop's first analysis of a bore-hole sample of the 3 ft. 9 in. seam has been given already, and his reports on the other seams shown above are almost equally satisfactory.

A second analysis of a sample of the 3 ft. 9 in. seam from which all extraneous impurities had been removed, by Professor Galloway, is worthy of record as evidencing the high commercial value of Kent Coal; thus :—

Proximate Analysis.—Volatile matters, 20.46 per cent.; fixed carbon, 77.21 per cent.; sulphur, 0.78 per cent.; ash, 1.55 per cent.

Evaporative Power.—16.03 lbs. of water from and at 212 deg. Fah.

Calories, as per Thomson's calorimeter=8,608.

> *Remarks.*—This is a steam and household coal of exceptional value, and if I may be permitted to invent a degree of classification I should put it in the super-superlative, since it is the purest and finest coal of its class which has yet passed through my hands, and probably through any other hands. It contains fully 95 per cent. of heat-producing elements, and therefore a small content of ash, oxygen and sulphur. It is essentially, therefore, an ideal coal.

It was in April, 1911, that Mr. John Hamilton, whose name has been mentioned in connection with the Tilmanstone Colliery, appeared upon the scene, and by way of introducing him to the shareholders Mr. Burr wrote :—

> "It is therefore with a feeling of great comfort and relief that I am able to announce that Mr. Hamilton has consented to take over my responsibilities in connection with the Tilmanstone Colliery, replacing me as managing director, for which purpose I have tendered my resignation."

My only comment is that although the word "camouflage" was then little known in this country, Mr. Burr was not unacquainted with its principles.

The borings to the north, in the neighbourhood of the River Stour, were indicating that the boundary of the Coal Basin in that direction was being rapidly approached. Consequently, at the end of April, Mr. Burr announced the "closing of the book," subject to some current negotiations for properties which would round off the boundaries of the allied companies' areas.

At this period Concessions was indebted to the Contract Company to the extent of £50,000. With a view to liquidating this liability, and to provide for the purchase of certain freehold minerals that were in the market, £150,000 of 6 per cent. debentures were created. They were redeemable in cash within three years at the rate of £12 per £10 debenture, or, at the option of the holder, in shares of the various parent companies at fixed prices.

This option is not at all likely to be exercised owing to the altered condition of the affairs of these companies; therefore it is not necessary for me to give details, which were of a very complicated nature. Holders of the debentures have agreed to waive payment of their interest and their principal until six months after the Declaration of Peace.

CHAPTER XX.

Intermediate Equipments. How its Capital was spent. Issue of Debentures. The Company passes out of Mr. Burr's Control. The Schneider Option. The Electric Power Co. Amalgamation simmering. Dr. Pearson's proposals. How they were rejected. Professor Bolton's Report. Boring results to end of 1911. List of Concessions Group of Companies with Capitals, etc.

"Pride is at the bottom of all great mistakes."
—RUSKIN.

1910 (*continued*).

Towards the end of the year 1910 the long list of companies working under the ægis of Kent Coal Concessions received yet another addition by the promotion of

INTERMEDIATE EQUIPMENTS, LIMITED

(Registered October 10, 1910.)

Capital.—£100,000 in 95,000 ordinary shares of £1 each, and 10,000 founders' shares of 10s. each, of which 62,654 and 9,638 respectively have been issued. This was another of Mr. Burr's companies with no board of directors, he himself being appointed managing-director at a remuneration of 20 per cent. of the profits.

The ostensible object with which this company was formed was to take up leases from the Concessions and South-Eastern Extension Companies of two mineral areas, with a view to selling them at a profit after a certain amount of development work had been done. This programme was partially carried out and the Company is responsible for the embryo collieries at Wingham and Woodnesborough. A start was made at the latter, but nothing more than the erection of some of the surface buildings was accomplished; while as regards Wingham, Intermediate Equipments promoted the Wingham and Stour Valley Collieries, Limited, to acquire the area, itself undertaking to sink the pits to a workable seam—the consideration for this being the right to call for allotments of fully-paid shares in the Company as the sinking progressed.

There are very few shareholders in this Colliery Company, nearly the whole of its issued capital being held by Intermediate Equipments, Limited, of which, in fact, the Wingham Company was to be but an appanage until its shafts had reached workable coal. Consequently there is little further to be said beyond that it is under the administration of Mr. Dewrance and his colleagues, and that the results, so far as the preferred ordinary shareholders are concerned, largely depend on whether or no Messrs. Schneider avail themselves of their option.

The work done at Wingham was not extensive. Boilers and winding engines were installed, and the surface equipment practically completed, but further than this only some 50 feet of sinking was accomplished. The fact is that Intermediate Equipments was as little competent, financially, to sink these pits as was the Contract Company to construct the East Kent Railway lines. In each case the provision of funds was dependent upon the selling of shares. This system of finance was a repetition of that employed by the old Kent Coalfields Syndicate in the early days of the Field, whose methods were so adversely criticised.

With the avowed intent of vigorously pushing on with the sinking, Intermediate Equipments issued £120,000 of 10 per cent. debentures in March, 1913, but most of the first proceeds were loaned to other companies of the group, and the Equipments Company made no really serious attempt to perform its obligations.

The debentures were to be redeemed within three years, and, although carrying interest at the rate of 10 per cent. per annum were offered under the usual extravagant discounts peculiar to the Burr group of companies. The issue price was £87 10s. per cent., "with a special allowance of a bonus of 5 per cent. in respect of underwriting taken firm." As a further bait, allottees had the right of an allotment at par of four fully-paid £1 deferred shares in the Wingham and Stour Valley Collieries, Limited, as well as to two 10s. founders' shares in Intermediate Equipments, Limited, also at par. The circular accompanying the application form stated that "These deferred and founders' shares have a present realisable value of at least £10 "

Assuming the accuracy of that statement, and allowing for the payment at par for these deferred and founders' shares, the net cost of the debentures, therefore, was reduced to £82 10s. per cent. on which interest at 10 per cent. per annum on the face value of £100, is equivalent to a return of 12 per cent. Further, their redemption at par in three years would have represented a bonus of £12 10s. on each £100 of debentures allotted at £87 10s. I have previously stigmatised such terms as appeals to the cupidity of human nature, and I do not suppose that any of my readers will quarrel with me for repeating myself in the present instance.

In August, 1914, when Mr. Burr's abdication was negotiated, meetings were held for the purpose of amending the Articles of Association in order that a regular board of directors might be appointed, with the result that Intermediate Equipments, Limited, together with practically all the other companies, passed under the control of Mr. Dewrance and his colleagues.

The accounts to June 30, 1914, showed that over £180,000 of shares and debentures had been issued, of which only £90,000 had been expended on the legitimate business of the Company. The items in the balance sheet which account for the disposal of the remainder of the capital are as follows:—

	£
Cost of issuing debentures	24,254
Purchase of East Kent Light Railway shares ..	15,391
Loans to allied companies	40,683
Interest on debentures, less interest on loans ..	10,365
	£90,693

The purchase of Railway shares was really a transaction designed for the purpose of transferring some of the proceeds of the debenture issue to the coffers of the Contract Company. As the debentures matured before the end of the war was in sight, a meeting was held at which the holders agreed to forgo repayment until six months after the declaration of Peace.

The directors issued a circular to the shareholders on July 1, 1918, informing them that it was proposed to include the Wingham and Woodnesborough areas in an option over 8,500 acres which the parent companies were arranging to give to an eminent French manufacturing firm (Messrs Schneider et Cie) with a view to their establishing and working collieries thereon.

The shareholders were advised that, in the event of this option being exercised, the purchase consideration would be insufficient to provide for repayment of both the debenture principal and accrued interest, but that the debenture holders had agreed to waive their claims in respect of any interest, accrued or to accrue. Owing to the liberal attitude of the debenture holders the directors expressed the hope that some return might be made on the ordinary shares, but stated that there could not possibly be anything left for the holders of the founders' shares.

Realising the position, the shareholders endorsed the proposal of the directors, and all Intermediate Equipments' interests in the Wingham and Woodnesborough minerals were therefore included in the Schneider option.

The situation created by the Sankey Commission naturally has had the effect of delaying any decision on the part of Messrs. Schneider with regard to this option, and it is obvious that they will not complete their proposed purchase unless and until the question of Nationalisation is definitely decided in the negative.

The next incident of importance in connection with the practical development of the Field was the passing by the House of Lords of a Private Bill, promoted by Concessions and its allies, under the provisions of which there was formed

THE SOUTH-EAST KENT ELECTRIC POWER COMPANY, LIMITED.

Nominal Capital—£1,000 in shares of £1 each, all of which were issued, but up to the end of July, 1911, only £100 had been paid up.

Directors—Mr. Arthur Burr, Sir William H. Crundall, Kt., J.P., Dr. Malcolm Burr, D.Sc., formed the original board, but Sir William Crundall, who took no active part in the administration, soon retired, and Messrs. Burr, *pere et fils*, managed the company conjointly.

The Parliamentary powers obtained extended over the greater part of East Kent, ranging from Herne Bay to Hythe, with the exception of the

Isle of Thanet, Canterbury and Sandwich, but taking in Herne Bay, Deal, Walmer, Dover, Folkestone, Shorncliffe, Sandgate and Hythe.

The power station erected at Tilmanstone was intended to be one of a series of units destined to supply power, first throughout the Coalfield and, later, to the above specified towns. The money was found by the East Kent Colliery Company, under an arrangement whereby their outlay was to be refunded when the Power Company issued its capital. Nevertheless, they were charged what the independent members of their board considered an extravagant rate for the current supplied. In this way the first accounts of the Power Company were made to show a substantial profit, of which, under the articles of association, the managing directors were entitled to receive 5 per cent. as remuneration for their services.

For reasons which perhaps I had better not set forth, Concessions took over the power house and the Power Company's debt, subsequently re-transferring the property to the East Kent Colliery Company, who, at a later date, paid for it by the issue of 4 per cent. income bonds. Upon the present realisable value of the bonds the transaction must show a substantial loss to Concessions.

The final result of these inter-company arrangements is that Tilmanstone Colliery gets its electric power plant for a song, whereas the Power Company, which contains the germs of a sound commercial undertaking, remains in embryo, possessing nothing but the Act of Parliament by means of which it came into being. It is now under the fostering care of Mr. J. Dewrance and his colleagues.

The idea that an amalgamation of the parent companies would be to the general interest had long been simmering, and various tentative negotiations had been initiated with certain financial groups with this object in view. Towards the end of May, 1911, however, definite proposals were submitted by a well-known Stock Exchange firm acting on behalf of the late Dr. Pearson, whose name was so prominently connected with large industrial undertakings in South America and elsewhere.

Shareholders will learn of these proposals now for the first time. They were never invited to consider them, nor indeed were they ever informed that any such proposals had been made.

At this time Dr. Pearson could command practically unlimited money for any enterprise he might take in hand, and he was a man of large ideas, who thought in millions. Had his proposition been accepted the Kent Coal enterprise, for the first time in its history, would have been backed by unlimited capital; not only would the separate interests of the various companies have been adequately safeguarded, but the value of their shares must have appreciated to a very material extent. It is indeed regrettable that the shareholders were not given the opportunity of considering Dr. Pearson's proposals, for I am confident that they would have been accepted—not to say jumped at.

However, under the then existing personal *régime* the shareholders were treated as a negligible quantity, and on June 15, 1911, Mr. Burr took upon himself the sole responsibility of rejecting the offer.

Explanation may be found in the fact that Dr. Pearson's scheme necessarily involved the control passing out of Mr. Burr's hands, though he was to have been appointed to the high-sounding, if purely nominal, office of president of the new company which it was proposed to establish. Thus, if the truth be told, the real reason of Mr. Burr's refusal is that he rated his *amour propre* higher than the interests of the companies over whose destinies he exercised such autocratic control.

In justification of my comment I will quote an extract from a Press report of a speech made by a very old personal friend of Mr. Burr, on the occasion of a banquet given to him at Dover on February 4, 1913. Proposing Mr. Burr's' health the Marquis of Winchester said:—

"During the time he was in those stormy seas he was constantly approached by the leviathans of finance. He (Lord Winchester) knew that, as they had approached Mr. Burr through himself. They had approached him through other channels, but to all of them he had said: 'No; I have taken upon myself to prove that coal exists in payable and commercial quantities, and in enormous quantities, in the district of East Kent, and no man shall touch or handle this business until I have brought the craft safely into port.'"

Replying to the toast, Mr. Burr, in the course of his speech, said that:—

> "Fortunately, it had not been a question of getting money, but had been a question of refusing money, which had been thrown at his head practically week after week in the last six or nine months, as the Marquis had told them."

The stormy seas to which Lord Winchester poetically referred were as nothing to the raging tempest that was to come. And it is beyond dispute that, to continue the simile, the barque "Kent Coal" might long since have been safely in port had its pilot steered a straighter course.

Although for some months hereafter "amalgamation" was ever present in the spoken and the written word, it was not until the middle of 1912 that a serious attempt was made to consolidate the various companies, as I will relate in detail in due sequence.

An important pronouncement concerning the geology of the Coalfield was made on November 18, 1911, by Professor H. Bolton, F.R.S.E., F.G.S., F.Z.S., of Bristol, who, after examination of the cores from the twelve borings on the allied areas, reported as follows:—

> "The list of fossil forms is not long, but the suite of remains is nevertheless a characteristic one, whilst the numerous horizons at which fossils have been proved to occur will provide useful and important datum levels in sinkings and the formation of roadways as coal seams are developed. The mode of occurrence of almost all the fossils demonstrates beyond all question, and in a fashion nothing else can do, what the character of the bedding of the rocks is. In nearly all cases, the fossils (as shown by the bea-

of *Anthracomya*, for instance) lie at right-angles to the course of the borehole, and thus show that the beds are horizontal. In very few cases has even a slight inclination from the horizontal been noted, and only in about three cases have feeble traces of contortion or puckering of the beds been seen. 'Slickensiding'—a sure sign of crushing movement—is exceedingly rare. These facts point fairly conclusively to the Coalfield being much less disturbed than is the case with that of Somerset, and augurs well for economy in development. They also indicate that the thicknesses of coal seams as revealed in the borings are likely to be true thicknesses, as the beds have been pierced as nearly as possible at right-angles. The correlation of the Coalfield with those of Somerset and South Wales on the one hand, and the French and Belgian fields on the other, is brought appreciably nearer by the determination of a definite fauna at well-established horizons, and that these horizons are likely to be fairly constant in character is shown by the constantly recurring phases where every stage from the smallest fry to old shells are seen packed together in great numbers, a condition hardly likely to occur except under conditions of great stability.

"A correlation of the beds of the various boreholes can only be attempted when all the details of strata, thicknesses, etc., are available. These details are also necessary to establish a correlation with the East and West Coalfields. That such correlations are likely to be obtained will, I think, be evident from the tabulated list of fossils appended to my interim report upon the faunas of the several borings.

"In conclusion, I may say that the results are distinctly good, and yield valuable data, whilst they also promise others even more valuable and useful."

The following tables giving particulars of the seams proved in the several borings, and of the capitals of the various companies of the Concessions group, graphically present the growth of the undertaking up to the end of 1911 :—

Summary of Boring Results on Concessions and Allied Companies' Areas to December 31, 1911.

Boring.	Total No. of seams.	Total coal proved. Ft.	In.	Seams comprised.	
Waldershare ..	6	17	3	3 seams	.. 1 ft. to 2 ft.
				1 seam	.. 3 ft. 4 in.
				1 ,,	.. 4 ft. 6 in.
				1 ,,	.. 5 ft. 2 in.
Fredville	3	7	4	2 seams	.. 1 ft. to 2 ft.
				1 seam	.. 4 ft. 4 in.
Barfrestone ..	10	32	11	3 seams	.. 1 ft. to 2 ft.
				4 ,,	.. 2 ft. to 3 ft.
				1 seam	.. 4 ft. 11 in.
				1 ,,	.. 6 ft. 1 in.
				1 ,,	.. 8 ft. 3 in.
Goodnestone ..	14	49	0	4 seams	.. 1 ft. to 2 ft.
				5 ,,	.. 3 ft. to 4 ft.
				3 ,,	.. 4 ft. to 5 ft.
				1 seam	.. 6 ft. 7 in.
				1 ,,	.. 7 ft. 10 in.
Walmestone ..	2	4	3	1 seam	.. 1 ft.
				1 ,,	.. 3 ft. 3 in.
Woodnesborough ..	8	25	1	2 seams	.. 1 ft. to 2 ft.
				2 ,,	.. 2 ft. to 3 ft
				3 ,,	.. 3 ft. to 4 ft.
				1 seam	.. 6 ft. 7 in.
Mattice Hill ..	4	9	3	2 seams	.. 1 ft. to 2 ft.
				1 seam	.. 2 ft. 10 in.
				1 ,,	.. 3 ft. 5 in.
Ripple	15	57	9	5 seams	.. 1 ft. to 2 ft
				4 ,,	.. 2 ft. to 2 ft. 4 in.
				2 ,,	.. 4 ft. and 4 ft. 8 in.
				4 ,,	.. 6 ft. to 10 ft.
Maydensole ..	17	60	7	6 seams	.. 1 ft. to 2 ft.
				1 seam	.. 2 ft. 6 in.
				1 ,,	.. 3 ft. 6 in.
				5 seams	.. 4 ft. to 5 ft.
				4 ,,	.. 5 ft. 8 in. to 7 ft. 6 in.
Trapham ..	10	29	9	4 ,,	.. 1 ft. to 2 ft.
				3 ,,	.. 3 ft. to 4 ft.
				3 ,,	.. 4 ft. to 5 ft
Stodmarsh	7	26	9	4 ,,	.. 1 ft. to 2 ft.
				1 seam	.. 2 ft. 10 in.
				1 ,,	.. 4 ft. 9 in.
				1 ,,	.. 13 ft. 8 in.
	96	319	11		

Of the above there are 64 seams of 2 ft. and upwards aggregating 277 ft. and showing an average of 4 ft. 4 in.

	Seams.	Aggregating.	Average.
In South Wales there are	73	120 ft.	1 ft. 6 in.
In Westphalia ,,	117	294 ft.	2 ft. 6 in.
In Mons ,,	110	250 ft.	2 ft. 4 in.
In Liège ,,	85	212 ft.	2ft. 6 in.
In Somerset ,,	35	98 ft.	2 ft.

KENT COAL CONCESSIONS, LIMITED, AND ALLIED COMPANIES.

Particulars as to Capitals authorised and issued as at December 31, 1911.

Name of Company.	Date of registration,	Authorised capital.	Par value.	Issued capital.	Debentures authorised.
		£	s.	£	£
Kent Coal Concessions, Ltd.	15 Apr., 1904	275,000	20	207,200	150,000 6%
Sondage Syndicate, Ltd.	7 Jan., 1905	5,000	20	5,000	nil
Fonçage Syndicate, Ltd.	18 Apr., 1906	20,000	20	20,000	nil
East Kent Colliery Co., Ltd.	28 Mar., 1907	490,000 10,000	5 1	208,642	25,000
South Eastern Coalfield Extension, Ltd.	6 June, 1907	80,500	20	40,500	nil
Guilford Syndicate, Ltd.	2 Aug., 1907	40,000	20	31,712	nil
East Kent Contract & Financial Co., Ltd.	13 Dec., 1907	50,000	20	42,033	nil
Snowdown Colliery Ltd.	25 Mar., 1908	250,000 1,250	20 1	178,274	nil
Extended Extension, Limited	26 Nov., 1909	50,000	20	45,094	nil
Intermediate Equipments, Ltd.	10 Oct., 1910	95,000 5,000	20 10	65,590	nil
Wingham & Stour Valley Collieries Ltd.	9 Feb., 1911	548,750 1,250	10 1	100,000	nil
South East Kent Electric Power Co., Ltd.	4 May, 1911	1,000	20	1,000	nil
East Kent Railways Co.	19 June, 1911	240,000	20	—	120,000
	Totals £	2,162,750	—	£1,035,045	£295,000

CHAPTER XXI.

Anglo-Westphalian Syndicate. Kent Freeholds and Minerals, Limited. North Kent Coalfield, Limited. Chislet Colliery. Its Sinking Record. Capital Increased by £120,000. All German Interests eliminated at the outbreak of War.

"Of which all Europe rings from side to side."
—MILTON.

1911—(*continued*).

The great wealth of coal proved within the areas of the Concessions group evidently impressed some of the Westphalian magnates with the possibilities of the field. Herr Stinnes and others had succeeded already in acquiring important areas in the old-established coalfields, and Kent was now to be the scene of further "peaceful penetration" on the part of the Germans, on whose behalf Dr. P. Krüsch, an eminent professor attached to the Geological Department at Berlin, made an exhaustive report on the Coalfield. Thus it came about that in conjunction with Sir John Lister Kaye and Mr. Woolley-Hart, Herr Carl Seitz, of Düsseldorff, was responsible for the registration on November 10, 1911, of

THE ANGLO-WESTPHALIAN KENT COAL SYNDICATE, LIMITED.

Capital, £25,000 in shares of £1 each.

Directors:—Mr. Arthur Woolley-Hart, Sir John Lister Kaye, Bart., Herr Carl Seitz (managing-director of Allgemeine Tiefbohr und Schachtban Aktiengesellschaft), and Herr Willi Peritz, of 356, Goldhawk Road, Hammersmith.

Solicitors:—Messrs. Minet, Perring Smith & Company.

Brokers:—Messrs. Wheatear, Cornwallis West & Company.

The Syndicate was formed for the purpose of acquiring from the Ecclesiastical Commissioners a lease of the coal under some 3,400 acres near

Chislet, and the terms accepted by that body from this quasi-foreign Syndicate were:—A dead-rental for the first three years of 2s. 6d. per acre; a dead-rental for the fourth to the sixth year of 7s. 6d. per acre; a dead-rental for the seventh to the ninth year of 12s. 6d. per acre; a dead-rental thereafter of 20s. per acre, merging into royalties at the rate of £28 per ft. of coal per acre. These terms, it should be noted, are considerably below those offered for other of the Commissioners' areas by the Concessions Company, and refused curtly and without explanation, as I have already described.

The granting of these minerals to a semi-foreign group was the subject of questions by Mr. Arthur Fell in the House of Commons on December 4, 1911, the answers to which were not more accurate than those usually given in similar circumstances. Messrs. Wheatear, Cornwallis West & Company were so disturbed at Mr. Fell's attempt to bring out the real facts concerning this transaction that they wrote a letter to "The Times" (December 11, 1911) which proclaims (and acclaims) the existence of the "Internationale" in finance; though when such a principle is sought to be established by Labour probably they would be the first to stigmatise it as a danger to the nation. The following extract from their letter is worth quoting:—

> "It is precisely this kind of thing which embitters the relations between two great nations who obviously depend on each other to an enormous extent for their progress and wealth. Surely there can be no greater guarantee of peace than the partnership in commerce of the subjects of the great nations. This is, in reality, the case to-day between the nations themselves, for there is no such thing as nationality in the world of finance and commerce."

On December 12 Mr. Fell returned to the charge with an inquiry as to whether the Commissioners' land at Lydden was also going to be leased to the Anglo-Westphalian Syndicate (that area which had been refused to Concessions), and Mr. Nicholson, who replied, stated:—

> "As to their land at Lydden, the Commissioners are not in negotiation for a coal letting

to any person or company. The special reason for entertaining the proposal of the Anglo-Westphalian Kent Coal Syndicate to explore the Chislet area, and work the coal, if found, was that they were the only applicants for that area, and the Commissioners were satisfied of their ability to provide the necessary capital."

It would be interesting to know in what way the Commissioners were satisfied of the Syndicate's ability to provide the necessary capital, for they might easily have learnt that its small capital was raised only on very onerous terms. According to the statement in lieu of prospectus, the Syndicate paid an underwriting commission of 50 per cent. at least to the directors, which is very greatly in excess of such commission given by any one of the previously established Kent Coal companies.

The following abstracts from the "Statement in Lieu of Prospectus" are worth reproducing:—

"Full particulars of the nature and extent of the interest of every director on the promotion of or in the property proposed to be acquired by the Company:—

"(1) Arthur Woolley-Hart has agreed with Messrs. Wheatear, Cornwallis West & Company to procure subscribers for 1,250 shares of this Company at par, and will receive 525 fully-paid shares in respect thereof, and will also be entitled to one-third of the benefit of the option to take up 5,000 further shares of this Company at par granted to them by the Contract No. 1 above referred to.

"(2) Sir John Lister Kaye, under Contracts Nos. 3 and 4, will receive £300 in cash and 800 fully-paid shares of this Company, and a further sum of £950 out of the first profits of this Company.

"(3) Willi Peritz will receive, under the Contract No. 4, the sums of £400 and £350 in cash above referred to, and also repayment of expenses incurred by him since September 13, 1911, estimated to amount to £125. He will also receive 2,950 fully-paid shares of this Company, and he is entitled to the benefit of the call on 5,000 shares of this Company at par for twelve months.

"(4) Carl Seitz is the managing-director of the Allgemeine Trefbohr und Schachtban Aktiengesellschaft, and holds shares for 2,000 marks out of the total issued capital of 1,200,000 marks. The Allgemeine Trefbohr und Schachtban Aktiengesellschaft will receive from Willi Peritz 1,875 shares, fully-paid, for procuring subscribres for 3,743 shares, and are also interested, as mentioned, in Contract No. 5."

In March, 1913, the Syndicate was transformed into the

ANGLO-WESTPHALIAN KENT COALFIELD, LIMITED.

Capital: £200,000 in 180,000 ordinary shares of £1 each and 40,000 deferred shares of 1s. each.

Directors: Messrs. A. Woolley-Hart (chairman), Joseph Shaw, K.C., F. L. Davis, Carl Seitz, and W. Peritz.

In consideration of the Austin Syndicate subscribing for 35,000 of the new ordinary shares at 35s. net, it was given the following options, viz.:—

To subscribe for 70,000 ordinary shares at 37s. 6d. net to January 1, 1914, and similarly with regard to a further 68,000 at 40s. net to July 1, 1914.

To acquire from the Company 3,500 acres of minerals for £30,000, plus an improved minimum rental of £500 per annum merging into 1d. per ton improved royalty.

To acquire from the Company 3,500 acres of areas on not less favourable terms, subject to the Syndicate's profits on such transactions being limited to 10 per cent.

The Anglo-Westphalian Kent Coalfield, Limited, in carrying out its settled programme, followed in the footsteps of its predecessors in the Field and formed a subsidiary company to act the part of intermediary and to share the profits arising from the purchase of freehold minerals. This offshoot was entitled the

KENT FREEHOLDS AND MINERALS, LIMITED.

(Registered June 12, 1912.)

Capital: £100,050 in 100,000 ordinary shares of £1 each and 1,000 deferred shares of 1s each.

Directors: Messrs. Woolley-Hart (chairman), A. A. Baumann, and R. C. Shaw.

This Company was formed with the chief object of acquiring and dealing with freehold mineral properties in Kent, which it undertook to lease to its parent, the Anglo-Westphalian Kent Coalfield, Limited.

We have seen that the latter Company had given the Austin Syndicate the option to deal with any of its acquired properties, so that the result of these arrangements has been the creation of a complicated system of inter-company transactions similar to those for which the "Burr" group achieved such notoriety.

Herr Willi Peritz established himself at Canterbury as local director of the Anglo-Westphalian Kent Coalfield, Limited, and was soon actively engaged in acquiring small areas within, what may be termed, the Kent Coal Concessions sphere of influence. One result of his activities has been that a deadlock has been created with regard to certain colliery areas; an impasse, however, that is likely to be removed, shortly, by legislation.

With the coming of war the German interests in Kent reverted to our own people; Herr Willi Peritz became the guest of the nation at Alexandra Palace, and the Anglo-Westphalian Kent Coalfield, Limited, assumed the guise of a true-born Briton in November, 1914, under the title of

NORTH KENT COALFIELD, LIMITED.

Directors: Messrs. A. Woolley-Hart (chairman) and Joseph Shaw, K.C.

In dealing with the activities of this new group I shall not attempt to discriminate between the operations of its several incarnations. Borings were made at Chislet, Rushbourne, Chitty, Beltinge and Reculver, not all of which were successful. In fact, two of them were put down about two miles beyond the northern boundary of the Coal Basin. Nevertheless, in addition to three 2-ft. seams, two workable seams, 5-ft. and 7-ft. 2-in. respectively, were proved at Chislet within quite reasonable depths, and in November, 1913, a Company was promoted to lease and work an area of about 2,500 acres, under the title of

THE ANGLO-WESTPHALIAN (CHISLET, KENT) COLLIERY, LIMITED.

The following particulars are abstracted from the Company's statement in lieu of prospectus:—

Capital: £230,000 in shares of £1 each, of which 120,000 shares have been subscribed for at par, and 48,000 shares will be issued as fully-paid.

Directors: Mr. Joseph Shaw, K.C. (chairman), Sir John Prescott Hewett, C.S.I., C.I.E.; Messrs. Charles B. O. Clarke, A. Woolley-Hart, W. Mewburn, and W. Peritz.

Mr. E. M. Hann, in the course of a "Report on the proposed Colliery," stated that:—

"The Chislet borehole has shown six seams of coal, each well over 2 ft. in thickness, and the cores of the shales and strata associated, forming the roofs and floors of these seams, impress me as good and sound. I do not think there need be any hesitation in embarking on a colliery there. As to resources, it is necessary in the present limited state of the available knowledge to speak with reserve . . . . . It seems to me a moderate estimate to take an area with a radius of a mile from the Pits and 20 ft. thickness of workable coal, and this would provide an output of 800,000 tons per annum for 80 years. Preparatory work will occupy from 10 to 16 months; sinking work will occupy, if dry, 10, if wet, 18 months; opening out at pit-bottom through pillar, 6 months; total time from the start to working a sufficient output to cover costs, from 26 to 40 months."

Mr. Hann's report deals at length with the questions of plant and general expenditure on sinking, etc.; he estimated that to provide for an output of 500 tons per diem £120,000 would suffice, and that for a further £40,000 the Colliery could be equipped to produce an output of 800,000 tons per annum.

It is, perhaps, scarcely necessary to remark that Mr. Hann's estimates as to time and cost have proved both to be on the wrong side. The Colliery being situated on the northern portion of the coalfield, the water-bearing strata that was such a bugbear at Tilmanstone is practically non-existent. The only real difficulty in the sinking was in getting through the loose sands of the Tertiary Period and through a fissured and water-bearing section of the Upper Chalk. As the site of the Pits had been settled somewhat to the south-east of that originally decided upon, the management, not being satisfied with the available records of the Secondary strata, considered it advisable to put down a check borehole, which was started on April 3, 1914, and had reached a depth of 1,124 ft. by May 15, 1914.

This boring, commencing at 68 ft. O.D., disclosed 70 ft. of running sand, 105 ft. of sandy clay, 560 ft. of chalk, and 336 ft. of gault, the Coal Measures being entered at 1,071 ft. from the surface.

Prof. Boyd Dawkins, it will be remembered, reported to Concessions in 1905 that at Waldershare the "Coal Measures are likely to be struck at this spot either directly below or within a short distance of the bottom of the Gault.'' But when the boring was made, 414 ft. of intervening Secondary strata were met with. It was not, therefore, until nine years later, and at a boring 10 miles distant, that the thinning-out of the Secondary strata, such as Boyd Dawkins had looked for at Waldershare, was established.

The boring at Chislet also proved that the Upper Chalk was much fissured and somewhat heavily charged with water. Consequently it was decided to adopt the cementation process with a view to consolidating this fractured strata, and on May 29, 1914, a start was made with a series of boreholes around each pit.

Complete success attended this work. The cement mixture, being forced into the strata at varying pressures up to 3,000 lbs. to the square inch, entirely filled not only the open fissures, but even minute ones no thicker than a hair, as I can testify from an examination of some of the chalk raised in the sinking.

Mr. Edmund L. Hann, in "The Times Engineering Supplement" for June, 1919, gives full details respecting the sinking of these Chislet pits, and publishes for the first time particulars of the cementation and shaft-lining system employed, of which Mr. C. Kearton, the then manager of the

Colliery (formerly manager of Snowdown Colliery) and himself are the joint patentees. Those interested in shaft-sinking in Kent might profitably consult Mr. Hann's article, in which, however, he goes out of his way to institute comparisons between Chislet and other collieries in Kent, disparaging the work of his predecessors on the field thus:—

> "The results obtained from colliery enterprise in Kent up to the formation of this (the Chislet) company in 1913 had been very disappointing from the view of both time and money expended unnecessarily in sinking and equipping the collieries.

As this statement might lead Mr. Hann's readers to assume that Chislet's sinking record was pre-eminently superior to that of any other colliery in the district, it would be only fair to examine the facts and see how far they warrant any such assumption.

From the registration of the Chislet Company to the date when both its 16-ft. diameter shafts were into the 5-ft. seam at 1,350 ft., a period of 5 years and 10 months elapsed. One of the shafts had in addition been sunk a further 86 ft. into the 7-ft. seam, so that the total footage sunk was 2,786 ft. Whereas at Snowdown Colliery both shafts were into the "Beresford" seam at 1,500 ft. within 4 years and 9 months from the registration of the company, the footage sunk being 3,000 ft. The work done at Snowdown was infinitely greater than the mere 214 ft., additional sinking would imply, for the shafts are 18 ft. in diameter, against 16 ft. at Chislet. Snowdown, therefore, shows an excess in excavation and walling of 130,000 and 56,000 cub. ft. respectively over Mr. Hann's company, notwithstanding which, and the extra footage sunk, the Snowdown shafts were put down in twelve months less time than those at Chislet.

I am aware that Chislet's work suffered some interruption during the war, but against this sinking was entirely suspended at Snowdown for one period of twelve months. There were also stoppages for lesser periods.

With regard to Mr. Hann's statement that money was unnecessarily expended in connection with sinkings elsewhere than at Chislet, my comment is that the facts do not support him. So far from having money to spend unnecessarily, both Tilmanstone and Snowdown were handicapped by a chronic lack of funds, it being generally difficult to provide for their essential requirements. However, Chislet has now arrived at the producing stage; it has a splendid surface equipment, a good clean seam of coal to work, and every prospect of taking a leading position in the Kent Coalfield.

The capital has recently been increased by the creation of a further 120,000 shares of £1 each. The Company is embarking upon a large housing scheme, and hopes to erect 800 cottages in close proximity to the colliery within the next two years.

All the German interests in this colliery were apparently eliminated in November, 1914, when the title was shortened to "Chislet Colliery, Limited." Herr Willi Peritz ceased to be a director, his place being taken by Col. Sir H. Mellis, K.C S.I.

CHAPTER XXII.

Several Borings Yield Rich Seams. Consolidation of the Allied Companies' Interests. United Coalfields of Kent, Limited. An Abortive Promotion. Snowdown Pits reach the Coal. Betteshanger Boring Company. Good Seams on Lord Northbourne's Estate. Canterbury Coal Company. Mr. Burr receives the Freedom of Dover. A Kent Coal Banquet. Share Values at End of 1913.

"So comes a reckoning when the feast is o'er."

—GAY.

1912.

A number of splendid seams were proved in quick succession by the various borings of the Concessions group in the early part of this year, viz.:—

January	15	a seam of	4 ft. 7 in.
,,	16	,,	6 ft. 2 in.
,,	27	,,	3 ft. 2 in.
,,	30	,,	4 ft. 8 in.
February	8	,,	4 ft. 2 in.
,,	13	,,	6 ft. 6 in.
,,	15	,,	5 ft. 4 in.
,,	29	,,	6 ft. 3 in.

This evidence further strikingly confuted the prognostications of those who for years had pooh-poohed the idea of coal being found in Kent, or who predicted that if found at all it would prove to be in thin seams of no commercial value.

It is, I think, beyond question that the slow development of this new Coalfield is due in a great measure to the extraordinarily uninformed criticism directed against it by a numerous body of pseudo-geologists throughout the country. I say nothing of the criticisms on the finance of the Field except to remark that these to a material extent actually created and intensified the evils complained of.

The number of seams proved up to the end of February, 1912, in all the borings of the Concessions group amounted to 111, with 373 ft. of coal. Seventy-four of the seams were of 2 ft. and upwards, aggregating 320 ft. of coal and averaging 4 ft. 4 in. in thickness. As I have stated previously, it has not been possible to determine the actual net coal contents of the Field by a correlation of these seams.

The principal event of the year 1912 undoubtedly was the attempt to consolidate the interests of Concessions and its allied parent companies in the undeveloped coal areas held by them, both freehold and leasehold. With this object in view an agreement was entered into whereby the Kolken Syndicate, Limited, undertook to form a company to take over and develop these areas to the extent of 44,000 acres.

The Kolken Syndicate was not in itself financially strong—its capital being only £45,000—but its shareholders were chiefly members of the Stock Exchange, who were able to command plenty of money for any approved scheme they might put forward, and many of them were already largely interested in the Kent Coal enterprise.

After several months' negotiation with Mr. Burr, the Syndicate was at last in a position to produce a prospectus with a view to getting the necessary capital underwritten. Brief particulars of so important a document must find a place in this narrative, for it establishes, on the written authority of experts of high standing in the colliery world, the then position of the Concessions group of companies, and indicates the future results likely to attend the vigorous exploitation of the Coalfield.

Preliminary to the public issue a private meeting of the shareholders in all the Burr group of companies was held in the Great Hall, Cannon Street Hotel, on June 13, 1912, at which the Marquis of Winchester presided. After Mr. Burr had given full particulars concerning the proposed New Company, which was to be entitled "The United Coalfields of Kent, Limited," Mr. A. H. Loring proposed and Mr. C D. Marson seconded the following resolution :—

> "Resolved,—That this meeting, having heard from Mr. Burr the explanation of the scheme relating to the new company, hereby approves the same."

The resolution was carried unanimously with acclamation. The shareholders were invited to underwrite a portion of the capital of the new company, and on June 24 a circular was issued to them covering advance particulars of the prospectus, the publication of which had been fixed for July 1.

UNITED COALFIELDS OF KENT, LIMITED.

Nominal Share Capital: £3,250,000, divided into 2,000,000 7 per cent. cumulative preference shares of £1 each, 1,250,000 ordinary shares of £1 each, and £260,000 of 7 per cent. income stock.

Directors—The Most Hon. the Marquis of Winchester (chairman); Messrs. G. B. Forrester (director of Albion Steam Coal Company, Limited, vice-chairman), Charles E. Allan (director of Workman, Clark & Company, Limited), Henry Armstrong, M.I.M.E. (director of the Seaton Burn Coal Company, Limited), W. Gascoyne Dalziel, J.P. (director of Locket's Merthyr Collieries (1894), Limited, Cardiff), Sir Henry Hall, I.S.O. (chairman, Cross, Tetley & Company, Limited, Wigan), and Mr. Arthur H. Loring (director, East Kent Light Railways Company). Mr. Arthur Burr, or, failing him, Dr. Malcolm Burr, had the right to join the board after allotment.

In addition to the mineral areas the Company was to acquire the Pluckley Clay Works, belonging to the East Kent Contract & Financial Company, Limited, the miners' villages, and a controlling interest in the South-East Kent Electric Power Company, Limited.

Mr. Maurice Deacon, under whose direct technical advice all future developments were to be carried on, reported that in his opinion there was an average thickness of 30 ft. of workable coal then proved under the areas to be acquired, or a total aggregate of 1,438,000,000 tons, including steam, house and gas coals of first-class quality, "apparently containing, in some instances, valuable coking and by-product properties." And he further stated: "I believe there is a great future for this Coalfield, and profit to those who invest their money in a properly capitalised and well managed company having for its object the development of what appears to me to be likely to prove to be a second South Wales coalfield within a short distance of London."

Mr. Arthur Lawrence stated that: "The vast area and resources of the property to be acquired promise an ultimate return out of all proportion to the price now asked for the undertaking."

Messrs. William Armstrong & Sons in their report state: "We are of opinion that if the evidence disclosed by the boreholes, and the analyses of the seams, are borne out by subsequent operations, the Coalfield may be found to present combined conditions which are not now possessed by any other in the kingdom, and such as justify a large concentration of capital for development and working, if properly expended."

The purchase price payable to the Concessions group was to be £1,322,500, and the proceeds of the public issue were expected to yield £1,000,000 for working capital. Thus it will be seen that the enterprise which had been started in 1904 by Kent Coal Concessions, Limited, with the small nominal capital of £50,000—but with considerably less than half that amount in actual cash—had grown, within the short space of eight years, to dimensions of no mean magnitude.

Unfortunately, the United Coalfields of Kent, Limited (which was registered with a merely nominal capital in order to safeguard the title), was born but to demonstrate once more the truth of the old adage, "the best-laid plans of mice and men gang aft agley." Through no fault of their own, the Kolken Syndicate found it impossible to proceed with the flotation in July as arranged, and the issue was indefinitely postponed. During the ensuing few months attempts were made to resuscitate the scheme, but without success; so this three-million-horse-power Company died the death, and its epitaph might well have been :—

"It is so soon that I am done for,
I wonder what I was begun for!"

Ignoring chronological sequence for a moment, I must interpolate here some extracts from Mr. Burr's circular to his shareholders in February, 1913, in which he refers to the defunct Company as "the not too attractive United Coalfields of Kent," and consoles the shareholders for its early demise by assuring them that " terms which were acceptable in January, 1912, when the contract was first discussed and settled, are to-day both out of date and, from our point of view, too unfavourable to even form the basis of discussion. In fact, the Companies had outgrown them even when the prospectus of the United Company appeared in print and the very justification for the arrangement had ceased to exist. I will now candidly confess that . . . . the net result will be to save for the shareholders some millions sterling "!

It may be noted here that the expenses incurred by the parent companies in connection with this abortive flotation amounted to considerably more than £5,000.

On November 20 of this year (1912) all the Kent Coal shareholders were advised that No. 3 shaft of Snowdown Colliery had reached the first of the 18-in. seams of the Fredville boring at a depth of 1,370 ft., as compared with 1,425 ft. shown in the borehole section. Also that Tilmanstone's shafts were being sunk rapidly through the Coal Measures. Thus, for the seven thousand shareholders who had adventured their money in the enterprise, the year drew to a close in an atmosphere of hope—" White-handed Hope, girt with golden wings."

The only substantial block of minerals within the ascertained boundaries of the Coalfield that had not come into the Concessions' fold were those underlying Lord Northbourne's Betteshanger estate. The Concessions' borings to the north, south, and west had in reality established the value of these minerals, but for the purpose of more closely determining the thickness of the seams and the character of the sinking ground in this locality there was formed the

BETTESHANGER BORING COMPANY, LIMITED.

(Registered September, 1912).

Capital: £20,000 in 200 shares of £100 each and 2,000 deferred shares of 1s. each. In 1913 the £100 shares were split up and the capital increased to £40,120 in 40,000 ordinary shares of £1 each and 2,400 deferred shares of 1s. each. The ordinary shares are entitled to a return of their capital in full, either out of the profits or the assets of the company, before the deferred shares rank for dividend. Thereafter the profits and assets belong to the holders of the ordinary and deferred shares in equal moieties.

Directors: Mr. Archibald Grove (chairman), the Hon. R. James, Messrs H. C. Embleton, N. P. W. Brady, A. Farquhar, and C. F. H. Leslie.

A boring was put down on the Betteshanger estate, which succeeded in proving a number of substantial seams of good quality. I am unable to give a complete section, but the following is a list of the seams met with:—

Ft.		ft.	in.	Ft.		Ft.	in.
At 1,208	a seam	2	6	At 2,364	a seam	4	1
„ 1,504	„	2	0	„ 2,403	„	3	0
„ 1,813	„	4	5	„ 2,513	„	2	7
„ 1,926	„	2	10	„ 2,562	„	4	6
„ 1,975	„	5	0	„ 2,592	„	2	3
„ 2,510	„	3	6	„ 2,632	„	7	9

Total, 44 ft. 5 in. in twelve seams. Average thickness, 3 ft. 8 in. As is the case throughout the Coalfield, the coals yield a decreasing amount of volatiles with depth. The first six seams range from 28.66 per cent. to 18.47 per cent. of volatiles; and the six deeper seams yield from 16.85 per cent. to 14.03 per cent.

Analysis of the 4 ft. 6 in. seam at 2,562 ft.:— Volatile matters, 14.03 per cent.; fixed carbon, 80.03 per cent.; ash, 4.97 per cent.; sulphur, 0.97 per cent.; calorific power, 14,414 B.T.U.

The general results of the analyses of the seams are entirely satisfactory, indicating, as they do, the existence of good steam coals suitable for locomotive bunkering and general manufacturing purposes. They also produce a good-grade coke.

In addition to the Betteshanger property, the company has obtained from H.M. Woods and Forests Department the right to exploit the undersea minerals in the neighbourhood of Deal. Including these, the total mineral area under the company's control amounts to about 10,500 acres.

Shortly before the outbreak of war three colliery sections had been mapped out and preparations made for their development, but so far (September, 1919) no actual work has been commenced.

The satisfactory outcome of bulk tests of the iron ore found in the Shakespeare Cliff pit, which has brought important steel interests into the Field (as I have already recorded) has resulted in the Channel Steel Company acquiring a substantial proportion of the Betteshanger minerals. But for the uncertainty as to the future of the coal industry consequent upon the now notorious Sankey Report, sinking would have been started as soon after the signing of the Peace Treaty as the necessary plant could have been got on to the ground.

The Betteshanger Company's prospects in normal times would be considered highly promising. It has a small capital and a large acreage of high-quality minerals. The royalties are on a moderate scale, and the general terms of the leases are favourable.

The future development of these minerals will, of course, largely depend upon what conditions the Government imposes on the coal industry. It is idle to suppose that the public will subscribe for new colliery undertakings under any of the schemes that, so far, have been suggested.

Although it has not done any serious work on the Field, I must record the formation of the

CANTERBURY COAL COMPANY, LIMITED

(Registered, December 10, 1912).

Capital: £167,500 in 150,000 "A" shares of £1 each and 350,000 "B" shares of 1s. each.

Directors: The Right Hon. the Marquis of Winchester, the Right Hon. Lord Sandys, both of whom have taken considerable interest in the Kent Coalfield; in fact, they had already acquired, through the medium of the Worcester Trust, Limited, the minerals under the Broome Park estate, but as these lie in close proximity to the south-western boundary of the coal basin, their value is, in my opinion, problematical.

While not strictly relevant to the affairs of the Canterbury Coal Company, I might, nevertheless, mention here that the purchasers of the Broome Park minerals were fortunate in securing the good offices of the East Kent Contract & Financial Company to pass on their bargain to Kent Coal Concessions, Limited, upon whom the Contract Company levied a toll of £5,000 for its services as intermediary. Of this sum the director-general of Contract claimed 10 per cent under his remuneration clause in the Company's Articles.

This Company was also interested in the Chilton boring, and owns some freehold minerals in that district.

1913.

This year opened with something more tangible than the promises with which, at the commencement of so many of its predecessors, shareholders had fain to be content.

The Snowdown shafts had entered the "Beresford" seam, those at Tilmanstone were in the Coal Measures, and within safe and negligible distance of workable coal. Hence it was but reasonable to suppose that the trials and tribulations of the past were buried in that past, and that the present achievement was to prove the harbinger of prosperity in the near future. These were undoubtedly the reflections of the general body of shareholders at this time, and in anticipation of so happy a state of things a movement had been initiated for the due celebration of the raising of coal, and for marking their appreciation of Mr. Burr's services. In this celebration the town of Dover decided to take part.

Although reaping a rich harvest from the earnings of the large body of men that the enterprise had brought into the district, Dover, hitherto, had been not only strangely sceptical of the potential wealth at its front door, but singularly unhelpful as regards its development. He would be a hardy man who would claim that the prophets of Kent Coal had been accorded any honour in their own county. However, there came a revulsion of feeling which found expression in the determination of the City Fathers to confer the freedom of the borough upon Mr. Burr. A special meeting of the Council was called, and the following resolution passed :—

"Resolved :—That the Town Council desires to place on record its sense of the eminent services rendered to the Borough by Mr. Arthur Burr in connection with the development of the East Kent Coalfield, and the benefits which have directly accrued to the Borough therefrom. And that this Council doth, at this special meeting, held under and in pursuance of the Honorary

Freedom of Boroughs Act, 1885, order that the above-named Arthur Burr be, and is hereby admitted, an Honorary Freeman of the Borough." The presentation of this honour was arranged to coincide with the gift of a loving cup, specially designed and made by the well-known artists in metal, Messrs. Omar Ramsden and Alwyn Carr, which was subscribed for by shareholders in the Kent Coal Concessions and allied companies, "to commemorate the uncovering of the Beresford seam at Snowdown Colliery." The ceremony took place at a banquet given to Mr. Burr in the Dover Town Hall on February 4, under the presidency of the Marquis of Winchester, supported by the late Right Hon. George Wyndham, M.P. The Mayors of Dover, Folkestone, Canterbury, Margate, Ramsgate and Deal were also present, together with a representative number of shareholders and a sprinkling of local notables.

This gathering witnessed the apotheosis of Mr. Burr, and the writing of my record would have proved a more congenial task had it not been my lot to chronicle his fall from the pinnacle to which he had been thus exalted. A gradual descent, but none the less humiliating. Had he been permitted to gaze with seeing eyes into the future surely he might have re-echoed Wolsey's foreboding:—

> "I have touched the highest point of all my greatness,
> And from that full meridian of my glory
> I haste now to my setting."

After this very natural ebullition in celebrating the advent of coal in bulk, things generally resumed their normal course. Interest was centred chiefly upon Snowdown and Tilmanstone, whose operations have been dealt with under the heads of their respective companies.

I might mention, *en passant*, that a number of colliery experts had been invited to visit Snowdown Colliery on the day of the banquet, and in this connection the "Coal and Iron and By-Products Journal" stated that:—

"Some of the experts were a trifle nonplussed at the curious appearance of the coal, and well they might be, for of its kind it is *sui generis*, and bears little resemblance to coal from seams in any other coalfield in this country. There was, however, something like a general agreement that it bore a striking resemblance to Forest of Dean coal. Like most of that mineral, it is undoubtedly of a somewhat composite character—exceedingly variable in texture, but withal singularly free from pyrites and other impurities."

As showing the values of the various shares of the Concessions group at this period I reproduce the following advertisement from the "Dover Standard," February 8, 1913:—

KENT COAL COMPANIES.

H. S. Simpson, Stock and Share Broker,
42, Castle Street, Dover.

SHARE LIST.

Name of company.	Share or stock.	Amount paid.	Middle Price. £	s.	d.
Kent Coal Concessions—					
Ordinary	£1	£1	3	17	6
Deferred	£1	£1	110	0	0
10 per cent. Preference ..	£1	£1	1	4	0
6 per cent. Debenture Bonds	£10	£10	14	0	0
South Eastern Coalfield Extension—					
Ordinary-	£1	£1	3	5	0
Extended Extension—					
Ordinary	£1	£1	3	7	0
Founders	£1	£1	16	0	0
Deal and Walmer Coalfield ..	£1	£1	1	8	9
Sondage Syndicate	£1	£1	16	0	0
Foncage Syndicate	£1	£1	4	0	0
East Kent Contract and Financial—					
Ordinary	£1	£1	3	5	0
Deferred	£1	£1	12	0	0
East Kent Colliery—					
Ordinary	5/-	5/-	0	5	7½
Vendors	1/-	1/-	0	17	6
Intermediate Equipments ..	£1	£1	1	1	3
Guilford Syndicate	£1	£1	2	0	0
Snowdown Colliery	£1	£1	1	12	6
Ditto Founders	1/-	1/-	1	15	0
Wingham and Stour Valley Collieries	10/-	10/-	0	10	0
East Kent Light Railways—					
Ordinary	£1	£1	1	2	6
5 per cent. Debentures ..	£100	£100	80	0	0

CHAPTER XXIII.

Details of the Latest Amalgamation Scheme. The Proposed New Company and its Directors. Its failure to materialise. The Year 1913 closes in gloom. The Adisham and Stonehall Colliery Companies. Section of Stonehall Boring. Whitstable and Canterbury Coalfield Company.

> "There is in the worst of fortune the best of chances for a happy change."
> —EURIPIDES.

The question of Amalgamation was still giving rise to endless discussions, but a serious attempt had been made to evolve an equitable scheme that would preserve the rights of all the shareholders in any form of consolidation that ultimately might be determined upon. Obviously it was desirable that any such scheme should bear upon it the hallmark of impartiality, therefore two firms of eminent accountants, Messrs. W. B. Peat & Co. and Messrs. Crewdson, Youatt & Howard, were engaged to deal with the financial matters involved. Professor W. Galloway and Mr. J. Loudon Strain were appointed to act similarly with regard to the geological factors, while Messrs. Worsfold & Hayward, the leading firm of estate agents in Dover, dealt with the question of acreages, and their figures in turn were audited by another well-known firm of accountants —Messrs. Thornton, Murray & Thornton. These details are important as showing the desire of the management that whatever scheme they might submit to the shareholders should be an honest and straightforward attempt to deal with an admittedly difficult and complicated proposition.

The general body of shareholders were advised by circular on April 9, 1913, that Nos. 1 and 3 Pits at Tilmanstone had reached their present objective, and were in a 5 ft. 2 in. seam at 1,548 ft. In this circular Mr. Burr stated :—

"Now that Tilmanstone has reached its first thick seam, there is no reason why the amalgamation of the Parent Companies should not be proceeded with. Superficially my plan is a simple one, as it will not include any financial proposals other than the redemption of the debentures, which will precede the actual agreements, and this presents no serious difficulties."

On May 3 Mr. Burr issued a very lengthy circular to the shareholders outlining, not a simple plan as indicated above, but a most complex project involving large financial arrangements, of which he wrote:—

"This would permit of the distribution of about £1,350,000 amongst the ordinary, and £650,000 amongst the deferred shares, or about the present market valuation of all the shares of the four companies, and leave £830,000, ample for converting the remaining 15,000 acres into a colliery undertaking with a combined output of 4 or 5 millions of tons of every class of coal, and with an earning capacity that had best be left to the imagination."

No immediate steps were taken towards bringing into being the Amalgamated Company, the advent of which was to be attended by the golden harvest so glowingly depicted. In fact, at the time Mr. Burr issued the circular from which I have just quoted, the auditors had not sent in their reports. It was not, indeed, until July 26 that the shareholders were advised that the respective rights of the amalgamating companies, viz., Kent Coal Concessions, Limited, South-Eastern Coalfield Extension, Limited, Extended Extension, Limited, and the Deal & Walmer Coalfield, Limited, had been determined. They were invited to attend an extraordinary general meeting on July 31, at which the resolution to be submitted recited that the various assessors "have reported that the proportions to be allocated to the said four companies are as under:—To Kent Coal Concessions, Limited, 1,966 units out of 3,962 units; to South Eastern Coalfield Extension, Limited, 902 units out of 3,962 units; to Extended Extension, Limited, 735 units out of 3,962 units; to Deal & Walmer Coalfield, Limited, 359 units out of 3,962 units."

The resolution proceeded:—

"Now it is resolved that the directors be and are hereby authorised to proceed with the amalgamation of the said four companies, embodying the above proportions as regards the mineral areas in the said schedules, and to submit formal contracts for such amalgamation with a new company to be formed for the approval of each of the said four companies, at separate meetings of those companies."

Shareholders turned up in large numbers at this meeting, and the directors were instructed to proceed with the scheme of amalgamation upon the basis of the accountants' report.

It will be remembered that in dealing with the affairs of the South Eastern Coalfield Extension, Limited, I stated that admittedly Concessions was entitled to be liberally dealt with in any settlement of joint accounts, having regard to its heavy expenditure, from which the other parent companies had derived such material benefit. This fact was not lost sight of by the accountants, as will be seen from their report subjoined :—

London, October 27, 1913.

To Kent Coal Concessions, Limited, South Eastern Coalfield Extension, Limited, Extended Extension, Limited, Deal & Walmer Coalfield, Limited.

Gentlemen,—In accordance with your instructions we have examined the scheme for the acquisition of the mineral areas of your companies on a leasehold basis. The scheme is framed upon formulæ prepared by Professor Galloway and Mr. J. L. Strain, the acreages forming the basis of which have been verified by Messrs. Worsfold & Hayward and Messrs. Thornton, Murray & Thornton.

In this connection we found that the Kent Coal Concessions, Limited, had incurred exceptional expenditure, the benefit of which will accrue to the new company. In our opinion it is equitable that a special sum should be allocated to the Kent Coal Concessions, Limited, in respect thereof. We have set aside accordingly a sum equal to 10 per cent. of the total purchase price payable to the four companies to be contributed by the three other companies *pro rata*.

After making provision for this in our calculations, and after apportioning the interests of the three companies in the properties purchased on joint account in accordance with the agreement defining the same, and making adjustments in respect of sales of areas prior to March 31, 1913, we certify that a purchase consideration of 800,000 shares and £100,000 in cash in the terms of the draft contracts submitted to us, should be allocated among the companies as follows :—

	Shares.	Cash.
To Kent Coal Concessions, Ltd. ..	517,743	£64,718
To South Eastern Coalfield Extension, Ltd.	145,963	18,245
To Extended Extension, Ltd. ..	95,552	11,944
To Deal and Walmer Coalfield, Ltd.	40,742	5,093
	800,000	£100,000

We further certify that after apportioning the interest of the Companies in the freehold mineral areas in accordance with the formulæ and taking into consideration the freehold properties on the basis of a valuation by Professor Galloway and Mr. J. L. Strain, the sum of £550,000 payable by the New Company (if it exercises its option, referred to in the draft contracts, to purchase such areas intended to be granted by the four Companies) should be allocated among the Companies as follows :—

	£	s.	d.
To Kent Coal Concessions, Ltd.	289,117	11	0
To South Eastern Coalfield Extension, Ltd.	80,996	15	8
To Extended Extension, Ltd.	136,841	13	0
To Deal and Walmer Coalfield, Ltd. ..	43,044	0	4
	£550,000	0	0

We are, yours faithfully,
Crewdson, Youatt & Howard.
W. B. Peat & Co.

A joint extraordinary general meeting of the four Parent Companies was held at the Cannon Street Hotel on October 30, 1913, to approve the draft agreement between themselves and the proposed new Company, based on the above report. Mr. J. Dewrance was in the chair, and in the course of his opening speech, commenting on the sales of areas that had been made to French groups, he said :—

"I believe myself that if to-day the whole Coalfield were put up for auction the greater part

> of it would go into the possession of foreigners, because they appreciate the value of our coalfield a very great deal more than our fellow-countrymen do, and I think that is rather a pity. . . . When we get the new board settled, as I hope we shall, with an honest intention to bring the finances and the arrangements of the different Companies into the most satisfactory condition—according to the wishes of the newspapers and the Stock Exchange if you like—then I say we shall be able to get that enormous sum of money which will be required to thoroughly develop the great Kent Coalfield."

Particulars of the proposed new company were then given by Mr. Burr, who stated that, with a view to keeping the capitalisation down, the sale price to the new company of the mineral areas on a leasehold basis was a purely arbitrary one. The consideration was to be £100,000 in cash and £800,000 in shares, and the new company was to have the option of acquiring the freehold minerals for a further sum of £550,000.

The directors of the proposed new company included Sir Henry McCallum, formerly Governor of Ceylon, Sir Arthur Yorke, director of the South-Eastern Railway Company, Mr. Charles E. Allan, whose name had appeared on the prospectus of the ill-fated United Coalfields of Kent, Ltd., Professor W. Galloway, who, Mr. Burr stated, was joining the board at the request of Lord Merthyr, Lieut.-Colonel R. H. F. Standen, who was described as a very old shareholder and a great enthusiast, and Dr. Malcolm Burr.

The resolution, with some unimportant modifications, was unanimously adopted by the shareholders of the several companies concerned. Thus another forward step had been taken towards putting the Kent Coal enterprise on a proper businesslike footing. But the end was not yet!

Under the date " Christmas, 1913," Mr. Burr issued another circular to the whole body of shareholders, which ran into no less than sixteen quarto pages, half of which were devoted to explaining the delay in bringing out the new company, and the remainder to a general review of the position of the subsidiary undertakings. Referring to the Cannon

Street Hotel meeting of October 30, Mr. Burr wrote :—

"I was in hopes that before this date effect would have been given to the resolutions then passed, and that the reins of administration would have passed out of my hands. I entertained dreams of wintering abroad, with an easy mind as to your interests, but no question of health or work will ever induce me to make those interests anything but my first consideration. . . . But the long delay, for which the holidays were mainly responsible, gave time for our enemies, including certain evening and financial newspapers, to circulate their anonymous and systematic attacks and misrepresentations, which, if not greatly influencing the minds of shareholders as a body, most certainly misled the general public."

As a matter of fact, during the preceding two months negotiations had been carried on with a well-known Stock Exchange firm for the sale of the whole of the Companies' undeveloped areas. These progressed to the point of embodiment in a draft agreement which had been approved by the boards of all the companies concerned on November 19, at Folkestone, where Mr. Burr resided. This arrangement was submitted also to the proposed board of the proposed new amalgamated company, by whom it was approved.

The procedure was somewhat Gilbertian—here were directors who were not directors performing administrative acts on behalf of a company that was not a company.

The first hint that any such negotiations were in progress was given by Lord Winchester, when presiding at a general meeting of New Rhodesian Mines, Ltd., which company, he claimed, was an interested party. This reference Mr. Burr considered to be ill-timed, but he felt that it was now incumbent upon him to issue some statement to his shareholders with respect to what was going on behind the scenes; hence the "Christmas, 1913" circular, from which I have just been quoting. Like the "Big Four" at the Peace Conference, Mr. Burr pleaded to be allowed to continue the negotiations free from the necessity of prematurely disclosing provisional and incomplete terms. Again I quote his own somewhat flamboyant language :—

"I am pledged to silence until every detail is agreed. Powerful influences are at work to spoil my work and destroy arrangements that will, if left alone, provide all the capital our Coalfield will ever require and settle our enemies once and for all. No important business negotiations can be conducted in the limelight."

The chief stumbling-block in all the varied negotiations that had been initiated with the object of placing the Concessions group on a sound commercial footing was the question of "control." If the presiding genius had been as willing to resign the cares of office as he so repeatedly professed himself to be, there is little doubt, in my mind, that the money so essential for the consolidation of the pioneer work would have been forthcoming. But the financiers who were willing to pay the piper quite naturally insisted upon calling the tune. Hence, although this year (1913) opened with brave promises for the future of the enterprise, promises, too, that expanded into a certain measure of fulfilment, advantage was not taken of the favouring conditions. The close of the year, consequently, found the whole undertaking suffering from the blight that so inevitably follows in the wake of neglected opportunities.

I must record the fact that in 1913 there were also registered two companies on behalf of French capitalists who had acquired colliery areas from Concessions. The first was entitled the

ADISHAM COLLIERY COMPANY, LTD.

(Registered as a private company June 23, 1913.)
Capital.—£120,000 in 24,000 shares of £5 each.
Directors.—Messrs. Jules Bernard & Arthur Capel, Sir Frederick Harrison, and Comte François de Beauchamp. The last-named gentleman was a young French engineer who had frequently visited the Coalfield. Those who had the pleasure of meeting him have learnt with great regret that he has since given his life "pour la patrie."

The Company was formed to take over and develop a mineral area adjoining Snowdown Colliery, for which an option had been granted to Monsieur Jules Bernard, but it has not yet commenced active operations.

The other company was entitled the

STONEHALL COLLIERY COMPANY, LTD.

(Registered July 9th, 1913.)

Capital.—£120,000 in 24,000 shares of £5 each.

The directors of the Adisham Colliery also constitute the board of the Stonehall Company, which was formed to acquire a colliery area from Kent Coal Concessions, at Lydden, some four miles out of Dover. The Concessions Company had expended about £25,000 upon surface buildings and equipment, but had not actually commenced sinking. The colliery site is connected by a siding with the South-Eastern & Chatham main line. The purchase consideration was £75,000 and half the profits after payment of a 10 per cent. dividend on the share capital, the Stonehall Company having the right to commute this half-share of profits upon payment of a lump sum of £75,000.

The purchasing company commenced sinking only a few months before the outbreak of war, since when all work has been suspended. There is a peculiar interest attaching to this sinking, and its future progress will be keenly watched, for the Stonehall boring, which was put down about 500 yards from the site of the pits, disclosed a most extraordinarily rich series of seams. The section is the more difficult to understand, inasmuch as there is no possibility of correlating with the seams in the Brady, Waldershare, and Chilton borings, which are within 4, 1¾, and 1¼ miles respectively.

Boring left off in Sandstone, with coal veins, at 3,691 ft.

Without taking into consideration anything below 2 ft., this section shows an aggregate of 112 ft. 11 in. of coal in eighteen seams, their average thickness being 6 ft. 3 in.

It is a wise proverb that tells us not to look a gift horse in the mouth, but it is difficult not to view askance this abnormal richness of coal, nor to distrust Nature's apparent lavishness in this instance. To account for it, one suggestion is that there must be one or more overthrow faults, and that several

Section of Stonehall Boring, O.D. 221.

	Ft.	in.		
Chalk	550	0		
Gault	165	0		
Wealden	121	0		
Oolites	454	0		Ft.
Coal Measures and	1	0	of coal at	1,291
Sandstone and Bind	216	0		
Coal seam	4	4	,,	1,508
Sandstone and Bind	334	0		
Coal seam	1	0	,,	1,842
Bind	76	0		
Coal seam	6	2	,,	1,918
Bind and Sandstone	140	0		
Coal seam	3	2	,,	2,058
Sandstone and Bind	56	0		
Coal seam	5	2	,,	2,114
Sandstone and Bind	95	0		
Coal seam	4	2	,,	2,209
Bind	82	0		
Coal seam	6	6	,,	2,291
Sandstone and Bind	115	0		
Coal seam	6	3	,,	2,406
Sandstone and Bind	248	0		
Coal seam	1	4	of coal at	2,684
Bind and Sandstone	105	0		
Coal seam	7	2	,,	2,789
Binds, Sandstone and Coal veins	196	0		
Coal seam	7	2	,,	2,985
Sandstone, Bind and Coal veins	94	0		
Coal seam	4	1	,,	3,079
Bind	16	0		
Coal seam	5	8	,,	3,094
Sandstone and Bind	98	0		
Coal seam	6	4	,,	3,192
Sandstone	48	0		
Coal seam	6	4	,,	3,240
Bind	33	0		
Coal seam	7	10	,,	3,273
Sandstone and Bind	70	0		
Coal seam	8	3	,,	3,343
Bind and Sandstone	62	0		
Coal seam	6	9	,,	3,405
Sandstone and Bind	148	0		
Coal seam	8	7	,,	3,553
Bind	102	0		
Coal seam	9	0	,,	3,655

of the seams have been bored through more than once. Such an explanation does not satisfy me altogether, for nowhere in the Field have any such disturbances been met with, and the other borings in the immediate neighbourhood give no confirmation to this theory. With a view to checking the original section, the Colliery Company started another hole about 200 yards away, which had just entered the topmost seams when work had to be suspended owing to the war. The borehole, however, has been carefully lined, and there will be no difficulty in continuing the exploration whenever the Company so desires.

Kent Coal Concessions, Ltd., and its allied Companies, having monopolised practically all available areas within the, so far, proven Coalfield, newcomers had perforce to seek for minerals in the only possible direction open to them. Hence the appearance on the scene of the

WHITSTABLE AND CANTERBURY COALFIELD, LTD.

(Registered July 8, 1913.)

Capital.—£40,125 in 40,000 ordinary shares of £1 each, and 2,500 deferred shares of 1s. each, of which all the deferred and about 12,000 of the ordinary shares have been issued. The ordinaries take all the profits until their capital has been repaid, after which each class of share is entitled to half the divisible profits.

Directors.—Messrs. Archibald Grove (chairman), Sydney Brown, W. R. Elgar, A. Farquhar, A. Woolley-Hart, and the Hon. R. James.

The Company was formed for the purpose of acquiring options over lands containing coal and other minerals.

A boring was put down at Harmansole (Lower Hardres) three miles to the south-west of Canterbury, and the same distance to the west of the Dover-Canterbury main road. Those who had knowledge of the many previous borings in this locality, which had proved failures, were not surprised to learn that another negative result had been obtained. Accordingly, in August, 1914, the directors issued the following statement to their share-

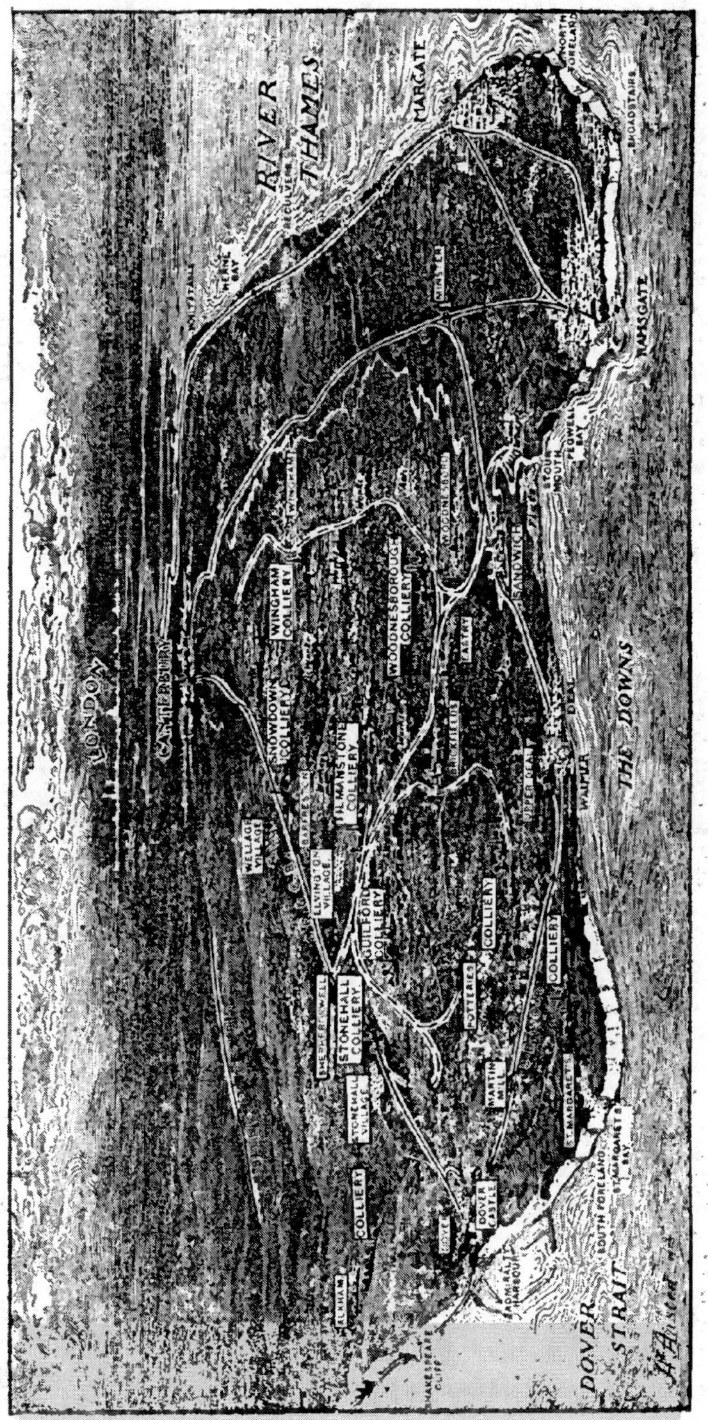

An "Aeroplane" View of the Kent Coalfield; by Alexander Ansted.

holders—it is rather a fearsome specimen of English composition, but I quote it as reproduced in the "Joint Stock Companies Journal" of August 19, 1914:—

> "It is with no little disappointment that the directors have to report that the boring at Harmansole has not proved satisfactory. It was carried to a depth of 1,767 ft. from the surface without proving coal. On the contrary, the Measures entered conclusively excluded the possibility of coal being found. The cores were submitted by the Company's engineers for verification to the staff of the Geological Survey, who have, unfortunately, confirmed the opinion formed by them. Of course, this result does not in any way mean that the whole of the Company's area to the south and east of the borehole is barren; and it does not prove anything one way or the other with regard to the area to the north. The board have fortunately been able to make arrangements with our neighbours by which the borehole will be put down to the north of Canterbury at a great saving of expense, and this work will be proceeded with as rapidly as present conditions will permit."

The site selected for the proposed boring to the north of Canterbury is at Tyler's Hill, on land held jointly with the North Kent Coalfield, Ltd. This work will probably be proceeded with now that the war is over, and it is likely that some coal seams will be discovered. It is improbable, however, that any large area of minerals will be found to exist, for all the borings in the direction of Canterbury indicate that the Coal Basin is running out to a point—exactly in the same manner as does that of the Pas de Calais.

CHAPTER XXIV.

A Financial Crisis. War brings relief. Shareholders taking Alarm. Committee of Control formed. Mr. Burr's retirement. Directors appointed. £100,000 required to carry on. Deep sinking at Snowdown. Mr. Dewrance on Amalgamation. Concessions' Assets and Liabilities. Housing. Shipping.

"Something is rotten in the State of Denmark."
—HAMLET.

1914-1919.

The early months of 1914 were occupied with the Stock Exchange group, who proposed to acquire the undeveloped areas of all the Parent Companies. There were various obstacles to be surmounted before this latest scheme could be brought to fruition; not only were there details of a personal nature to be agreed, but it was highly desirable—if, indeed, not absolutely essential—that provision should be made for the redemption of the outstanding debentures. Meanwhile the financial position of Concessions was steadily growing worse, and yet another grandiose scheme for raising the wind failed to materialise.

When dealing with the affairs of the Guilford Syndicate I showed how completely its interests had been sacrificed, and how a large slice of Concessions minerals was also involved. The only possible explanation for this transaction is that the management must have realised that a financial crisis was impending. It was hoped, apparently, that the £60,000 deposit, payable on the signing of the contract with the Forges de Chatillon, would enable the critical situation to be tided over. Had the war not intervened to hold up this payment some temporary relief would certainly have been secured, but, at best, the threatened *débâcle* would have been merely postponed for a few months.

As events proved, this Guilford-Concessions joint transaction had the effect of opening the eyes of some of the more important shareholders, to whom it appeared as the red light betokening danger ahead. Taking alarm, they held conferences and decided to invite Mr. Burr to meet them privately and give an account of his stewardship. A meeting, accordingly, took place at Folkestone towards the end of May, and resulted in the formation of an advisory committee, who agreed to advance £30,000 for the general purposes of the undertaking, as a measure of temporary relief, to enable immediate and pressing demands to be satisfied. A condition was that Mr. Burr should undertake not to dispose of any more of the companies' property nor to enter into any business engagements without first obtaining the sanction of the committee. They further insisted that, as soon as the necessary legal formalities could be completed, both Mr. Burr and his son, Dr. Malcolm Burr, should resign their managerial and administrative positions, and that the other members of Concessions' board should also retire.

The first of the series of extraordinary general meetings to amend the Articles of Association was held on August 7, 1914, when the committee—Messrs. John Dewrance, Stuart Greig, Lieut.-Col. J. P. Dalison, William P. Studholme, G. N. Scarfe, and the Earl of Darnley—were elected directors of Kent Coal Concessions, Ltd., without fees. The same procedure was adopted in respect of the South-Eastern Coalfield Extension, Limited, Extended Extension, Limited, Deal and Walmer Coalfield, Limited, and the East Kent Contract and Financial Company, Limited.

It has been suggested that the troubles of the Parent Companies would have been successfully surmounted but for the outbreak of war. The exact contrary, however, is the fact. The moratorium was the one and only thing that could have saved them from passing into the hands of a receiver for the debenture-holders.

Upon examination it became apparent to the new board that the various companies were not only unable to pay their creditors, but were without funds for carrying on their business. Consequently they submitted a scheme of arrangement to the shareholders on October 27, which was as follows:—

"(1) The companies' landlords, or most of them, should forego their dead rents during the war and three months thereafter, or until his Majesty should by Order in Council determine the operation of the Courts (Emergency) Powers Act, 1914, or limit its effect.

"(2) The debenture-holders of the various companies should agree to postpone their claims during the war and six months thereafter.

"(3) The unsecured creditors of over £100 each should bind themselves by a scheme of arrangement to postpone their claims during the war and six months thereafter.

"(4) The unsecured creditors of under £100 each should be paid in full.

"(5) The sum of £100,000 should be raised by the joint and several bonds of Kent Coal Concessions, Limited, South-Eastern Coalfield Extension, Limited, Extended Extension, Limited, and Deal and Walmer Coalfield, Limited, bearing interest at 6 per cent. per annum, redeemable at a premium of 25 per cent. in cash six months after the conclusion of the war."

The board advised the shareholders in a circular dated January 20, 1915, that—

"It is intended to spend this money in sinking one of the shafts at Snowdown to the seams below that known as the 'Snowdown Hard' (this, it is estimated, will cost £40,000 and occupy nine to 12 months), in administration expenses, maintainence of railway, completing existing contracts for the acquisition of certain mineral rights, in respect of which large sums have already been paid, and generally for the purposes of the above Companies."

The directors, being anxious that the necessity for raising this £100,000 should be clearly appreciated, called a combined meeting of shareholders in the Concessions group of companies, which was held at the Cannon Street Hotel, London, on January 28, 1915.

Mr. J. Dewrance, who presided, stated that Mr. Maurice Deacon (the eminent colliery engineer) was of opinion that if the proposed deep shaft at Snowdown confirmed the accuracy of the boring records, it would establish the existence of 1,400,000,000 tons of coal within their boundaries. Mr. Dewrance also made it clear that had it not been for the action of himself and his colleagues in May, 1914, the Companies would have gone into bankruptcy; now that another emergency had arisen he impressed upon the shareholders that they must come forward and do their share, and that if they could not—or would not—then, Mr. Dewrance said, "You have got to efface yourselves, and you have got to stand aside for others who are waiting until you do so, and then they will come in and make the fortune that rightly belongs to you."

Resolutions approving the programme of the directors were passed unanimously at this meeting, and in due course the bonds were issued. Although only £90,000 was subscribed, the Court sanctioned the directors' scheme, which was at once put into operation.

I have already given the results of the deep sinking in question when dealing with the affairs of the Snowdown Colliery, Limited. The seams of the Barfrestone boring were met with at their expected depths in the shaft, which terminated with the cutting of a very fine 4 ft. 5 in. seam of coal at 3,000 ft. Thus any latent doubts respecting the reliability of the boring sections were entirely removed.

At the time the new directors took up their burden the Amalgamation scheme was still in the evolutionary stage, and in the already quoted circular, which covered application forms in respect of the £100,000 bond issue, the directors stated:—

> "In making the necessary financial arrangements for the development of the field we will use our best endeavours to secure an allotment of shares in the new Amalgamation Company on the best terms we can arrange for those subscribers of the present issue who may wish to exchange their bonds.
>
> "It is impossible to set out the details of this exchange without committing ourselves to an extent that would hamper future negotiations. Moreover, the terms and the conditions of the

MINERS' COTTAGES AT WOLLAGE VILLAGE, NEAR SNOWDOWN COLLIERY.

new Company would manifestly be influenced by the results obtained from the sinking of the shaft at Snowdown."

Nothing further was heard about this Amalgamation scheme until the question was raised by a shareholder at the general meeting of the Deal and Walmer Coalfield, Limited, held at the Cannon Street Hotel, London, on February 26, 1917. Mr. J. Dewrance, speaking from the chair, is reported to have replied thus:—

"He thought the best arrangement would be to sell to a new company. To work the field £1,000,000 to £2,000,000 of actual cash would be required. Probably the new company would offer to existing companies so much in its shares and so much in cash as purchase consideration, which it would be the duty of the directors to apportion among the selling Companies. They had been working on the proportions laid down by the old administration and accepted at a very large meeting of shareholders. Having made this apportionment, the directors would go to the shareholders of each of the Companies concerned, saying: 'This is your proportion of the purchase consideration in shares and cash. Will you accept it or not?' He did not think there was any real ground for revising the apportionment accepted by the shareholders, and it was the basis upon which the expenses were being apportioned."

In response to other questions Mr. Dewrance dealt at greater length with the Amalgamation scheme, and shareholders desirous of obtaining further information may be referred to the "Joint Stock Companies' Journal" of February 28, 1917, in which his speech is fully reported.

When dealing with the affairs of the other Parent Companies I have referred to the option granted to Messrs. Schneider et Cie., in which Concessions naturally included such of its minerals as were suitably situated. I have also reproduced the official statement of the assets and liabilities of those companies, and I now subjoin similar particulars regarding Kent Coal Concessions, Limited, given at a meeting of shareholders at the Cannon Street Hotel, London, on July 10, 1918:—

Assets.

	£
1341 acres of freehold minerals at £40 ..	53,640
5619 acres of leasehold minerals at £21 ..	147,499
Miners' Villages (Cost £50,000.)	30,000
Interest in properties purchased by all the Parent Companies on joint account ...	63,667
Income bonds in East Kent Colliery, Ltd. ..	11,000
Prior lien bonds in Snowdown Colliery, Ltd.	9,250
Castle Hill House and furniture	2,500
Consideration for Stonehall area	125,000
Do. for area sold to Forges de Chatillon ..	50,000
Amounts owing by Allied Companies ..	15,700
Sundry Debtors, etc.	3,827
Shares in Allied Companies	1,100
	£513,183

Liabilities.

	£
Debentures	149,955
Accrued interest	51,253
Premium on redemption	30,000
Sundry creditors	31,680
Amounts due to Allied Companies	61,544
East Kent Contract Company, mortgage and interest	33,000
Proportion of bonds issued on joint account and interest	51,750
Premium on redemption of these bonds ..	11,250
Advances against security	8,718
5 Years' interest on Cumulative preference shares	15,000
	£444,150
Surplus of assets	69,033
	£513,183

Amongst the above assets is an item of £30,000 for miners' villages, which sum is certainly an under-valuation, as they cost over £50,000 in pre-war days.

HOUSING.

It was early appreciated that if the better type of miner was to be attracted to Kent, a good class of house would have to be provided. It was realised, also, that if the rental yield should prove inadequate, the producing companies could well afford to make up any deficiency, and that, in fact, it would be sound policy for them to do so.

A large building scheme was, therefore, projected, and a start was made, even before the coal had been reached, in order to provide for the prospective requirements of the Snowdown, Tilmanstone, Stonehall, and Guilford collieries. There have been constructed, so far, twenty-five cottages and an Institute to serve Tilmanstone, twenty-four cottages to serve Snowdown, and forty-nine cottages to serve Guilford and Stonehall.

The accompanying illustration shows that due regard has been given to external appearances, while the arrangement of the interior accommodation has received no less attention. The cottages are not all of the same type architecturally, but all are equally artistic, and the following particulars and dimensions of the rooms are typical :—

Ground Floor—

Living room ...	13 ft. × 11 ft.	
Parlour ...	12 ft. × 11 ft.	
Scullery ...	11 ft. × 7 ft.,	with cooking range, copper, and sink.
Yard		
Larder.		
Coalshed, etc.		

First floor—

Bedroom ...	12 ft. × 11 ft.	
,, ...	11 ft. × 9 ft.	
,, ...	11 ft. × 10 ft. 6 in.	
Bathroom ...	7 ft. × 5 ft. 5 in.,	with hot and cold supply.

The housing question, so prominent in all parts of the country, is particularly acute in Kent, and the lack of money that restricted the building of miners' cottages before the war is responsible for much of the delay in the development of the Coalfield. Unless, in the near future, suitable dwellings for colliery workers are provided, not in tens or hundreds, but in thousands, it will not be possible for the Field to produce the annual tonnage that might, within a few years, be brought to bank. The potential riches of East Kent would thus remain dormant for the benefit of another generation.

The East Kent Colliery Company have recently put up a dozen concrete houses for their workers, but these are a veritable drop in the ocean compared with their requirements.

The Chislet Company has leased, as a temporary measure, a number of houses at Ramsgate. They are, however, taking steps to make provision for their men nearer to the colliery.

Where the Guilford colliers will be housed when that colliery enters upon the producing stage, it is difficult to see, unless that Company also sets to work on a building programme of its own.

Any scheme within the scope of the powers recently conferred upon local authorities will be hopelessly inadequate for the requirements of the mining community. At best such schemes can but serve the necessities of those who will follow in the wake of Kent Coal developments. It is, therefore, incumbent upon the colliery owners to make provision for their own workers.

SHIPPING FACILITIES.

To anyone having practical knowledge of the capacity of the lines serving the Kent Coalfield it is obvious that without a large amount of capital expenditure the railways cannot successfully handle anything like the prospective output.

From its proximity to the Continent there should grow up in Kent a large export trade, and here again the Field is likely to be seriously handicapped owing to the absence of suitable harbours on its coasts.

Dover.—The Admiralty has a strangle-hold on Dover, and has ever been obstructive towards the commercial usage of the port. Moreover, Dover Harbour is physically unsuited for dealing with anything approaching the tonnage that is shipped from such ports as, say, Cardiff or Hull. The approaches to the town are by way of a series of tunnels, and, further, the line runs along a valley the contours of which preclude the provision in this direction of the extensive siding accommodation which is a *sine qua non* for a coal exporting port.

An attempt was made a year or two before the war, by the Dover Harbour Board and the South-Eastern & Chatham Railway Company, to improve the inner Harbour so that a certain amount of export trade could be done. The scheme involved the taking in of some of the foreshore, and the inhabitants of the town, at the instigation of the leading local paper, offered such factious opposition that it was abandoned. It is patent to the unprejudiced observer that the townsfolk eventually must be the sufferers if this short-sighted policy is maintained.

Another effort is about to be made by the Harbour Board and the South-Eastern Railway, in conjunction with Lord Cowdray, to create a commercial port. This scheme is on much more ambitious lines than its predecessor, and Parliamentary powers are being sought in the present session to give effect to it. Probably the local Municipal Council will take a more common-sense view of these proposals than they did of the last. At any rate, it is to be hoped that the townspeople will not again be misled into opposing an undertaking that cannot fail to materially increase the prosperity of Dover. Otherwise the shipping trade that might, and should, be theirs will pass them by to the enrichment of one, or other, of the neighbouring towns.

Sandwich, on the same coast, is well situated so far as proximity to the Coalfield is concerned, but it is incapable of any but a small type of barge.

Richborough.—During the war the Government spent a great deal of money in creating harbour facilities at Richborough, two miles nearer the outlet of the Stour than Sandwich, but even here the draught of vessels is restricted to something between 10 and 12 ft. Moreover, the channel through Pegwell Bay to deep water has necessitated an expenditure on dredging that the commercial possibilities of the port could not sustain. Under the most favourable conditions a very limited barge traffic is all that can be looked for at this point.

Deal possesses nothing at all in the shape of a harbour, and, although lying under the lee of the Goodwin Sands, which give a certain protection from the northerly gales, yet anyone who has seen the waves breaking over the sea-front will realise that it would take a very large sum of money to create a port. A scheme has, however, been mooted for making inland docks on the site of the golf-links, similar to those constructed at Immingham. This is an ambitious plan which could be profitable only when the production of the Field has attained very large dimensions.

Whitstable.—Several thousand tons of coal have been exported to France in small sailing barges from this port, but there are no facilities whatever for loading, and at present it takes about two days to despatch a 150-ton vessel. A moderate expenditure would provide for a small export or coastal trade from here, but the local conditions are such as to make it impossible that anything worthy of the title of "port" could be established.

Faversham.—From Faversham Creek also a certain amount of coal has been shipped to France in small sailing barges. The conditions here could easily be improved and a much larger tonnage dealt with, but under even the most favourable circumstances the quantity, in relation to the product of the Field, would be negligible.

Queenborough.—This is the only locality where existing conditions could be readily adapted for an extensive overseas trade. At the present time vessels drawing 16 ft. of water can be loaded alongside the wharf, but the port is capable of being developed to deal with an almost unlimited amount of export coal. The greatest—if not the only—objection that can be urged against Queenborough as the chief outlet for Kent Coal is its distance from the collieries. If, however, the Coalfield is rapidly and systematically developed, it is quite reasonable to anticipate that a direct line might be constructed for the mineral traffic.

Birchington.—With a view to securing a harbour easy of access from the centre of the Coalfield, a scheme has been under serious consideration for the construction of a jetty in the open-sea between Birchington and Reculver. It is claimed by the competent engineers who are responsible for the proposal that there is a possible site where the protection offered by sandbanks would enable sea-going vessels to load at all seasons of the year.

Shipping facilities are essential if the Field is to advance in importance; not only is the export trade to be provided for, but the very large London market must be taken into consideration.

While a substantial tonnage might be carried by rail, particularly when a good household coal is being raised, an extensive barge traffic will be necessary in order to supply the manufacturing establishments on the banks of the Thames with slack. All these works are already equipped for taking their supplies from small vessels and barges, and the large quantities they require should ultimately be drawn from Kent.

CHAPTER XXV.

Borings by Channel Collieries Trust. No workable coal found. Geological records enriched. Later Borings of the Concessions Group. The "Ash" boring yields good seams.

"He gets knowledge cheaply who gets it at another's expense."

—PLAUTUS.

The Channel Collieries Trust, Ltd., which had acquired mining rights over an extensive range of under-sea minerals, commenced work in 1913 on what is known as the

BERE BORING (396 ft. O.D.),

the site of which is on the Deal-Dover road, a little under two miles north-east of Dover, and 1¼ miles from the foreshore at Langdon Bay. The following is an abridged section of this boring :—

	ft.	in.	ft.
Chalk	825	0	
Gault	123	0	
Folkestone and Sandgate beds	62	0	
Atherfield clay	22	0	
Weald clay	35	0	
Hastings beds	7	0	
Corallian	80	0	
Oxford clay	80	0	
Kellaways	23	0	
Cornbrash	18	0	
Forest Marble	10	0	
Great Oolite	67	0	
Coal Measures			at 1,358
Coal seam	2	4	,, 1,701
Coal seam	1	8	,, 1,993
Bottom of borehole ...			,, 3,005

The boring left off in hard Grey Sandstone, containing coal pebbles, and it is somewhat surprising that it was not continued down to the Carboniferous Limestone. At Oxney (135 ft. O.D.), the nearest boring of the Concessions Group, the base of the Coal Measures was reached at 3,742 ft., which equals 3,067 ft. below O.D., whereas boring at Bere was stopped at only 2,609 ft. below O.D. The stretch of unexplored ground in all probability contains the 50 ft. of coal that was proved within the same horizon at Oxney. As there was, I understand, no physical obstacle in the way, it surely would have been wiser, after boring so far, to have continued to the end. Messrs. A. C. Potter & Co. were the contractors, and the work occupied over two and a-half years.

Notwithstanding the lack of success attending the numerous borings put down to the west of the Dover-Canterbury road during the past seventeen years, the Channel Collieries Trust, Ltd., adventured into this unpromising region early in 1914. For reasons best known to themselves, they selected a site so near to that of the Brabourne Boring, which was well known to be outside the limits of the Coalfield, as to reduce the prospect of a successful issue to the vanishing point.

This boring was located alongside the Elham Valley Railway line, close to the station—from which it took its name, and consequently is known as the

ELHAM BORING (275 ft. O.D.).

The chisel having been used down to 1,400 ft., the given thicknesses of the various strata, to that depth, should be regarded as approximate only. From 1,400 ft. to the bottom of the hole, at 2,346 ft., cores were secured. The following is an abridged section :—

	ft.	in.
Chalk	287	0
Gault	116	0
Folkestone and Sandgate beds	130	0
Atherfield clay	30	0
Weald clay	80	0
Hastings beds	73	0
Kimmeridge clay ...	199	0
Corallian	252	0
Oxford clay	130	0

	ft.	in.	ft.
Kellaways, Cornbrash, and Forest Marble ...	68	0	
Oolites	131	0	
Lias	99	0	
Coal Measures			at 1,598
Coal seam	1	8	,, 1,828
,, ,, ...	2	0	,, 1,867
,, ,, ...	3	2	,, 1,920
,, ,, ...	2	8	,, 1,951
,, ,, ...	1	4	,, 2,014
,, ,, ...	1	10	,, 2,155
,, ,, ...	1	6	,, 2,168
,, ,, ...	1	3	,, 2,179
,, ,, ...	1	5	,, 2,207
Carboniferous Limestone			,, 2,289
Bottom of borehole (reached June, 1915)			,, 2,346

Having regard to the thickness of the bad sinking ground, it is not at all probable that any attempt will be made to win the coals of the very poor seams shown above for a great many years to come.

The indifferent results of this boring led the Channel Collieries Trust to make another attempt to discover workable coal. The site selected was some six miles to the south-east of Elham, adjoining the Martello Tower that—since Napoleon's days—has stood sentry on the low cliff overlooking East Wear Bay, a little to the east of Folkestone. It is known as the

FOLKESTONE BORING (113 ft. O.D.).

This borehole, started towards the end of 1915, was carried down to 3,400 ft., at which depth the work was stopped after 1,913 ft. of Coal Measures had been penetrated. The shales in these measures were decidedly more sandy than those at Elham, and there were also some comparatively thick beds of hard grey Quartzose Sandstone, but for all practical purposes the coal itself was non-existent. Here, also, the chisel was employed for the passage of the Secondary Strata, so that the records are none too exact. Sufficient evidence was, however, forthcoming to show that, even if good seams of coal had been met with, the cost of sinking would have been extremely great, if, indeed, not prohibitive. The following is an abridged section of this boring:—

	ft.	in.	ft.
Chalk	85	0	
Folkestone and Sandgate beds	210	0	
Atherfield clay	40	0	
Weald clay	165	0	
Hastings beds	53	0	
Kimmeridge clay ...	210	0	
Corallian	327	0	
Oxford clay	172	0	
Kellaways, Cornbrash, and Forest Marble ...	38	0	
Oolites	113	0	
Lias	112	0	
Coal Measures			at 1,487
Coal seam	2	0	,, 1,676
,, ,, ...	1	2	,, 1,727
,, ,, ...	1	2	,, 2,487
The boring terminated in Coal Measures ...			,, 3,400

Unless the Company was actuated by philanthropic motives, and desired to enrich the records of the Geological Survey at the shareholders' expense, it is difficult to appreciate what inducement prompted them to the expenditure involved in this boring. The evidence as to the thinning of the coal seams, and the thickening of the Secondary Rocks, to the westward of Dover was so strong that I cannot see what justification there was for the work, other than, perhaps, the very laudable desire to add another page to the rapidly accumulating record of the strata of East Kent.

The two following borings, "Ash" and "Bourne," pertain to the Concessions group, and if their relative positions are studied on the map, the sections will be found to confirm much that I have written regarding the contours of the Coal Basin.

THE ASH BORING (25 ft. O.D.).

This boring has been generally known as the "Fleet" Boring, but owing to its being confused with that at Ebbsfleet, it was decided to adopt the name of the neighbouring town of Ash. The boring is situated a little to the east of Richborough Castle, and 1¾ miles south-west of Ebbsfleet, with the exception of which, it is the most northerly exploration in this portion of the Coalfield. Its proximity to the northern confines of the Basin is adduced by the fact that the Carboniferous Limestone was met with at only 1,909 ft. from the surface. The Coal Measures, which are all of the Middle Series, are only 819 ft. in thickness, and although a number of thin seams of no commercial value were met with, yet it will be seen that there are several of nice workable thickness within easy sinking distance. Analyses show all these seams to be of excellent quality, giving every promise of proving highly remunerative to work. The following is an abridged section of the boring:—

	ft.	in.	ft.
Eocene	85	0	
Chalk	753	0	
Gault	157	0	
Lower Greensand ...	36	0	
Wealden	58	0	
Coal Measures			at 1,089
Coal seam	3	1	,, 1,446
,, ,, ...	3	1	,, 1,485
,, ,, ...	4	3	,, 1,515
,, ,, ...	2	2	,, 1,737
,, ,, ...	7	2	,, 1,776
,, ,, ...	2	4	,, 1,844
Carboniferous Limestone			,, 1,909
Bottom of borehole ...			,, 1,966

The Tréfor Company were the contractors, work starting on August 18, 1913, and finishing on December 29, thus averaging 360 ft. per month.

THE BOURNE BORING (176 ft. O.D.).

This boring was put down by the Concessions Company at a site 100 yards to the west of the Canterbury-Dover road, within less than four miles of the Trapham, Fredville, and Ropersole borings. The Coal Measures here show unmistakable evidence of having been affected by faults of some magnitude, and, according to Dr. Arber, this faulting is doubtless due to the proximity of the western boundary of the Field. That the boundary cannot be far removed is indicated by the absence of Coal

Measures, already noted, at the Harmansole boring, which is only three miles to the west of Bourne. The following is an abridged section of this boring:—

	ft.	in.		ft.
Chalk and Gault ...	937	0		
Lower Greensands ...	24	0		
Oolites	327	0		
Lias	25	0		
Coal Measures			at	1,313
Coal seam	2	5	,,	1,383
,, ,, ...	2	7	,,	1,490
,, ,, ...	3	6	,,	1,504
,, ,, ...	2	0	,,	1,834
,, ,, ...	2	3	,,	2,100
,, ,, ...	2	0	,,	2,252
,, ,, ...	2	1	,,	2,637
,, ,, ...	3	1	,,	2,806
,, ,, ...	5	10	,,	2,838
Carboniferous Limestone			,,	3,169
Bottom of borehole ...			,,	3,235

The Coal Measures were penetrated through a thickness of 1,856 ft., in which were a large number of thin bands of coal of no commercial value, in addition to the seams enumerated above. Dr. Arber assigns about the first 800 ft. of these Measures to the Transition Series, and the remainder to the Middle Measures, the evidence being insufficient to more exactly define each horizon.

The results from this boring are far from satisfactory. The 2 ft. 5 in. seam—the first met with—is out of court owing to the fact that it is only 70 ft. below the junction bed, and no mining engineer having acquaintance with this coalfield would, I think, take the responsibility of working under so slight a cover. The next two seams, 2 ft. 7 in. and 3 ft. 6 in., are really one seam with a 10 ft. parting, so far as the available data permits one to judge. This parting will probably increase in thickness and the seams correspondingly diminish westward of the bore hole. Further, while so many thousands of acres of much more valuable minerals are crying out for development, it is not to be expected that the large sums that would be required to exploit the 5 ft. 10 in. seam at 2,838 ft. will be forthcoming. Another factor militating against the profitable working of this area is the fact that the absence of Coal Measures at Harmansole indicates a rapid rise of all the seams at Bourne to the outcrop westward. The borehole being on the extreme eastern boundary of the property there is no coal available in that direction, therefore I am afraid that the shareholders must not look upon the Bourne area as a probable revenue producer. In fact, the conditions here do but confirm my previously expressed conviction that west of the Canterbury-Dover road there is no coal of commercial value under present-day working conditions.

THE CHILTON BORING (150 ft. O.D.).

This boring, which was initiated by Mr. Arthur Burr, in conjunction with the Canterbury Coal Co., Ltd., was completed in 1913. The site is on the Alkham-Folkestone road, a mile west of the Dover-Canterbury road, and $1\frac{1}{4}$ miles south by east of the Stonehall boring. The results do little more than add to the difficulty of resolving the underground structure of the Coalfield in this neighbourhood. They do, however, furnish still further evidence as to the poverty of the Coal Measures in the direction of the south-western boundary of the Field. The following is an abridged section of the boring:—

	ft.	in.		ft.
Chalk and Gault ...	400	0		
Lower Greensands ...	128	0		
Wealden	289	0		
Oolites	424	0		
Lias	19	0		
Coal Measures			at	1,260
Coal seam	2	8	,,	1,295
Coal seam (with 2 partings)	4	8	,,	2,411
Coal seam (with 1 parting)	3	0	,,	2,918
Coal seam	3	8	,,	3,018
Coal seam	2	1	,,	3,184
Boring terminated in Sandstone			,,	3,348

There are no fewer than seven bands of coal from 8 in. to 1 ft. in thickness between 2,858 ft. and the bottom of the hole. The boring penetrated 2,077 ft. of Coal Measures, the whole of which pertain to the Transition Series. A great deal of faulted ground was passed through, and the seams proved offer no inducement for the sinking of a colliery in the vicinity.

Boring was begun on August 22, 1912, and finished on June 19, 1913. The contractors were the Internationale Bohrgesellschaft; their rate of progress—334 ft. per month—was satisfactory; but their records of the Secondary Rocks were not such as to justify any great reliance being placed on the figures I have given of their respective thicknesses.

CHAPTER XXVI.

A concealed coalfield. Waldershare boring proves its extension. Similar explorations in Yorkshire. The inertia of coal magnates. Schedule of Analyses.

"Melt and dispel, ye spectre doubts."—CAMPBELL.

We have seen that in 1891 the Brady boring under Shakespeare Cliff proved that there was a concealed coalfield in Kent, and that it was not until 1906 that its extent and value were confirmed by the successful results at Waldershare.

The concealed coalfield of Kent, however, is not the only one that was permitted to lie fallow for years after geologists of authority had prognosticated that exploration might become the parent of exploitation. A similar state of things obtained in Yorkshire, where, after the South Carr boring had proved the Barnsley seam, 4 ft. 7 in. thick at 3,181 ft., in 1893, eleven years elapsed before this pioneer work was followed up on practical lines. It was not until 1906, when the Thorne boring also proved this celebrated seam (9 ft. thick at 2,754 ft.), that active development of the extension of the Coalfield really started.

It cannot be successfully maintained, therefore, that in these instances the magnates of the coal industry exhibited to any marked degree that spirit of private enterprise upon which so much stress was laid during the recent Coal Inquiry before Mr. Justice Sankey. Indeed, so far as concerns Kent, they had no part nor lot in its discovery, nor, until quite recently, in its development. It is a fact, and one that has aroused considerable adverse comment, that, notwithstanding all that has been written on the subject of Kent Coal during the past twenty years, the majority of these "coal kings" remain lamentably uninformed on all matters concerning the Kentish Field. The chief recognition of the potentialities of East Kent came from the representatives of the coal industry in France, under whose control the greater part of the Coalfield bids fair to pass.

The accompanying schedule of analyses of the principal seams proved by the Concessions group (the correlation of which has not yet been possible), deserves careful study. The disappointment consequent upon the seams now being worked at Snowdown and Tilmanstone not having proved good household coal, owing to their friability, has led to much and very widespread misconception as to the intrinsic values of the Kentish coals. The schedule should, however, convince even the most sceptical of critics that there are seams in Kent of quality equal to the best in the kingdom. It is to be hoped that the realisation of this fact may conduce to their early exploitation by our own people.

Kent Coal Concessions, Limited, and Allied Companies. Schedule of Analyses of Seams of 3 ft. and upwards in order of Carbon Contents.

Boring.	Thickness of Seam.	Depth.	Volatile matter.	Carbon.	Sulphur.	Ash.	Evaporative power.	Class of coal.
	Ft. ins.	ft.	%	%	%	%	%	
Ripple	10 0	2761	10.71	84.26	0.63	4.40	15.56	Steam
Oxney	9 0	3271	10.02	83.91	0.82	5.25	15.21	Smokeless Navigation Steam
Do.	7 10	3376	10.23	83.50	0.77	5.50	15.23	Smokeless Navigation Steam
Do.	6 6	2613	13.71	83.20	0.99	2.10	15.25	Smokeless Navigation Steam
Maydensole	5 9	3626	11.25	83.17	0.73	4.85	15.32	Steam
Oxney	5 7	2431	13.97	82.32	1.03	2.68	15.06	Navigation Steam
Woodnesborough ...	4 0	2242	14.01	82.21	0.90	2.88	14.92	Steam
Ripple	8 0	2873	10.70	82.03	0.64	6.63	15.05	Steam
Oxney	11 4	3195	10.81	81.50	0.93	6.76	14.88	Smokeless Navigation Steam
Ripple	4 8	2698	13.48	81.23	0.69	4.60	15.30	Steam
Maydensole	4 9	3569	13.54	81.17	0.88	4.41	15.15	Steam
Ripple	6 10	2177	13.62	81.13	0.89	4.36	14.94	Steam
Do.	4 0	2405	14.25	80.96	1.34	3.45	15.34	Steam and general heating
Barfreston	9 6	3318	15.95	80.63	0.50	2.92	15.18	Steam

Goodnestone ...	4	6	2827	16.30	80.31	0.56	2.83	15.34	Navigation steam
Maydensole	7	6	3721	12.86	79.84	0.85	6.45	15.04	Steam
Goodnestone ...	7	10	2881	15.83	79.33	0.79	4.05	14.75	Steam
Maydensole	4	1	3097	14.72	79.33	1.83	4.12	15.02	Navigation Steam
Mattice Hill	3	5	1629	14.96	79.30	0.55	5.19	15.11	Steam
Trapham	3	5	2315	18.01	79.16	0.71	2.12	15.28	Navigation steam
Stonehall	9	0	3655	15.64	78.77	0.76	4.83	14.89	Steam and house
Maydensole	4	4	2979	17.08	78.66	1.13	3.13	15.23	Steam and house
Barfreston	8	3	2754	18.28	78.65	1.02	2.05	15.72	Steam and general heating
Maydensole	4	6	2862	16.30	78.50	0.70	4.50	14.93	Steam
Oxney	4	9	3392	15.51	78.44	0.66	5.33	15.34	Smokeless navigation steam
Goodnestone ...	3	6	2642	17.35	78.41	0.78	3.46	15.36	Smokeless navigation steam
Barfreston	4	7	2939	19.02	78.10	0.89	1.99	15.41	Steam and house
Goodnestone ...	6	7	2802	18.38	77.97	0.64	3.01	15.78	Steam and house
Ripple	6	2	2062	16.61	77.87	0.77	4.75	14.81	Steam and furnace
Mattice Hill	2	10	1541	16.82	77.87	0.92	4.39	15.38	Smokeless navigation steam
Woodnesborough ...	6	7	2294	16.30	77.68	0.82	5.20	14.84	Steam
Maydensole	6	8	3235	15.19	77.51	1.25	6.05	14.95	Navigation steam
Barfreston	4	0	3260	15.47	77.22	0.65	6.66	14.64	Steam
Stonehall	7	2	2790	19.98	77.22	0.80	2.00	15.54	Steam and house
Goodnestone ...	3	9	2426	20.46	77.21	0.78	1.55	16.03	House and steam
Do.	4	6	2353	18.48	76.14	2.32	3.06	14.85	Steam, house, general heating
Trapham	3	5	2541	19.79	75.91	0.85	3.45	14.82	Steam and house
Woodnesborough ...	3	6	1901	21.24	75.78	1.12	1.86	15.24	Navigation, Steam, house and general
Trapham	4	1	2635	20.79	75.06	0.85	3.30	14.91	Steam and house

Boring.	Thickness of Seam. Ft.	ins.	Depth.	Volatile matter.	Carbon.	Sulphur.	Ash.	Evaporative power.	Class of coal.
	Ft.	ins.	ft.	%	%	%	%	%	
Stonehall	8	7	3554	19.39	74.74	1.05	4.82	14.92	Steam, house, general heating
Woodnesbrough ...	2	3	1606	24.22	72.65	.67	2.46	15.48	Steam, house, general heating
Barfreston	2	9	1365	22.70	72.46	1.57	3.33	15.48	Steam and house
Walmestone	6	3	1948	21.04	72.30	0.86	5.80	14.47	Steam and house
Barfreston	4	11	2197	22.81	72.27	1.40	3.52	15.42	Steam and house
Walmestone	7	2	1978	22.81	72.13	0.70	4.36	14.78	Steam and house
Stonehall	6	4	3240	20.60	72.11	1.15	6.14	14.56	Steam
Do.	6	4	3192	19.69	71.92	1.13	7.26	14.65	Steam and general heating
Do.	6	3	2419	23.30	71.26	1.49	3.95	14.65	Steam and house
Walmestone	5	10	2003	20.78	71.08	1.01	7.13	14.27	Steam and house
Stonehall	3	2	2055	25.65	70.64	1.12	2.59	14.83	Steam and house (a)
Do.	5	2	2109	24.23	70.55	1.67	3.55	14.74	Steam and House
Barfreston	6	1	1452	25.84	70.07	1.19	2.90	15.50	Steam and house
Trapham	4	9	2479	21.31	74.45	0.97	3.27	14.93	Steam and house
Stonehall	6	9	3405	17.83	74.40	0.82	6.95	14.52	Steam and house
Woodnesborough ...	3	0	2127	18.96	74.30	0.82	5.92	14.50	Steam and house
Do.	5	4	2544	12.98	74.12	4.69	8.21	13.91	Steam
Maydensole	3	6	1751	21.65	74.09	0.94	3.32	14.80	Steam and house
Stonehall	5	8	3094	19.59	73.40	0.95	6.06	14.68	Steam and general heating
Do.	4	1	3080	19.95	73.26	1.03	5.76	14.63	House and steam

Walmestone ...	3	5	1910	20.12	73.25	0.52	6.11	14.53	House and steam
Woodnesborough	3	9	1755	23.44	73.06	1.14	2.36	15.71	House and steam
Maydensole ...	4	4	2158	19.18	72.58	1.51	6.73	14.36	House and steam
Stonehall ...	7	2	2985	23.18	70.05	1.44	5.33	14.97	Steam and house
Do. ...	6	2	1912	26.02	70.01	1.51	2.46	15.28	Gas and Coking (*b*)
Walmestone ...	3	1	1825	21.12	69.93	0.94	8.01	14.76	Steam and house
Trapham ...	3	10	2075	27.01	69.60	0.91	2.48	15.12	Gas and coking (*c*)
Stodmarsh ...	13	8	1925	24.45	69.14	1.04	5.36	14.48	Steam and house (*d*)
Stonehall ...	7	10	3274	22.19	69.11	1.50	7.20	14.51	Steam and house
Stonehall	6	6	2284	24.14	69.04	1.77	5.05	14.35	Steam
Fredville ..	4	4	1506	28.34	68.12	.84	2.70	15.34	Gas, steam and house (*e*)
Do. ...	4	2	2205	23.90	67.50	1.83	6.77	14.02	Steam, house and gas
Do. ...	4	4	1504	26.88	67.05	2.12	3.95	14.51	Gas and coking (*f*)
Walmestone ...	3	3	1434	27.82	66.63	1.30	4.25	14.53	Gas and coking (*g*)
Trapham ...	4	2	1900	27.81	65.88	1.23	5.08	14.58	Gas and coking
Waldershare ...	5	2	2372	40.23	52.66	—	1.90	14.73	Gas manufacturing (*h*)

(*a*)	Gas per ton	11,000	cub. ft..	Candle power	16.5.
(*b*)	,,	11,500	,,	,,	17.0.
(*c*)	,,	12,250	,,	,,	16.5.
(*d*)	,,	11.000	,,	,,	16.0.
(*e*)	,,	11,450	,,	,,	15.4.
(*f*)	,,	11,800	,,	,,	17.0.
(*g*)	,,	12,000	,,	,,	17.5.
(*h*)	,,	13,000	,,	,,	23.5.

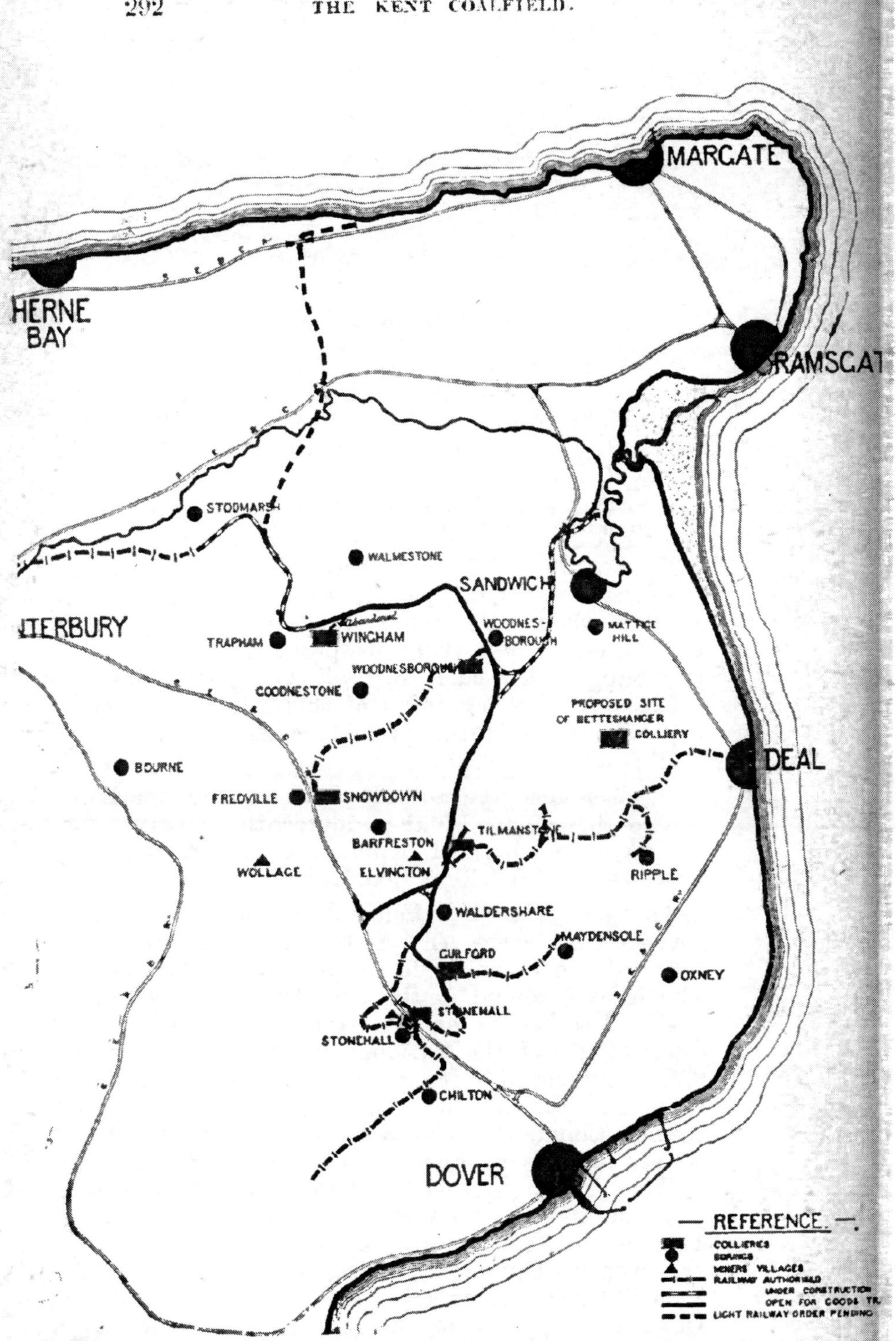
MARGATE
HERNE BAY
RAMSGAT
STODMARSH
WALMESTONE
SANDWICH
TERBURY
TRAPHAM
WINGHAM
WOODNES-BOROUGH
MATTICE HILL
WOODNESBOROUGH
GOODNESTONE
PROPOSED SITE OF BETTESHANGER COLLIERY
DEAL
BOURNE
FREDVILLE
SNOWDOWN
BARFRESTON
TILMANSTONE
WOLLAGE
ELVINGTON
RIPPLE
WALDERSHARE
MAYDENSOLE
GUILFORD
OXNEY
STONEHALL
STONEHALL
CHILTON
DOVER
— REFERENCE. —
COLLIERIES
BORINGS
MINERS VILLAGES
RAILWAY AUTHORISED
UNDER CONSTRUCTION
OPEN FOR GOODS TR.
LIGHT RAILWAY ORDER PENDING

CHAPTER XXVII.

The uncertain future. Difficulties of the Pioneers. Recognition of their work. Kent Coal Concessions ranks first. Summary of Borings. Schedule of Analyses. Nationalisation applied to Kent. L'Envoi.

"Who ever knew truth put to the worse, in a free and open encounter."—MILTON.

Having now dealt with the affairs of the various companies operating on the Kent Coalfield up to a date when, impending legislation threatening to entirely change their prospects, their future is trembling in the balance, I will bring my story to a close. At the beginning of this historical record I quoted the following pronouncement of Professor Hull :—

> "Amongst the solved problems and remarkable discoveries of the nineteenth century will rank, as not least of importance, that of the real existence of a 'Kent Coalfield.'"

All those who have followed my narrative must concede that later events and discoveries have fully justified the claim made in the quoted statement. The Kent Coalfield in the near future is certainly destined to become an important factor in the industrial life of the nation, even to the extent of "shifting the whole centre of commerce and manufacture in this district," as prognosticated by Sir Arthur Conan Doyle at a time anterior to his so closely identifying himself with the spirit world.

When I first contemplated the mass of material at hand, the accumulation of years, without which I could not have attempted to tell the story of this Kentish Cinderella, I became fully aware that I should have to exercise the utmost discrimination. It has been my aim to omit none of the salient facts in order that my readers might have a clear conception of the vicissitudes through which this great industrial undertaking has passed. These vicissitudes are by no means ended, but it is beyond question that the Kent Coalfield, regarded by the Royal Commission on Coal Supplies in 1905 as a negligible quantity, ranks to-day amongst the recognised commercial assets of the nation.

The pioneers of the Field, whose mental vision pictured busy scenes of industrial activity supplanting the rustic life of the Garden of England, never would have surmounted the great and varied obstacles by which they were confronted, but for the enthusiastic optimism that inspired and sustained them. The lure of gold, potent though it be, is not always all-sufficing. Great enterprises are born of imagination—nursed by enthusiasm—and faith in the future is the support of their adolescence.

Within the limits of the coal-basin as defined by the exploratory borings of Kent Coal Concessions and its allies, there is room for the establishment of some 20 collieries which, when fully developed, should raise at least 15 million tons of coal per annum and give employment to about 60,000 colliery workers—not to mention the many thousands of other classes of labour that would follow in their wake.

Thus in the coming years this Coalfield is bound to bulk largely on the industrial horizon, and to become of no mean importance in commercial and shipping spheres. In those days prophets will arise that knew not Joseph, and a short-memoried public will be apt to esteem them as the true discoverers of the Promised Land. Already the stars lately appearing in the Kent Coal firmament are assuming the dignity of suns.

This record of mine at least sets forth, in a spirit of impartiality, the actual events that have operated to transform a scientific theory into an acknowledged and epoch-making fact. I have shown that the *kudos* due to the discoverers of the Field belongs to the Concessions group of companies, and however successful later comers may be, their success will always be built upon the foundations laid by the pioneers. It is the fact that no workable coal has yet been discovered by any of the later explorers the existence of which had not already been established by one of the Concessions companies. A reference to the map of the Coalfield will show that the few seams proved under a restricted area beyond the Stodmarsh and Trapham borings are merely the continuation of others previously proven. The only other successes have been achieved at Lydden and at Betteshanger, which lie well within the area shown to be coal-bearing by one or other of the pioneer companies.

The following table clearly sets forth the respective importance of the boring operations of the various groups durng the past twenty years :—

Summary of Coal Borings in East Kent, 1890-1919.

Borings.	Depth in ft.		Coal proved in seams of 2 ft and upwards. Ft.	in.
The "Brady" Boring at Shakespeare Cliff ..	2,300	..	20	0
By the old "Burr" group, associated with the Shakespeare Cliff enterprise ..	12,206	..	nil.	
By the KENT COAL CONCESSIONS and its assoated companies	47,677	..	561	5
By the Anglo-Westphalian group	11,645	..	31	9
By the Channel Collieries Trust, Ltd...	8,751	..	15	2
By the Ebbsfleet Coal Syndicate, Ltd.	3,401	..	20	10
By the Betteshanger Boring Co., Ltd.	2,930	..	47	9
By the Medway Coal Exploration Syndicate, Ltd. ..	2,314	..	nil.	
By the Whitstable and Canterbury Coalfields, Ltd. ..	1,767	..	nil.	
Totals	92,991	..	696	11

The true contents of the Kentish Coal Measures cannot be determined until the seams are accurately correlated.

Geological Data Concerning 16 Borings by Kent Coal Concessions and its Associated Companies.

	Waldershare.	Fredville.	Goodnestone.	Barfrestone.	Woodnesboro'.	Mattice Hill.	Walmestone.	Trapham.	Stodmarsh.	Ripple.	Maydesnsole.	Oxney.	Ash.	Bourne.	Chilton.	Stonehall
Height above O.D. (feet).	335	259	136	193	51	11	74	59	87	68	253	135	10	175	150	221
	Ft.	Ft.	Ft.	Ft.	Ft.	Ft.	Ft.	Ft.	Ft.	Ft.	Ft.	Ft.	Ft.	Ft.	Ft.	Ft.
Drift and Eocene	—	—	9	$4\frac{1}{2}$	19	14	137	23	41	—	2	21	85	—	12	—
Chalk and Gault	976	948	952	879	949	906	915	877	977	793	927	779	910	938	407	738
Lower Greensands	70	52	42	46	37	53	17	} 98	—	} 89	76	65	36	} 23	198	98
Wealden	42	35	43	33	37	2	5		—		40	39	58			
Oolites	301	316	142	257	30	—	—	126	48		} 152	93	—	367	424	} 394
Lias	5	24	—	—	—	—	—	—	—				—	25	28	
Coal Measures at below O.D. ..	1059	1116	1052	1031	1022	964	1001	1065	981	814	944	862	1079	1138	1119	1007
Transition Coal Measures ..	1469	461	312	1614	—	—	—	—	—	518	1156	778	—	800	2077	1669
Middle Coal Measures	—	—	1406	489	1547	1076	1201	165	1195	1769	1409	1927	766	1056	—	792
Total Coal Measures penetrated	1469	461	1718	2103	1547	1076	1201	165	1195	2287	2565	2705	766	1856	2077	2461
Total Coal in seams of 2 ft. and upwards	13	4′4″	45	48	27	6	36	$22\frac{1}{2}$	22	46	54	62	22	27	16	113
Carboniferous Limestone* ..	—	—	—	—	2569	2040	2202	2716	2176	3101	—	3567	1845	2994	—	—
Depth of Boring from Surface	2863	1836	2906	3227	2633	2075	2285	3226	2263	3316	3762	3743	1966	3236	3346	3691

*At below O.D.

Nationalisation.

In normal times I should have given my views concerning the future of the Kent Coalfield, particularly as affecting the destinies of the existing companies, but it is obviously impossible to assume the Prophet's mantle when the intentions of the Government are still indefinite. So far as can be gathered from the Premier's last utterance on the subject—which strikes me as having been purposely vague as to details—a scheme founded somewhat on the lines laid down by Sir Arthur Duckham is contemplated.

I cannot see what is going to attract the large amount of capital necessary for the rapid development of the coalfield unless some greater inducement is offered than anything yet suggested. I am of opinion that half-measures in this case will fail to achieve the possibilities of the situation, and I do not contemplate with any satisfaction the prospect of this Coalfield being allowed to stagnate, when it could so easily be established upon a sound industrial and commercial basis.

Earlier in this narrative I have drawn a comparison—to our national disadvantage—between the results following upon the discovery of coal in Kent, and in the Pas de Calais. I have also commented upon the lack of enterprise of even so large and powerful a body as the shareholders in the South-Eastern Railway, in failing to respond to the appeal of their Chairman, Sir Edward Watkin, to join him in putting the boring results at Shakespeare Cliff to the practical test.

Therefore, as private enterprise has proved so inadequate, and notwithstanding that I am opposed to the principle of nationalisation being applied to the old-established coalfields, I believe that the experiment might well be made in Kent. In fact, no better opportunity could be found for such an experiment than is here, and now, presented.

Nationalisation of the whole coal industry, to my mind, would be a national calamity, but I am convinced that an isolated and practically virgin coalfield, such as Kent, might be worked under such conditions to the general good of the community. Nevertheless, I must qualify this statement with an " IF." Success would be possible only if the organisation were established on purely commercial lines, and if those responsible for its working were entirely free from political influences and intrigues.

The nationalisation of minerals is almost universally regarded as a necessity of the times, and I cannot imagine anyone connected with collieries —not being also a royalty-owner—who would not welcome the elimination of the individual landlord, subject, of course, to an equitable scale of compensation.

The nationalisation of collieries is another matter, and a most debatable proposition. Could it be proved that such would be in the national interest, nothing should be allowed to stand in its way. So great an industrial revolution, however, would be truly a leap in the dark—it might prove of substantial good to the community or it might be followed by the disastrous consequences its opposers so emphatically predict.

My suggestion, therefore, is that the question might be put to a really practical test under conditions that could not possibly involve the Government in any monetary loss. Conditions, too, that would not cause any disorganisation or financial embarrassment in the commercial world, and that would give the miners the opportunity for which they are clamouring of proving whether or no their theories are well founded.

Having said so much, it might be as well for me to set forth the reasons why I believe that a system which I regard as inapplicable generally should be worth considering in connection with a restricted area. In my opinion the suitability of the Kentish Coalfield for such a legislative adventure is established by the following facts:—

(1) It is an entirely isolated and self-contained entity, the centre of which is situated about 150 miles from the nearest developed coalfield.

(2) It has a proven area of approximately 200 sq. miles, and within its boundaries there are estimated to lie some 6,000 million tons of coal. The existence of this coal has been proved by a large number of borings down to a depth of 3,700 ft.

(3) The seams vary in thickness from 2 ft. to 13 ft. 8 in. and exist under geological conditions more advantageous for working than is the case in the Pas de Calais or Westphalian coalfields.

(4) The coal is of varying classes and qualities, including gas and coking coals, ordinary steam coals, and, as analyses of borehole samples show, smokeless navigation steam coals of Admiralty standard.

(5) The developments so far are not on a large scale, and consequently State purchase would not have any far-reaching effects on either the financial or industrial worlds.

(6) The effective exploitation of the Coalfield would relieve to an enormous extent our already over-burdened railways. This fact is evidenced by the following table showing the respective rail mileage to the London market from all our coal-fields :—

	Miles.		Miles.
Kent	65	South Wales ...	180
Gloucester & Somerset	120	North Wales ...	185
Worcester & Warwick	115	Lancashire	198
Staffordshire	146	Durham	245
Derbyshire	130	Northumberland ...	275
Yorkshire	175	Cumberland ...	310

(7) 1,500,000 tons of coal could be raised annually from Kentish collieries within a period of from three to five years.

(8) The production even of only 1,500,000 tons in East Kent would result in a saving in haulage of not less than 150 millions of ton-miles.

(9) The saving in rolling stock would be on an equally imposing scale. At present wagons coming into Kent do not average more than one and a half trips a month, thus 8,000 ten-tonners are required for the transport of 1½ million tons of coal. If this tonnage were raised in the County the wagons would make on an average one trip per week; the number required, therefore, would not be more than about 3,000, thus releasing 5,000 wagons for general goods traffic.

These calculations have reference only to an output that can be reached within the next few years, but it is evident that the future annual production of the Coalfield will be limited only by the expenditure upon its development.

If the State is to sink a large amount of capital in acquiring the mineral rights, it is obviously to the national interest that the exploitation of the field should be speeded up, in order that the maximum revenue may be achieved with as little delay as possible. Assuming that this proposition were handled by the Government on the lines I visualise, there is no reason why it should not prove as profitable an investment as Disraeli's celebrated purchase of shares in the Suez Canal.

L'Envoi.

Thus we have followed the march of events from those far days when the question of Coal in Kent was but in the realm of abstract hypothesis, onwards through the 'fifties of last century, when the prophetic voice of Godwin-Austen proclaimed that the answer would be an affirmative, and thence through nearly three-quarters of a century up to the present moment.

We have seen Kent Coal emerge from the region of shadows into the light of day, and, whatever trials and tribulations may be still in store, one thing is certain—the worst of its troubles lie buried in this Romance of Industry which I have endeavoured to chronicle. With Marcus Aurelius we may say:—

"As for the rest, the past is gone, the future yet unseen."

APPENDIX. I

List of Coal Borings in Kent, 1886 *to* 1919.

Bore.	Commenced	Finished.	Depth in feet.
Dover (Brady)	1886	1890	2,300
Brabourne	1897	1899	2,204
Ropersole	1897	1899	2,129
Penshurst	Aug., 1897	Feb., 1899	1,867
Pluckley	July. 1897	Apr., 1900	1,699
Ottinge	May, 1898	Oct., 1899	840
Old Soar	Aug., 1898	Oct., 1899	858
Hothfield	July, 1898	Oct., 1899	809
Ellinge	1900	1902	1,800
Waldershare	Jan., 1905	Sep., 1907	2,883
Fredville	Aug., 1905	1907	1,835
Goodnestone	Dec., 1906	July, 1907	2,902
Barfrestone	Dec., 1907	May, 1912	3,327
Woodnesborough ..	Mar., 1908	Mar., 1909	2,633
Walmestone	Oct., 1908	Feb., 1913	2,288
Mattice Hill	June, 1909	July, 1912	2,075
Oxney	April, 1910	Nov., 1912	3,742
Trapham	Oct., 1910	July, 1911	3,225
Maydensole	Nov., 1910	Nov., 1911	3,760
Stodmarsh	Dec., 1910	July, 1911	2,262
Chilham	1910	1911	1,154
Ebbsfleet	1910	1912	1,389
Bobbing	1910	1911	1,160
Ripple	Feb., 1911	Nov., 1911	3,316
Stonehall	Nov., 1911	July, 1912	3,691
Chilton	Aug., 1912	June, 1913	3,346
Lydden Valley	1912	1914	2,012
Herne	1912	1912	1,180
Chislet	July, 1912	May, 1913	2,901
Chitty	Oct., 1912	April, 1913	2,015
Rushbourne	Dec., 1912	Aug., 1913	2,490
Betteshanger	Feb., 1913	Dec., 1913	2,930
Bourne	Mar., 1913	Jan., 1914	3,236
Harmansole	1913	Aug., 1914	1,767
Hoades	July, 1913	Nov., 1913	1,246
Herne Bay	July, 1913	Oct., 1913	1,964
Beltinge	July, 1910	Oct., 1313	1,964
Ash	Aug., 1913	Dec., 1913	1,966
Bere Farm	Mar., 1913	Oct., 1915	3,005
Reculver	May, 1914	June, 1914	1,029
Elham	April, 1914	June, 1915	2,346
Folkestone	Oct., 1915	Dec., 1916	3,400

APPENDIX II.

List of all Kent Coal Companies Registered between the years 1896 and 1919.

Names of Companies.	Registered Capital.
	£
Kent Coalfields Syndicate	200,000
Kent Collieries Corporation	1,500,000
Kent Coal Exploration Co.	250,000
Kent Coal Finance and Development Co. ..	251,000
Mid-Kent Coal Syndicate	12,000
Colliery and General Contract Co.	50,000
Consolidated Kent Collieries Corporation ..	1,250,000
Kent Collieries, Ltd.	400,000
Channel Collieries Trust, Ltd.	750,000
Channel Steel Company, Ltd.	750,000
Dover Coalfield Extension, Ltd.	25,000
Kent Coal Concessions, Ltd.	275,000
Sondage Syndicate, Ltd.	5,000
Foncage Syndicate, Ltd.	20,000
East Kent Colliery Co., Ltd.	500,000
Snowdown Colliery, Ltd.	301,250
South-Eastern Coalfield Extension, Ltd. ..	80,500
Guilford Syndicate, Ltd.	40,000
East Kent Contract and Financial Co., Ltd. ..	50,000
Extended Extension, Ltd.	50,000
Deal and Walmer Coalfield, Ltd.	100,000
East Kent Light Railways Co.	240,000
Medway Coal Exploration Syndicate, Ltd. ..	12,500
Ebbsfleet Coal Syndicate, Ltd.	20,850
South-East Kent Electric Power Co., Ltd. ..	1,000
Intermediate Equipments, Ltd.	100,000
Wingham and Stour Valley Collieries, Ltd. ..	550,000
Anglo-Westphalian Kent Coal Syndicate, Ltd.	25,000
Anglo-Westphalian Kent Coalfield, Ltd. ..	200,000
Kent Freehold and Minerals, Ltd.	100,050
Anglo-Westphalian(Chislet, Kent)Colliery, Ltd	350,000
Betteshanger Boring Company, Ltd.	20,000
Canterbury Coal Company, Ltd.	167,500
Adisham Colliery Company, Ltd.	120,000
Stonehall Colliery Company, Ltd.	120,000
Whitstable and Canterbury Coalfield, Ltd. ..	40,125
Guilford Waldershare Colliery Co., Ltd. ..	240,000
Kentol Syndicate, Ltd.	1,000
Kent Outcrop Coal Syndicate, Ltd.	50,000
Canterbury Drillers, Ltd.	2,550
Total	£9,220,325

In addition there are Debentures issued by the Concessions group to the extent of about £800,000.

INDEX.

S.

T.

U.

W.

Z.

Printed for and Published by
THE IRON AND COAL TRADES REVIEW,
Bessemer House, Adelphi, Strand,
London, W.C.2

Lightning Source UK Ltd.
Milton Keynes UK
UKOW011941160712

196076UK00008B/133/P